What Worries Parents

The most common concerns of parents explored and explained

Kristina Murrin & Paul Martin

Vermilion
LONDON

3 5 7 9 10 8 6 4

First published in 2004 by Vermilion,
an imprint of Ebury Press, Random House,
20 Vauxhall Bridge Road, London SW1V 2SA
www.randomhouse.co.uk

Random House Australia (Pty) Limited
20 Alfred Street, Milsons Point, Sydney,
New South Wales 2061, Australia

Random House New Zealand Limited
18 Poland Road, Glenfield,
Auckland 10, New Zealand

Random House South Africa (Pty) Limited
Endulini, 5A Jubilee Road,
Parktown 2193, South Africa

The Random House Group Limited Reg. No. 954009

Papers used by Vermilion are natural, recyclable products
made from wood grown in sustainable forests.

Printed and bound in Great Britain
by Biddles Ltd, King's Lynn, Norfolk

A CIP catalogue record for this book
is available from the British Library

ISBN 0-09-189487-5

CONTENTS

Acknowledgements   vi
About the Authors   vi

PART 1
About this Book   1
How the Book Works   2
How to Worry   3

PART 2
Your Top 40 Worries   6
I am concerned that my child ...
 1 Might be knocked over by a vehicle   7
 2 Might be abducted or murdered   12
Face the Facts 1 – The Top Ten Risks   16
 3 Eats too much sugar and sweet foods   17
 4 Spends too much time watching TV or
    playing computer games   21
 5 Is growing up too fast   26
Face the Facts 2 – Alcohol   31
 6 Might be the victim of crime   32
 7 Eats too much junk food or convenience
    food   37
 8 Has friends who are or could be a bad
    influence   43
Face the Facts 3 – Smoking   48
 9 Might get a serious illness   49
10 Might be the victim of physical violence   55
11 Might be abused by an adult   60
12 Will only eat a narrow range of foods/
    has food fads   66
13 Has difficulty concentrating/
    paying attention   71

What Worries Parents

14 Will not be successful in adult life if he/she does not do well at school 76

15 Does not get enough sleep 81

16 Doesn't tell me what he/she is really thinking or feeling 86

Face the Facts 4 – Working Parents 91

17 Won't go to bed 92

18 Is at risk if he/she goes on a school trip 97

19 Is reckless and not sufficiently aware of dangers 102

Face the Facts 5 – Drugs 107

20 Has tantrums 108

Face the Facts 6 – Divorce 113

21 Won't get up, get dressed and get ready in the mornings 114

22 Is shy/lacks confidence 119

23 Squabbles with/is too jealous of his/her siblings 123

24 Won't listen to me/is disobedient 129

Face the Facts 7 – Smacking 133

25 Doesn't eat enough 135

26 Isn't reading or writing as well as he/she should 140

27 Is bored or under-stimulated at school 146

28 Is being bullied 151

29 Is disorganised/loses things 157

30 Might be harmed by mobile phone masts or overhead power cables 161

Face the Facts 8 – Mobile Phones 165

31 Might have an accident in the home 166

32 Does not get enough physical exercise 171

33 Won't help with household chores 176

34 Is always asking for things or money 181

35 Doesn't get enough vitamins from his/her normal diet 187

36 Won't do his/her homework 193

37 Is not safe on public transport 198

38 Might get into trouble with the authorities or commit a crime 203

Face the Facts 9 – The Law 208

39 Isn't as good at maths as he/she should be 209

40 Is only assessed on narrow academic achievements, not on broader abilities 215

And Ten Questions from Us 220

Do I spend enough time with my child? 221

Are we communicating as well as we can? 222

Am I allowing my child to be a child? 223

Am I providing a sufficiently stable and loving environment? 224

Do I really understand the world my child lives in? 225

Am I practising what I preach? 226

Am I laying the foundations for good health? 226

Am I helping my child to develop a lifelong love of learning? 227

Are my beliefs about boys and girls correct? 227

Am I enjoying being a parent? 228

Final Thoughts 230

PART 3

About our Research 232

Our Advisory Panel 235

Selected References 236

Index 244

Acknowledgements

We would like to thank Gillon Aitken, James Baderman, Helen Bird, Julie Jessop, Louise Newberry, Suzi Stephenson, our families and all the partners at ?What If! for helping us with this project. We are especially grateful to our amazing research assistant Nancy Milligan, who did a brilliant job in hunting down and collating information on a huge range of subjects.

About the authors

Kristina Murrin is a partner at ?What If!, the world's largest specialist innovation and creativity organisation. She was educated at Cambridge University, where she read Social and Political Sciences, specialising in child psychology. She worked for several years in marketing before helping to establish ?What If! in the early 1990s. She now splits her time between researching and developing new children's products, and working as a government advisor. She is co-author of *Sticky Wisdom* and is married with three young children.

Paul Martin was educated at Cambridge University, where he read Natural Sciences and took a PhD in behavioural biology, and at Stanford University, California, where he was Harkness Fellow in the Department of Psychiatry and Behavioral Sciences. He lectured and researched in behavioural biology at Cambridge before leaving academia to pursue other interests, including science writing. He is the author of *The Sickening Mind* and *Counting Sheep*, and co-author of *Measuring Behaviour* and *Design for a Life*. He is married with three teenage children.

PART 1

About this Book

Who is it for?

This book is aimed primarily at the parents, teachers and carers of children in the UK aged from four to 14 years. These are crucial years in every child's development, spanning the start of formal schooling to the early years of secondary school (Foundation Stage and Key Stages 1–3).

Why did we write it?

Bringing up children is probably the most important and satisfying thing that most of us will ever do. Yet none of us gets taught how to do it, and parents receive relatively little support or guidance once their children reach school age. Any parent, regardless of their background, can find it hard going at times.

Many excellent books have been written for parents of babies or toddlers, and many others have been written about specific issues such as learning, discipline or nutrition. But in our research we found remarkably few books that offered a broad range of advice for parents of children in the crucial 4–14 age range. These parents, it seems, have had to rely mainly on information gleaned from the media, relatives, friends and other parents. While well-intentioned, some of that information is out of date and some of it is plain wrong.

The media can give parents a distorted picture, not because they report things inaccurately (though they certainly do that sometimes) but because they often publicise a single research finding simply because it is newsworthy. And, of course, a research finding is often judged to be newsworthy because it appears to conflict with what many experts believe, with the result that people can become confused about the picture.

In the light of this we set out to create a reliable source of knowledge and evidence-based guidance. Rather than constructing a book around our own personal experiences or opinions, we have researched each topic to find the most trustworthy information that is currently available from academic research literature and other authoritative sources.

Our aim is not to preach to parents about how they should raise their children, but rather to provide them with the knowledge to help them do the job. Our preliminary research before starting to write the book showed that parents don't want to be told what to do. However, many feel they would be better equipped to make the right choices if they were armed with more reliable information, together with guidance about how to translate that information into practical action.

In summary, then, we have tried to write a book that is:

- shaped by the actual needs and interests of parents
- based on evidence rather than opinion
- wide-ranging in its choice of subjects

Who are we?

We both have professional training and experience in relevant areas, including psychology, behavioural biology, science writing and public sector policy, but we do not claim to be child development experts. We are both parents, but we do not claim to be parenting experts. Our expertise, such as it is, lies in collating, filtering and presenting knowledge. Our aim has been to listen to the worries of real parents and then try to find the best possible answers to help them.

How the book works

What Worries Parents grew out of a year-long research programme to establish the specific issues on which parents wanted more information and guidance. The top 40 worries of British parents were revealed by a national survey conducted especially for us by MORI, in which more than 1000 parents of four- to 14-year-old children were interviewed to find out the issues they felt most worried, concerned or uncertain about.

The topics that emerged from this survey – determined not by us, but by the parents themselves – encompass a very wide range of subjects including accidents, nutrition, discipline, schooling, health, the family, sleep, crime and physical development. All are covered in the main section of the book, Part 2, which consists of 40 short chapters, each tackling a top worry or concern – followed by ten additional issues in the form of questions that parents might like to ask themselves. The latter are intended to draw together the main themes that emerged from our research. Finally, Part 3 of the book deals with the research itself – how it was conducted, and what else it revealed in terms of parents' concerns.

This book is not designed to be read from cover to cover, although there's no reason why you shouldn't do this, but, rather, is intended to be a source of information and advice that you can dip into according to your own particular needs and interests. The beginning of each 'Worry' chapter deals with a summary of the findings, followed by a system of assessing real-life risks and their likelihood of happening (see page 4) that we hope will be helpful in terms of directing worries in the right direction. Information related to topics of general concern that may not have been covered in the specific 'Worry' chapters has been added in the form of Fact Boxes that appear throughout the book.

We confess that this is a rather British book (if not an English one). The choice of topics was determined by British parents, and much of the factual information and research evidence we have cited refers to the UK. In some cases it relates specifically to England, or to England and Wales, which have different legal and educational systems from Scotland and Northern Ireland. Nonetheless, children are children the world over. So, while some of the details may differ between countries, the general principles tend to remain the same.

How to Worry

To help parents direct their worries in the right directions, we've devised a simple system for assessing real-life risks in terms of their likelihood (Chances), their impact (Consequences) and the extent to which parents can do something about them (Control).

Managing risk

If you are a parent you will know that everyday life is stuffed full of potential reasons for worrying about your children, ranging from the mundane to the exotic. Junk food, drugs, disobedience, mugging, academic failure, obesity, unpopularity, murder, accidents, illness, anorexia, mobile phones, bullying, untidiness, bad behaviour, crime – the list of things you *could* worry about is endless. How, then, can you distinguish between those that are really worth worrying about and those you can afford to be more relaxed about? The answer lies in the concept of risk.

People worry because bad things might happen, or because things that have happened might have bad consequences. Another way of saying this is that worry is all about *risk*: parents should worry most about the situations that would expose their children to most risk.

Parents who don't think in terms of risk sometimes end up worrying about the wrong things. They may:

- worry too much about things that are, in reality, very unlikely ever to happen to their children
- worry too much about things that would not matter very much even if they did happen
- worry too much about things over which they have little or no practical control

- not worry enough about things that in fact pose a surprisingly big threat to their children

We found real examples of all these. For example, our national survey showed that far more parents are concerned about their children being abducted or murdered than about accidents in the home. In reality, the average British child is more likely to be killed or seriously injured in a domestic accident than to be murdered. And the risk of being murdered by a *stranger*, which lies at the heart of many parents' worries, is actually very small indeed: in fact, more children die each year from drowning in garden ponds. Of course, the horrifying cases of children being murdered by strangers receive much more attention from the media than the everyday tragedies of domestic accidents or road traffic fatalities, so it's not surprising that these more unusual types of risk tend to be more prominent among parents' worries.

When thinking about a particular type of risk, parents should start by asking themselves two basic questions: (1) How likely is it to happen to my child? and (2) How much harm would it do if it did happen? If something is very unlikely ever to happen to your child, and wouldn't matter much even if it did happen, there seems little point in worrying about it.

Another question to ask yourself when thinking about risks is How much can I practically do to control or reduce them? Some risks are much easier to reduce or eliminate than others. By all means worry about things you can actually do something about: worry can be a crucial spur to action. But there is little point in endlessly fretting about a risk if you are powerless to change it; you would be better off conserving your time and energy for those issues where you can make a difference.

Controlling risks is not a straightforward matter, however, and when thinking about how to protect your child you will need to consider the wider consequences of your actions. Anything you do to protect your child from one particular type of risk will inevitably have other consequences, and in some cases those consequences might be even worse than the original risk. In other words, by trying to eliminate a risk you could actually make things worse.

Again, we came across several examples. For instance, many parents worry about their children being attacked by strangers, and, in response, will insist on driving their children around rather than letting them walk by themselves, thus restricting their freedom to play outdoors with friends. However, this well-intended response has some distinct downsides – notably, by depriving children of opportunities for social interaction, physical exercise, play, developing independence and learning how to be safe pedestrians. It also introduces a new source of risk – that of being killed or injured while travelling in a car.

Chances, consequences and control

In Part 2 of the book we have assessed each of the top 40 worries of British parents in terms of three risk-related dimensions, called *Chances*, *Consequences* and *Control*.

Chances refers to the likelihood (or probability) of the worry coming true – as in *What are the chances that it will actually happen to my child?*

For each worry we have made a crude judgement about the chances of that situation actually happening to the average British child, based on the available statistics. We have rated the Chances as High, Medium or Low, as follows:

LOW means a probability of less than 1 in 100,000
MEDIUM means a probability of less than 1 in 100 (but more than LOW)
HIGH means a probability of 1 in 100 (1 per cent) or higher

Unless otherwise specified, these categories refer to the probability of the worry coming true over the course of a year. To put it another way, LOW means that the risk is unlikely to affect more than one child a year in a city the size of Gloucester, whereas HIGH means it might well affect at least one child in each year-group of a typical secondary school.

We should stress that our ratings are only crude estimates. Moreover, they refer to the *average* child – which does not mean *your* child. The chances of a particular worry coming true for an individual child may be substantially lower or higher than this average figure, depending on factors such as the child's age, sex, family background and so on. Conclusions based on averages do not apply to every individual; for example, men are taller on average than women, but many women in the population are taller than many men.

To give a more practical feel for what is meant by LOW, MEDIUM and HIGH probabilities, here are some real-life illustrations. On our rating scale, the chances of being struck by lightning within the next year, which are somewhat less than one in a million, are LOW. (And the chances of winning the National Lottery on a single ticket are lower still.) If you are a 40-year-old man, the chances that you will die within the next 12 months (about 1 in 500) are MEDIUM. And your chances of developing some form of cancer during your lifetime (about 1 in 3) are HIGH.

Consequences refers to the impact on the child if the worry does come true – as in *What would be the worst consequences if it did happen to my child?*

For each worry we have made a crude judgement about the *worst* likely consequences for the average child if the circumstances referred to in the worry came true. We have rated the Consequences as High, Medium or Low, as follows:

LOW means no serious, life-threatening or long-term consequences; at worst, there should be only a short-term and relatively minor impact

MEDIUM means significant but not life-threatening; at worst, there would be a significant negative impact on the child's physical or mental well-being, lasting for an appreciable period of time

HIGH means life-threatening; at worst, the child could die or be seriously injured

Control describes the extent to which a parent could reasonably do something to protect their child without making matters worse – as in *How much could I do to reduce or eliminate the risk, such that my actions would be feasible, reasonable and unlikely to do more harm than good?*

We have added the important qualification that the protective measures must be *feasible, reasonable and unlikely to do more harm than good*, for the reasons explained above. It would often be possible (at least, in theory) to reduce or eliminate a particular risk by doing *un*reasonable things which would make matters worse overall. For example, one way of eliminating the risk of your child being murdered by a stranger would be to keep your child permanently locked up in a cupboard. But of course, that would not be reasonable (or legal) and it would do more harm than good. The solution would be worse than the problem.

For each worry we have rated Control as High, Medium or Low, as follows:

LOW means there is little or nothing you can reasonably do; the risk stems largely from factors you cannot control by taking steps that would be feasible, reasonable and unlikely to do more harm than good

MEDIUM means there are some things you can reasonably do to improve matters; you have significant scope to reduce the risk by taking steps that are feasible, reasonable and unlikely to do more harm than good

HIGH means there is a lot you can do; you can substantially reduce or even eliminate the risk by taking steps that are feasible, reasonable and unlikely to do more harm than good

To summarise: when thinking about a particular type of risk to your child, you need to consider its likelihood (Chances) and its impact on your child if it does happen (Consequences). You also need to consider the extent to which you can reasonably do something to reduce or eliminate the risk without making matters even worse (Control).

PART 2
Your Top 40 Worries

I am concerned that my child …

WORRY **1**

Might be knocked over by a vehicle

45% of parents worried

....

Chances: MEDIUM   **Consequences: HIGH**   **Control: MEDIUM**

Parents are right to worry about this: being knocked over by a vehicle is the leading cause of death and injury to school-aged children. Each year, about 15,000 child pedestrians receive some form of injury and about 100 are killed.

The chances of a child in the UK being killed by a vehicle are at least ten times greater than the chances of being murdered by a stranger. Those most at risk are boys, children aged around 10–12 years, and children playing or walking near their own home.

The largest single factor is speeding. If drivers kept within speed limits and drove with more care, especially in built-up areas, fewer children would be killed or seriously injured. Parents can help by teaching children road awareness when they are young.

Withdrawing children from the risk by driving them everywhere may not be the best solution, as it deprives them (among other things) of the opportunity to learn how to be a safe pedestrian.

Our national survey found that this was the biggest single concern of parents in the UK. Parents sometimes worry about things that in fact pose relatively little danger, but in this case they are right to worry. Being knocked over by a vehicle is the principal cause of death and injury among school-aged children. Vehicles certainly pose a much bigger threat to children than violent strangers do. In fact, the average British child is more than ten times as likely to be knocked over and killed by a vehicle than to be murdered by a stranger.

Each year in the UK, vehicles cause at least minor injuries to about 15,000 children under the age of 16. Of these, approximately 3000 are seriously injured and around 100 are killed. Most accidents involving child pedestrians occur close to their homes and in residential areas. In many cases the accident happens when the child is crossing a road while masked by parked or stationary vehicles.

Child pedestrians are about four times more likely to be injured or killed than adult pedestrians. That statistic is even more shocking if you consider that children generally have much less exposure to traffic than adults and therefore have fewer 'opportunities' to be knocked down.

For a child, being a pedestrian is considerably riskier than travelling in a car: a child is at least three times more likely to be killed or seriously injured when walking than when travelling in a vehicle.

Which children are most at risk? Statistics show that boys are twice as likely as girls to be knocked over: two-thirds of child pedestrians who are killed or seriously injured each year are boys. Children from economically deprived homes are also at greater risk: they are five times more likely to be killed on the roads than children from the most affluent backgrounds. Among other reasons, this is because they tend to live near more dangerous roads, have fewer safe places to play, and spend more time out on the streets.

Age is another important factor. The likelihood of a child pedestrian being killed or seriously injured rises with age and peaks at around 10–12 years. Pre-teen children are physically mobile and increasingly want to be independent, but they often lack the experience and judgement needed to be safe pedestrians. Few children below the age of ten have the ability to make consistently accurate judgements about the speed, distance and behaviour of traffic.

Moreover, young children often have dangerous misconceptions about traffic. For example, they may believe that if they can see the driver then the driver must be able to see them, or that cars can stop instantly. The small size and unpredictable behaviour of young children also make them harder for drivers to see and avoid. Parents tend to over-estimate the ability of young children to behave safely as pedestrians.

Child cyclists are vulnerable too. Each year about 25 children are killed while riding bicycles and several hundred are seriously injured, mostly as a result of being hit by a vehicle. More than two-thirds of fatal cycling accidents involve head injuries. Wearing a suitable helmet can greatly reduce a child's risk of head injury, but less than 1 in 5 children actually wear one.

The vast majority of all these deaths and injuries to child pedestrians and cyclists could be avoided if children and adults behaved differently. Drivers must shoulder much of the blame here, since the biggest single factor in pedestrian deaths is driving too fast. A speeding car is not only far more likely to hit a child in the first place, but also far more likely to kill that child when it does hit them.

The evidence shows that reducing vehicle speeds by only 1 per cent reduces the number of accidents by 5 per cent. On top of that, relatively small differences in a vehicle's speed make surprisingly big differences to the likelihood of it killing a pedestrian. A child who is hit by a car travelling at 20mph has a 95 per cent chance of survival and may sustain only minor injuries, but at 40 mph they have only a 15 per cent chance of surviving and, if they do survive, their injuries are likely to be severe. To put it another way, a car travelling at 40 mph is 17 times more likely to kill a child than one travelling at 20 mph.

So, one way we could all help to reduce the numbers of children being killed or injured on our roads is to drive more carefully and keep within the speed limits, especially in built-up areas.

Another way of saving children's lives would be to drive cars that do less damage to pedestrians. The design of a car has a substantial effect on the level of danger it poses to pedestrians: a vehicle with a carefully designed bumper and bonnet leading edge, plus a soft or yielding bonnet, will do much less damage to a child's legs and head than one whose designers have given no consideration to pedestrian protection.

All new cars sold in Europe must satisfy stringent safety criteria, which are intended to ensure the safety of their occupants in a crash. Most new cars now score four or five stars, out of a maximum of five, in the crash tests conducted by the independent European New Car Assessment Programme (EuroNCAP). In contrast, most cars still perform poorly on tests that measure the injuries they would cause to pedestrians.

In the EuroNCAP pedestrian test, which simulates the effects of hitting child and adult pedestrians at 25 mph, the majority of new cars score only one or two stars out of a possible four. EuroNCAP has described the pedestrian protection provided by some vehicles as 'dire'. Among the worst offenders are some models of large 4x4 'off-road' vehicle, which are often favoured by urban parents for the school run. Their high, sharply angled and unyielding bonnets can cause severe injuries to child pedestrians, even at low speeds. When it comes to choosing a new car, most people are far more concerned about protecting themselves and their own family than they are about not killing children or other pedestrians they might hit.

The rate of child pedestrian casualties has fallen in the UK over the past 30 years. However, it still does not compare especially favourably with other countries: the number of accidents involving child pedestrians (relative to the number of children in the population) remains above the average for other European countries, even though the children in these countries spend just as much time near roads. Moreover, the decline in child pedestrian casualties does not necessarily prove that Britain's streets have become much safer. To some extent, it is simply a reflection of the fact that British parents have increasingly withdrawn their children from the streets.

Responding to the risk

Parents who are concerned about the threat posed by vehicles have tended to respond by removing their children from the source of risk. They do this by keeping their children indoors and driving them everywhere rather than allowing them to walk or cycle by themselves. The most visible consequence has been a large increase over the past 30 years in the proportion of children who are driven to school. Less than half of school-age children now walk to school, and only 1 in 50 cycle to school. This decline in walking has reduced children's independence and their opportunities for physical exercise.

The continuing growth in the numbers of children being driven to and from school has had other undesirable effects too. The most obvious of these is traffic congestion, with its associated air pollution. At around 8:50 am, which is the peak time for the school run, 1 car in every 6 on British roads is carrying children to school. Being driven to school, rather than walking with friends, also deprives children of valuable opportunities for social contact.

But driving children everywhere does not reduce the overall risks as much as some parents may think. Each year more than 14,000 children are injured while travelling in vehicles, and around 70 are killed. Unsurprisingly, some of these accidents occur while children are being driven to or from school.

Indeed, in the longer term, parents might actually be exposing their children to more risk by driving them rather than walking with them. As well as facing the immediate risk of travelling in a car, children who are driven everywhere have fewer opportunities to learn the vital skills of being a safe pedestrian.

When they do eventually start walking to places on their own – as they inevitably will – they may actually be at greater risk because they lack the awareness of more experienced and street-wise child pedestrians.

What can you do?

◆ **Think about your immediate environment.**

Don't assume that your child is safe just because he or she is in your driveway or close to the house. Most child pedestrian accidents occur close to the victim's home, often when the child is masked by parked or stationary vehicles.

◆ **Teach your child how to be a safe pedestrian.**

Walk with your child as often as you can and show him or her how to be a safe, streetwise pedestrian; the more they do it, under adult supervision, the safer they will become. Research has shown that simply telling children about road safety is not enough; the best way for children to develop safe pedestrian skills is through guided practice at the roadside.

◆ **Set a good example.**

Practise what you preach by demonstrating good road awareness and following the pedestrian code. Stop, look and listen before you cross.

◆ **Choose a safe route.**

Make sure your child takes the safest route when walking to and from school or other regular destinations, even if that means walking a bit further. A safe route is one that avoids unprotected crossings. Don't assume that a road is safer just because it has less traffic. Crossing a busy road using a proper pelican crossing, or where there is a lollypop person, can be safer than crossing a quieter road unaided.

◆ **Help your child to be vigilant and visible.**

Try to ensure that your child is not distracted by listening to a personal stereo or chatting on a mobile phone while crossing the road. Children are also safer if they are easily visible, so consider getting them to wear some reflective material on an outer garment, especially in winter. (That said, fashion-conscious children may be reluctant to have fluorescent strips on their clothes: if so, consider putting some on their school bag instead.)

◆ **Cyclists should wear helmets.**

If your child rides a bike, make sure they learn about safe cycling and insist that they always wear a helmet. Ensure that the helmet fits and is worn properly. The risk of head injury is greatly increased if the helmet is worn pushed back on the head or with the strap unbuckled.

◆ **Drive safely.**

Don't put the lives of other people's children at risk by being a bad driver. Drive carefully and keep within the speed limit, especially in built-up areas. Slow down and be extra careful if there are ▶

children about – you might be in a hurry, but that is no excuse for putting lives at risk. Stop and think about how you would feel if you crippled or killed a child.

◆ *Drive a more pedestrian-friendly car.*

When you next buy a car, consider choosing one that is more pedestrian-friendly in its design. Check out the EuroNCAP pedestrian impact ratings and avoid models with the worst scores for pedestrian protection (0 stars out of 4).

◆ *Share lifts.*

If you have no alternative to driving your children to school, think about sharing lifts with other parents. Car pooling would make everyone's lives a little better by reducing the numbers of cars on the road.

Further advice

Child Accident Prevention Trust

Tel: 020 7608 3828

E-mail: safe@capt.org.uk (to register personal questions)

www.capt.org.uk

Factsheets, information and advice on all aspects of road safety.

The Royal Society for the Prevention of Accidents (RoSPA)

Tel: 0121 248 2000

E-mail: help@rospa.co.uk (to register personal questions)

www.rospa.com

Advice and information on children using the roads.

Department for Transport: Hedgehogs Campaign

www.hedgehogs.gov.uk

Games and exercises to help motivate and inform children about road safety.

European New Car Assessment Program (EuroNCAP)

www.euroncap.co.uk

Crash test data for the occupant and pedestrian safety performance of different models.

Related worries

19. Is reckless and not sufficiently aware of dangers

32. Does not get enough physical exercise

37. Is not safe on public transport

Might be abducted or murdered

42% of parents worried

....

Chances: MEDIUM   **Consequences: HIGH**   **Control: MEDIUM**

Many parents worry about the nightmare possibility of their child being abducted and murdered. Our research showed that for most parents this fear is driven by a concern that their child might be abducted or murdered by a stranger. In reality this threat is tiny. While a depressingly large number of children are killed every year in the UK, most of them are killed by their parents or family members, not by strangers.

On average, one or two children aged 0–16 are murdered each week in the UK. Eight out of ten of these murders are committed by the child's parents. Those at greatest risk are babies under the age of one. Amongst children in the 4–14 age range the murder rate is much lower, running at one or two a month.

The likelihood of a child in the UK being abducted and killed by a stranger is very small, and not much different now from 30 years ago. Fewer than ten children a year are killed by strangers, making the chances less than one in a million for an individual child.

If you have a baby or a young child, think carefully about the suitability and mental state of whoever is looking after them – including yourself.

Dramatic TV and newspaper stories can some-times create an impression that the abduction and murder of children by strangers is a common and growing threat in the UK. It is partly as a consequence of this fear that most British children now have less independence and freedom to play outside and less independence than their parents did as children. Three out of four parents cite a fear of strangers as the main reason for keeping their children indoors.

The reality is somewhat different. The chances of a child in the UK being murdered by a stranger are very small, and they have not changed much over the past 30 years. The number of children murdered by strangers has been fewer than ten a year for decades and shows no sign of rising. In the year 2000, for example, there were seven cases among 12 million children in the UK. Statistically, the chances of a child being murdered by a stranger are less than one in a million – a level of risk that most statisticians would regard as negligible.

Another popular belief that fails to stand up to scrutiny is that girls are more likely to be murdered than boys. In fact, the opposite is true. Almost two-thirds of all child murder victims are boys. This is true at all ages, but particularly for the under-fives.

The number of children murdered by strangers might be small, but the *total* number of child murders in the UK is higher than many people would expect – about 80 a year on average. This death toll is not far short of the 100 or so children who are knocked over and killed by vehicles each year (see Worry 1, page 7). But the great majority (80 per cent) of all these child murders are committed by parents. Of the remainder, nearly all are committed by a carer, relative or family friend. Strangers are responsible for only a tiny proportion.

The children who are at greatest risk of being murdered are those under one year of age. A baby or infant under one is at least five times more likely to be murdered than a child in any other age group. Among children in our 4–14 age range the murder rate is much lower, running at one or two a month rather than one or two a week. Moreover, while murders among older children have remained static, the murder rate for the under-ones has risen substantially over the last decade, for reasons that remain uncertain.

Research by the NSPCC suggests that the true number of child murders in the UK might be higher than the official statistics report. Many deaths of babies and very young children happen within the family home, and this can sometimes make it difficult to establish the exact circumstances of their death. A small number of children whose deaths were thought to have been natural or accidental might actually have been murdered.

The uncomfortable fact that more than 60 children a year are killed by their own parents is seldom discussed publicly. Despite the fact that murders by parents outnumber those committed by strangers by almost 10 to 1, these cases receive far less media attention – perhaps reflecting a general taboo. After all, how could a parent possibly murder their own child?

Responding to the risk

Anyone who has looked after a young baby will know that it can be a lonely and stressful experience. About half of all parents feel they receive inadequate support during their first year of parenthood, and it is not hard to see why. The decline of the extended family has left many parents without the practical help that previous generations could rely upon. Official help has also declined – the number of postnatal visits to new mothers by midwives and health visitors, for example, has fallen by a quarter in the last decade.

The strain is just too much for some parents, especially if their circumstances are already difficult for other reasons. Research has found that three out of four mothers have shaken or hit their infant by the time it is one year old, the most common reason given being that it would not stop crying. On top of this, up to 15 per cent of new mothers experience postnatal depression. For many women, this will amount to a relatively short, if unpleasant, period of 'baby blues', with no lasting effects, but for others it can be a full blown psychiatric illness which makes them deeply unhappy and desperate.

Where does all this leave us? One conclusion is that parents of young children should perhaps focus more on managing their own stress and frustrations, and those of other people caring for their children, than on worrying about random strangers murdering their child.

A more general point is that protecting children from real or imaginary risks can often have downsides that should also be taken into account. If the protective measures are excessive, and the true risks are small, then the downsides might even outweigh the benefits.

Parents who become excessively worried about 'stranger danger' often restrict their children's freedom, refuse to let them outside the confines of the house or garden to play, or insist on driving them everywhere instead of letting them walk. As a result their children have fewer opportunities to develop independence, interact with their peers, or be physically active. They get less exercise and are therefore at greater risk of becoming overweight or obese, which in turn can seriously threaten their health. Obesity is now a major public health risk.

Over-protected children are also deprived of opportunities to develop an awareness of the dangers posed by traffic, and are therefore at greater risk of being run over when they do eventually walk on their own. They spend more time in cars and are therefore at greater risk of being killed or injured in a vehicle accident. And so on.

Over-protectiveness can also have undesirable psychological and emotional effects. Children are highly sensitive to their parents' thoughts, attitudes and anxieties, and will pick up and absorb these fears, even if they are unspoken. Parental anxieties about the danger from strangers can sometimes convey to children a distorted view of the world, in which serious threats to their personal safety lurk around every corner and other people are not to be trusted. This can sap a child's sense of confidence and control. Moreover, there will be situations in every child's life when their safety or well-being may depend on their being able to trust a stranger who is trying to help them.

In our opinion, raising children to be deeply suspicious and distrustful of everyone is undesirable, both for the children and for society as a whole.

What can you do?

◆ **Apply the three Ws: Where, Who and When.**

Try to ensure that you always know *where* your child is, *who* they are with, and *when* they will be back. Keeping in touch with parents of your children's friends can provide useful additional information and the opportunity to do some discreet cross-checking.

◆ **Think carefully about anyone who helps to look after your child.**

If you leave your child in the care of someone else – even a partner, relative or friend – think carefully about his or her suitability and trustworthiness. Are they stressed or depressed? Do they drink excessively or take mood-altering drugs? Are they capable of being violent?

◆ **Check the background and credentials of any paid carer.**

Child minders must be registered with your local authority. Nannies and baby-sitters, for whom there are no legal requirements, should come through a reputable agency or with the personal recommendation of someone you trust. ▶

Anyone whose job gives them access to children, including teachers and scout leaders, must be cleared by the Criminal Records Bureau.

◆ *Think twice before leaving young children in the sole care of someone under 16.*

Looking after children, especially young ones, is a big responsibility and can be demanding. The guidelines published by the Royal Society for the Prevention of Accidents (RoSPA) and the National Society for the Prevention of Cruelty to Children (NSPCC) suggest that parents should not leave their children in the care of anyone who is under the age of 16. If a child is harmed while in the care of someone below this age, the parents might be found legally negligent.

◆ *Teach your child never to accept sweets, gifts or lifts from strangers.*

Teach your child to be polite but firm in saying no. But try not to convey an excessive sense that the world is full of hostile, dangerous people. It isn't.

◆ *Teach your child how to dial 999 in an emergency.*

If you leave your child with someone, make sure he or she has a contact number for you. Consider getting them a mobile phone for emergencies when older.

◆ *Teach your child not to reveal information about themselves or the family to strangers.*

Addresses and home numbers should never be given out over the phone or on the Internet.

◆ *Ask for help if you need it.*

Far more children are killed by their parents or carers than by strangers. If you are a parent or carer and feel you cannot cope, seek help from your GP, health visitor, local hospital, or from a support charity such as Parent Line. It's obviously far better to admit you need help than to harm a child. If you are the partner, spouse or friend of a depressed parent, and you think they may be reaching breaking point, do something: talk to them about it, listen to how they feel, and encourage them to get help.

Further advice

NSPCC
Helpline: 0808 800 5000
www.nspcc.org.uk
Advice on keeping your child safe, dealing with parental stress, and recognising the signs of abuse.

Reunite
Tel: 0116 255 6234
www.reunite.org
E-mail: reunite@dircon.co.uk

Fact sheets on preventing abduction and what do to if you think your child has been abducted.

Related worries

6. Might be the victim of crime
10. Might be the victim of physical violence
11. Might be abused by an adult
37. Is not safe on public transport

The Top 10 Risks Worldwide

◆ Research by the World Health Organisation (WHO) shows that for humanity as a whole, the top ten risk factors worldwide are:

1. Being underweight
2. Unsafe sex
3. High blood pressure
4. Tobacco consumption
5. Alcohol consumption
6. Unsafe water, sanitation and hygiene
7. Iron deficiency
8. Indoor smoke from solid fuels
9. High cholesterol
10. Obesity

◆ These ten risk factors account for more than a third of all deaths globally among adults and children.

◆ At least 170 million children in developing nations are underweight, and more than three million die each year as a consequence.

◆ At the same time, more than one billion adults elsewhere in the world are overweight and 300 million are clinically obese. More than half a million people die each year in North America and Western Europe from obesity-related diseases.

◆ The biggest threats to health in industrialised countries like the UK are high blood pressure, smoking, alcohol, high cholesterol and obesity. These are all risk factors for cardiovascular disease, which is now the leading cause of death worldwide.

◆ Unsafe sex is the main risk factor behind the spread of HIV/AIDS, which is the fourth biggest cause of death worldwide. Nearly three million deaths a year, mostly in Africa, are attributable to unsafe sex.

◆ Unsafe water, sanitation and hygiene lead to almost two million deaths a year, primarily among children in developing countries.

◆ Iron deficiency causes almost a million deaths a year.

◆ Half the world's population is exposed to indoor air pollution, mainly from burning solid fuels, causing respiratory infections, asthma and lung cancer.

WORRY 3

Eats too much sugar and sweet foods

38% of parents worried

Chances: HIGH   **Consequences: MEDIUM**   **Control: MEDIUM**

We British – adults and children alike – consume large amounts of added sugar in our diets. We do this because it is pleasurable, not because it is necessary. The average schoolchild consumes tens of kilograms of added sugar a year, much of it hidden in savoury foods and fizzy drinks.

Excessive sugar consumption contributes to obesity, which can have a profound long-term impact on health. It also contributes to tooth decay. Most British children (and adults) would be better off with less sugar.

When people refer to 'sugar' they usually mean sucrose – the white, granulated substance extracted from sugar beet or sugar cane that we use to sweeten drinks and foodstuffs. All sugars are carbohydrates. Refined white sugar is 99 per cent pure sucrose, but there are several other sorts of sugar that occur naturally in our diets, including fructose – present in plants and abundant in honey – and lactose, which is the main sugar found in milk.

In Britain one of the most popular sources of sugar is chocolate. The British have the largest chocolate intake in Europe, accounting for almost a third of total European consumption. We eat nearly 600,000 tonnes of chocolate every year, which works out at about 10 kilograms (22 pounds) of chocolate for every man, woman and child. The average British schoolchild consumes 30 kilograms (66 pounds) of sugar a year. And 30 kilograms of sugar contains about 120,000 Calories[1] of energy.

Refined white sugar is a relatively recent addition to the British diet. The earliest sugar refineries existed in London as long ago as the 1540s. Nonetheless, sugar remained a rare and highly valuable commodity until the first half of the 18th century, when merchants started to import it in large quantities from Caribbean sugar plantations. Even then, high taxes meant that it remained a luxury item. It wasn't until the 1870s that it became a cheap and common component of the British diet.

We consume sugar and sugary foods mainly for the pleasure of their taste, not because we need to. Refined white sugar provides plenty of energy (Calories), but nothing else. It contains no protein, no vitamins, no essential fatty acids and virtually no minerals. Unrefined brown sugar does, admittedly, contain tiny traces of protein and some common minerals, but nothing like enough to make it healthy. The only reason for preferring it to white sugar is that it tastes slightly different.

In moderation sugar does little or no harm, but excessive consumption can contribute to tooth decay. Far more importantly, it can also lead to obesity, which most experts now regard as one of the leading threats to public health in the UK. The health hazard is made worse because many foodstuffs that are high in sugar, such as cakes, biscuits, puddings, pastries, chocolate and ice cream, are also high in saturated fats and low in vitamins and minerals. Conversely, some purportedly healthy foods contain surprisingly large amounts of added sugar. Certain brands of flavoured yoghurts marketed at children, for example, contain as much as 25 per cent sugar. Large amounts of added sugar are also found in some fruit drinks and breakfast cereals.

The risk of high sugar consumption

One of the biggest-ever scientific studies of the eating habits of British children and teenagers, conducted in the late 1990s, found that sugar was providing at least 16 per cent of their total daily energy intake. This is well above the recommended maximum of 11 per cent of total energy intake. The main sources of all this sugar in children's diets are soft drinks, chocolate, sweets and biscuits. Children aged 7-10 consume an average of more than half a kilogram of sugary foods every day, with soft drinks forming the biggest single element. A standard can of cola drink contains about nine level teaspoons (35 grams) of sugar.

High levels of sugar consumption are associated with obesity, which has increased dramatically among children in the UK, USA and Western Europe. Currently, at least 1 in 5 of all British primary school children is overweight, and at least 1 in 10 is classified as obese. Fat children usually grow into fat adults, which means that the proportion of adults who are obese will also continue to rise.

---

[1] The terminology of calories is confusing. Diet books still commonly give the energy contents of foodstuffs in Calories, where 1 Calorie (with a big C) = 1000 calories (with a small c). Scientists and doctors use a unit of energy called the joule, where 1 Calorie = 4200 joules = 4.2 kJ.

Obesity is far more than a just a cosmetic problem: it is a life-threatening illness. Being overweight or obese increases the long-term risks of developing diabetes, raised blood pressure, coronary heart disease and some forms of cancer. According to research by the World Health Organisation (WHO), obesity is one of the top ten risk factors for death and disease worldwide (see The Top 10 Risks Worldwide, p. 16). (Ironically, the biggest risk factor for humanity as a whole is being *under-weight*.)

Another risk associated with consuming lots of sugary drinks and foods is tooth decay, or dental caries – caused when bacteria create acid which eats into the enamel of the tooth. More than half of all British children and teenagers show signs of tooth decay. Research evidence shows that those with the worst problem are the ones who eat sweets at least once a day, frequently drink non-low-calorie soft drinks, or frequently drink coffee or tea sweetened with sugar. In particular, children who drink sugary drinks at night are far more likely to have tooth decay than those who only drink water after they go to bed.

The main factor behind tooth decay is not so much the total sugar intake, as the number of occasions during the day when it is consumed. The more often sugar is consumed, the bigger the risk. That is why the habit of grazing on sugary snacks and drinks throughout the day is particularly harmful to teeth. Children would probably be better off pigging-out on sweets a few times a week than nibbling smaller amounts every day.

Obesity and tooth decay are the most obvious health concerns associated with sugar, but they are not the only ones. Many parents and teachers believe that sugar also has adverse effects on children's behaviour, contributing, in particular, to hyperactivity.

Although this view is often echoed in the media, the scientific evidence is not clear-cut. Many rigorous studies have failed to uncover conclusive evidence that eating sugar causes adverse changes in children's behaviour, or that eliminating sugar from children's diets produces significant improvements. Even when scientists have looked specifically at children who are hyperactive or sugar sensitive they have still failed to find firm links between sugar intake and behaviour.

On the other hand, research has found that people's reactions to certain food substances and additives can be highly idiosyncratic, with some individuals reacting very differently. The safest conclusion is that sugar is probably not by itself a direct cause of hyperactivity or disruptive behaviour in the majority of children.

Standard soft drinks are sweetened with sugar, corn syrup, or a combination of the two. In the past, health concerns about sugar led to the development of artificial sweeteners such as aspartame, saccharin and sucralose, whose sugary taste, but calorie-free content, made them a popular addition to diet soft drinks and other health-conscious foods. Today, most low-calorie soft drinks are sweetened with aspartame, otherwise known as Nutrasweet or E951, which is 200 times sweeter than sugar.

Various media stories have in the past cast doubt on the safety of aspartame, with claims that it causes headaches, seizures, mood changes and allergic reactions, for example. However, numerous scientific studies have failed to find conclusive evidence that it poses a significant health threat. In Europe, the official Acceptable Daily Intake (ADI) for aspartame remains set at 40 milligrams per kilogram of body weight per day. To exceed this safe dose, the average British adult would have to consume more than 14 cans of low-calorie soft drinks every day.

The long-term health of most British children would benefit from reducing both the total amount of added sugar they consume and the frequency with which they consume it. If both these measures were adopted they would be less likely to become obese or develop tooth decay. However, trying to prevent children from having *any* sugary foods, sweets or soft drinks is unlikely to work and could store up problems for the future. Children need to learn how to control their own intakes.

What can you do?

◆ **Try to limit your child's total intake of sugary drinks and foods.**

Encourage your child to drink water, rather than always reaching for sweet drinks. Consider whether they would be better off eating a school lunch rather than dining off a packed lunch containing sugary snacks. Find out whether your child's school has vending machines selling chocolate and fizzy drinks: if it has, consider asking the school to remove them.

◆ **Discourage grazing.**

Try to reduce the number of times during the day when your child consumes sugary snacks or drinks. Grazing and snacking are bad for teeth.

◆ **Set a good example yourself.**

Children learn a lot from the eating habits and attitudes of their parents.

◆ **Think about what you buy.**

When food shopping, check labels to see if there is any added sugar. You will find it in surprising places, including soup, baked beans and tomato ketchup. Many breakfast cereals marketed for children contain large amounts of added sugar. Some fruit drinks are also high in added sugar.

◆ **Make sure your children clean their teeth.**

And don't let them drink fruit juice or any other sugary drink after they have cleaned their teeth at bedtime.

Further advice

British Nutrition Foundation
Tel: 020 7404 6504
www.nutrition.org.uk
Information on the nutritional needs of school children and adolescents.

Food Standards Agency
Tel: 020 7276 8000
www.foodstandards.gov.uk
News, information and advice on all aspects of food safety and nutrition.

The Food Commission
Tel: 020 7837 2250
www.foodcomm.org.uk
Independent advice and information on healthy eating.

Related worries

7. Eats too much junk food or convenience food
12. Will only eat a narrow range of foods/has food fads
35. Doesn't get enough vitamins from his/her normal diet

WORRY 4

Spends too much time watching TV or playing computer games

36% of parents worried

Chances: HIGH   **Consequences: MEDIUM**   **Control: HIGH**

Most children spend much more time watching TV or playing computer games than being physically active. Watching too much TV has various undesirable effects. The lack of physical activity, combined with the exposure to adverts for high-calorie foods and soft drinks, is helping to fuel an epidemic of childhood obesity. Furthermore, staying up late to watch TV or play computer games can deprive children of sleep, with adverse effects on their mental and physical wellbeing. Children who watch more than two hours of TV a day also tend to perform worse at school, especially in reading.

The evidence that violent TV programmes or computer games cause individuals to become more violent is inconclusive. But, at best, violent images are unlikely to do children any good.

For most children watching TV is a major part of life. They spend an average of three hours a day doing it – more than they spend on anything else apart from going to school and sleeping. And when they are not watching TV, there is a good chance they may be playing computer or video games instead.

Nearly all British homes (99 per cent) have at least one TV, and three-quarters have two or more; more than four out of ten homes have a computer. Households with children are significantly more likely than adult-only households to have two or more TVs, a video recorder, games console and access to the Internet. Moreover, TV is now available 24 hours a day from more than 150 TV channels. Compare this with the 1980s, when only four channels were broadcasting, and only from 6 am to midnight.

Does any of this matter? Parents express a number of different concerns. The first is that TV programmes or computer games might have a harmful influence on their children's attitudes and behaviour, and in particular that repeated exposure to images of violence could encourage some individuals to become more aggressive or violent themselves. Many parents certainly seem to regard violent TV programmes as a problem. For example, one 2001 study found that 6 out of 10 British parents had intervened at least once to change the channel their child was watching after judging that a programme was unsuitable.

A second concern is that when children are watching TV or playing computer games they are not doing other things that could be more beneficial to them, such as engaging in social activities or physical exercise.

A third concern is that children who stay up late to watch TV or play on the computer won't get enough sleep. Research in this area is notoriously difficult to conduct. Scientists investigating the effects of TV find it hard to collect accurate data on children's viewing habits, and harder still to separate the specific impact of watching TV from a host of other factors affecting children's behaviour.

The connection between TV viewing and violent or anti-social behaviour remains controversial, and the research evidence is far from consistent. Experts really are divided on this issue. Nonetheless, there are some grounds for at least mild concern. In the USA, research has shown that by the time children leave primary school they will have seen several thousand murders and countless other violent acts portrayed on television. Saturday morning TV, despite being intended for child viewers, exposes them to an average of 25 violent acts an hour. In addition, more than three-quarters of computer games are based on violent themes and at least a fifth portray violence towards women.

Of course, the mere fact that children are exposed to violent images doesn't prove that they will become more violent as a consequence. Children have been exposed to violent ideas or images for generations; you only have to think of classic children's stories such as *Little Red Riding Hood*, for example. What some experts argue, however, is that TV is a far more immediate and powerful medium and hence its effect may be greater. And there is some evidence to suggest that this may be the case.

Many studies over the past decade have found that watching TV can have a short-term effect of promoting aggressive thoughts and behaviour. While the behavioural changes found in these studies have often been small and temporary, they have been consistent with the practical experience of many teachers and parents. Many primary school teachers, for example, know that after a popular action film has been shown on TV, some children will be acting out the characters and plots in the playground the next day. It is usually clear to everyone that both the film and the children's play-acting are in the realm of fantasy rather than reality. Nonetheless, the suspicion remains that, for a few children at least, the dividing line between fantasy and reality might occasionally become blurred.

Perhaps more worrying are the results from one of the few large-scale studies to track the consequences of TV-watching over a long period of time.

Researchers monitored children's TV viewing habits and then assessed the same individuals 17 years later. They discovered that people who had watched three hours or more of TV a day when they were children were subsequently five times more likely to commit a violent act resulting in serious injury, compared with those who had watched less than one hour of TV a day.

Findings like this must be interpreted with caution. Do they really prove that TV is the direct cause of violent behaviour, or might it be that naturally aggressive individuals also tend to watch more TV? Social and economic factors must also be taken into account. Growing up in a low-income household and having a poor education might tend to make someone more likely both to be aggressive and to spend a lot of time watching TV. In other words, the TV-watching might be a symptom of other factors rather than a direct cause of violent or anti-social behaviour.

The consequences of too much TV

One of the few things that many researchers do agree upon is that if children are affected by violent images then some individuals will be more strongly affected than others, both because of their personality and their circumstances. For example, the evidence suggests that individuals with risk-taking or excitement-seeking personalities respond more strongly to TV images. The link between TV watching and violence also seems to be generally stronger in boys than in girls. Parents of boys who show tendencies towards violence are the ones who perhaps should think most carefully about this issue.

Whether or not TV and computer games are positively harmful, there is no doubt that while children are engaged in these pastimes they aren't doing other things that would be more beneficial to them. To use the business jargon, watching TV and playing computer games have 'opportunity costs'. They are essentially solitary and sedentary pastimes.

While they are sitting in front of a TV or computer screen, children do not get any physical exercise. And people who are physically inactive are more likely to become overweight or obese, with potentially damaging consequences for their health. A large proportion of British children now have sedentary, inactive lifestyles. A third of boys aged 7–14 don't get the recommended minimum of one hour of moderate physical activity a day. Girls are even more inactive, with half of all seven- to 14-year-olds falling below the recommended minimum. At the same time, a large and increasing proportion of British children are overweight or clinically obese.

Clearly, television can't take all the blame for childhood obesity, but it does seem to be a contributing factor. Research has found that children who watch relatively little TV are less likely to be overweight than children who watch it a lot. The differences are considerable: children who watch less than one hour a day of TV are 40 per cent less likely to be overweight than those who watch four hours or more.

Television also has a significant influence on children's diets. Children who watch a lot of TV are found to be more likely to choose the food products they see advertised there. (Advertising really *does* work, which should come as no surprise in view of the £14 billion a year spent on it in the UK.) Many of the food products and drinks that are advertised on TV are high in sugar and/or fat, and this is especially true of many products aimed at children.

Staying up late at night to watch TV or play computer games can also deprive children of sleep, with potentially damaging consequences for their mental and physical well-being. Many children and teenagers don't get enough sleep anyway, and anything that adds to this problem should be avoided if at all possible (see Worry 15, page 81). More than half of eldest children have a TV in their bedroom, a third have a games console and a quarter have a video recorder. In our view, no child's bedroom should contain a TV. Bedrooms are for sleeping in.

Perhaps most worrying of all, however, is the relationship between TV-watching and school performance. There is evidence that children who watch more than two hours of TV a day tend to perform worse at school, possibly because of tiredness. Reading appears to be the area worst affected: children who watch more TV do less homework and read less while at home.

At worst, then, watching too much TV could make your child violent, obese, sleep-deprived and perform poorly at school. But, surely, you may be thinking, TV also has positive aspects; it helps us to relax and feel better. Even here, though, the evidence is not entirely positive.

Research suggests that watching TV is not a sure-fire recipe for happiness. If anything, it is correlated with *un*happiness. One study found that adults who watched a lot of TV were less happy on average than those who watched only a little. This might be because people who watch a lot of TV tend to have less satisfactory social lives. One of the biggest causes of personal happiness is our relationships with other people, and someone who spends a lot of time watching TV will probably be spending less time interacting with others. Curiously, the one exception seems to be people who regularly watch a lot of TV soaps, who were found to be slightly happier.

So, are we suggesting that children should not watch TV? Definitely not. TV can be stimulating and educational in the broadest sense, while computer games can help to improve hand eye co-ordination and spatial skills. We all need to spend time relaxing and unwinding, even if that involves vegetating in front of the telly for a while. However, watching several hours a day of mindless pap is unlikely to do children any good. It will certainly deprive them of opportunities to do other things that would be better for their social, emotional and physical development.

What can you do?

◆ *Plan what you're going to watch.*

Encourage your child to make positive choices about the TV programmes they watch. Talk to them about TV and ask why they like some programmes more than others. Discourage them from channel hopping and get them to switch off when their chosen programme has finished. Don't leave the TV on as permanent background: if no one is really watching, switch it off.

◆ *Think carefully before putting a TV or computer in your child's bedroom.*

You cannot easily control how or when your child will use a TV or computer in their bedroom. TVs and computers in bedrooms compete with sleep.

◆ *Have firm rules about bedtime.*

Try not to let your child's desire to stay up and watch TV, or play on the computer, eat into their sleep. They will suffer for it the next day.

◆ *Try to avoid eating meals in front of the TV.*

Most of us like to do this from time to time, but it shouldn't become a normal way of life. If nothing else, it removes a valuable time in the day when parents and children can talk to each other.

◆ *Watch TV together sometimes.*

Watching TV together allows you to discuss the programme with your child. It also allows you to point out the differences between TV and reality.

◆ **Don't be a slave to the TV schedule.**

Record favourite programmes and view them at a convenient time when they will not get in the way of other activities such as socialising or taking exercise. Recording programmes will also give you more scope to control what your children watch.

◆ **Try not to over-use TV as an easy substitute for a baby-sitter.**

It's OK to do this once in a while, to give yourself a break, but try not to make it a way of life.

◆ **Set a good example yourself.**

Don't slob out in front of the telly for hours every night and then complain when your children do the same. Research has shown that one of the key factors affecting the quantity and type of TV that children watch is the TV-viewing behaviour of their parents.

◆ **Make a plan for the holidays.**

You may need to impose stricter rules during school holidays. For example, you might consider imposing a rule such as no TV before 4 pm. That might encourage your children to go out and do something active or social. Find other things for them to do, and encourage them to invite their friends around to the house.

◆ **Encourage other hobbies.**

Support and encourage your child to engage regularly in sports and other physically active pastimes. If children are given attractive alternatives to TV they will often pursue them.

Further advice

LifeBytes

www.lifebytes.gov.uk

Health advice for 11- to 14-year-olds, with suggestions for how much and what kind of exercise they should do.

Broadcasting Standards Commission

Tel: 020 7808 1000

www.bsc.org.uk

Handles complaints about TV programmes.

Related worries

7. Eats too much junk food or convenience food

15. Does not get enough sleep

32. Does not get enough physical exercise

34. Is always asking for things or money

WORRY 5

Is growing up too fast

33% of parents worried

....

Chances: HIGH   **Consequences: LOW**   **Control: MEDIUM**

Young people are becoming sexually active younger, although the age of puberty has not fallen much in recent decades. The average boy has his first sexual experience at 13, while for girls the average age is 14. However, it is not clear that children's social and emotional development has kept pace with their more precocious behaviour. They may be dressing and behaving like adults at younger ages, but they do not necessarily think or feel like adults.

Society exerts many pressures on children and adolescents to emulate the ways of adults. However, children have in some respects become less independent in recent decades. One reason is that parents increasingly restrict children's freedom, and hence their opportunities for learning about life, out of concern for their safety.

The notion that children are growing up faster nowadays has been around for generations and to some extent says more about parents than it does about children. Watching them grow up, become independent and leave home can be hard for any parent.

The most obvious sign of growing up is puberty. The first physical sign that a girl is entering puberty is when her breasts start to develop and pubic hair starts to grow, which typically happens at around the age of ten. The start of menstrual periods usually follows about three years later. However, the timing varies considerably, with some girls developing much earlier (or later) than others. A variation of two to three years either side of the average should be no cause for concern. A substantial minority of girls have their first period before leaving primary school.

The ages at which mothers and daughters start their periods are to some extent correlated, which means that a girl whose mother started earlier than average is more likely to start early herself. There is also research evidence that earlier puberty in girls is associated with family conflict, particularly the absence of a father.

On average boys reach puberty a year or two later than girls. The first physical sign that a boy is entering puberty is an increase in the growth rate of his scrotum and testicles (though of course this change may not be apparent to even the most observant of parents). Pubic hair and facial hair appear later, followed by the production of sperm and deepening of the voice. By the age of 15, the average boy's voice will have broken and he will have discovered masturbation.

Many parents believe that their children are reaching puberty far younger than they did. This is, however, a myth. While a typical young woman in the 19th century would have started her periods at the age of 17, the weight of evidence shows that this historical trend towards earlier puberty has bottomed out. The biggest drop occurred between the 19th century and the mid-20th century, and the age of puberty has not continued to fall dramat-ically over the past few decades. Indeed, research in the UK has found that the age at which girls have their first period has changed little, if at all, since the 1960s. There does, however, appear to be greater recognition that a few girls show very early development of breasts or pubic hair, a fact that probably went unreported in the past.

Scientists are uncertain as to why children in wealthier nations reach puberty earlier now than they did a century ago. Among the possible explanations are better nutrition, lack of physical activity and chemicals in the environment that mimic the effects of hormones. Another factor may be the trend towards smaller families, since the evidence shows that the fewer brothers or sisters a girl has, the earlier she is likely to start menstruating.

Growth and sexual activity

As well as growing faster, children also end up bigger than they once did. The adult height in wealthier nations has been increasing at the rate of about 2 centimetres every decade. The average British man is now 5 feet 9 inches (1.75 metres) tall, and almost a third of young men under the age of 25 are 6 feet (1.8 metres) or taller. The average British woman is now 5 feet 4 inches (1.62 metres) tall.

Probably the most dramatic sense in which children *are* growing up faster is that they are becoming sexually active younger. Boys now typically have their first sexual experience when they are 13 years old, and girls when they are 14, while the most common age at which both sexes have full sexual intercourse for the first time is now 16. Not many years ago it was 17, and 50 years ago the average Briton was aged 20 before they lost their virginity – at least, according to the available evidence. (Incidentally, the sharpest drop in the average age at which people lost their virginity occurred during the 1950s, not the 'swinging sixties'.)

More than a quarter of young people nowadays have full sexual intercourse before the legally sanctioned age of 16, and the vast majority have done it before the age of 20. Statistics show that an individual is more likely to have sex before the age of 16 if they reach puberty earlier than average, if they come from a low-income or disrupted home, if they leave school without any qualifications, or if they learned about sex from their friends rather than at school.

Although young people are becoming sexually active younger, there is no clear-cut evidence that their social and emotional development has kept pace with their behaviour. Just because they dress and behave in some respects like adults does not mean they always think and feel like adults. The result can be a phase during adolescence when some individuals have the bodies of young adults but the minds and emotions of children. Their desire for independence and maturity can co-exist with a continuing need for parental security and guidance.

The risks of growing up too fast

Problems can arise for some individuals who become sexually active at an age when their physical development has temporarily run ahead of their emotional maturity. In line with this, researchers have found that 2 out of 5 young women and 1 out of 5 young men regret having sex when they were too young. (Of course, this also means that three-fifths of young women and four-fifths of young men do not regret it. Some may even wish they had started younger.)

One consequence of teenage sex can be unplanned pregnancy. Each year, around 8 out of every 1000 girls under the age of 16 become pregnant. A teenage girl is statistically more likely to become pregnant if she is the daughter of a teenage mother, or if she leaves school early with no qualifications. More than a quarter of sexually active girls who have no qualifications become pregnant before they are 18.

In one rather curious respect, children appear to be getting smarter. Over the past century, people's IQs have been increasing. Average IQ (intelligence quotient) scores in industrialised nations have been rising at the rate of about five points every decade. More specifically, what has been increasing is abstract reasoning ability – that is, the capacity to solve mental problems. There has, however, been no accompanying increase in people's factual knowledge, vocabulary, numerical ability or other aspects of mental capacity.

Scientists are not sure why IQ scores have been rising in this way, and various theories have been put forward to account for it, including better nutrition and more mental stimulation. According to one idea, children's brains receive more stimulation thanks to smaller families and the faster pace of modern urban life. Another suggestion is that children's brains are becoming increasingly agile because of their early exposure to the various complex stimuli in today's world. However, the simplest explanation is that people have just learned, through plentiful experience, to perform better on written tests.

The rate at which an individual grows up, in the broader sense of their social and emotional development, can be heavily influenced by their experience and the demands placed on them. To take an extreme case, the 'street children' who live rough in many developing nations in Asia, Africa and South America are forced to become physically and financially independent at an age when most British children would be regarded as incapable of looking after themselves. About 150 million street children all over the world work every day to support themselves and, often, other family members. Some are fending for themselves before they are five years old.

Even in the UK, difficult circumstances force some children to behave more like adults from an early age. For example, around 50,000 children under the age of 16 are caring for elderly, ill or disabled relatives. Many children in distressed families have a very strong sense of their responsibility for a needy parent or sibling. Caring for someone can help a child to develop independence, giving them a veneer of maturity and coping. But the price may be losing part of their childhood. Teachers can often detect clear signs of physical and emotional stress in children who are caring for sick or disabled relatives.

Society exerts many subtle, and not-so-subtle, pressures on children to emulate the ways of adults and to aspire to the trappings of adult life. British children are subjected to continual influence from the media – and hence also from their peers – to dress, talk and behave in adult-like ways.

TV, newspapers, magazines and advertising repeatedly expose children to adult fixations about beauty, fitness and sexuality. Young girls are bombarded with images of thin, perfect bodies; they are given detailed advice in magazines about dating and sex, and they are encouraged to adorn themselves with make-up and the latest fashions. 'Teen' magazines ostensibly aimed at 16- and 17-year-olds are actually read mostly by girls who are considerably younger. And the most glamorous careers to which many young people aspire, such as football, pop music, modelling and acting, often require deep commitment from an early age.

Some parents appear to have double standards about childhood and maturity. They would be rightly squeamish about encouraging their little girl to start wearing high fashion and make-up at the age of 12, let alone starting to have sex. Yet they would be delighted if she passed her GCSE maths four years earlier than normal. Some parents and schools push children to be academically precocious, in the dubious belief that faster always means better. But they tend to take the opposite view when it comes to social and sexual precocity.

That said, a few parents do encourage precocious sexuality – for example, by giving pre-pubertal girls bras before they have breasts.

So, are children *really* growing up faster these days? You could argue that the opposite is true. Despite the teen sex, the fashion-consciousness and other trappings of adulthood, British children are in some ways becoming *less* independent. In recent decades, parents have increasingly restricted children's freedom out of concern for their safety. Far fewer children now walk to school, travel independently or play outdoors freely with their friends than was the case 30 years ago. They may be somewhat safer as a result (though this is far from certain), but they are also deprived of valuable childhood experiences that would have contributed to their social and emotional development. And whereas 40 years ago many teenagers were earning a living, the majority of young people now remain in education or training until they are at least 18.

Children have always wanted to emulate aspects of adult life. In our view, there is no inherent harm in this – provided it does not intrude too much into childhood or lead young people into objectively risky behaviour such as smoking, drinking, using drugs or having unprotected sex. Parents can help by not pushing children to be precocious in other ways, such as academically, and by not placing unnecessary restrictions on their freedom. Children should be allowed to be children.

What can you do?

◆ *Value childhood.*

Give your children the time, space and support to be child-like when they want to be. Let them play childish games when they feel like it. Don't always direct their attention to the future world of exam grades and careers; childhood is more than just a preparation for adult life. Point out to them the benefits of being a child, such as having someone else to pay for everything, cook their food, provide them with free accommodation and buy them clothes.

◆ *Enjoy your child's childhood.*

Enjoy being with your child when he or she is young. Many adults have a lot to learn from the playfulness and creativity of ▶

children. Show your child that even parents are still capable of deriving pleasure from being playful.

◆ *Try to be consistent in your attitudes towards maturity.*

Don't push your child to be academically precocious in school whilst at the same time resisting their desire to be socially precocious outside school. When choosing a school, consider other things besides its record of academic attainment. In particular, think about how well the school would respect your child as an individual and help them to develop socially and emotionally.

◆ *Be honest with yourself.*

If you are worried about your child growing up too fast, think about why you are worried. Is it because your child is genuinely being pressured into inappropriate forms of adult behaviour?

Is it because they are shouldering more adult responsibilities than they should have to at their age? Or is it because you just don't want to lose them?

◆ *Encourage your child to think for him/herself.*

Be aware of the cultural and social pressures on children to adopt adult styles of dress, thought and behaviour. You couldn't entirely insulate them from these pressures, even if you wanted to, but you can at least encourage them to think critically and form their own views.

◆ *Make your child aware of the facts of life.*

Start talking to your child about sex, pregnancy, smoking, alcohol and drugs when they are young, as this will improve your chances of influencing their attitudes. Children sometimes find it easier to talk about sex 'in theory' – i.e., when the discussion is not specifically about them.

Further advice

Brook Advisory Centres

Helpline for young people: 0800 0185 023
www.brook.org.uk
E-mail: information@brookcentres.org.uk (for individual questions)
Walk-in centres, phone lines and website offering advice and information for young people regarding sex and relationships.

Sex Education Foundation

Tel: 020 7843 6052
www.ncb.org.uk/sef
Advice and information on sex for young people and parents.

NHS Direct

Tel: 0845 4647
www.nhsdirect.nhs.uk
Offers information on puberty.

Children's Play Council

Tel: 020 7843 6016
www.ncb.org.uk/cpc
Advice about better play and safe play for children.

Related worries

4. Spends too much time watching TV or playing computer games
14. Will not be successful in adult life if he/she does not do well at school

Alcohol

◆ Around a quarter (24%) of children aged 11–15 have had an alcoholic drink within the past week, and more than half have drunk alcohol at some time.

◆ The proportion of children who drink regularly has not increased consistently since the late 1980s. However, the *amount* of alcohol consumed by those who do drink has almost doubled: the average consumption has risen steadily from 5.3 units a week in 1990 to 10.5 units a week in 2002.

◆ Drinking is strongly related to age. Only 1 in 20 (5%) of 11-year-olds have drunk alcohol within the past week, compared with nearly half (47%) of 15-year-olds. The amount consumed also rises sharply with age. Among 11- to 13-year-olds who drank within the past week, the average alcohol consumption was 6.8 units, compared with 12.9 units for 15-year-olds.

◆ 1 in 20 (5%) of 14- to 15-year-olds regularly exceed the maximum intakes recommended for adults (21 units a week for men and 14 for women).

◆ Most children who have drunk alcohol within the past week have done so on only one or two days. Only a small minority (2%) have drunk on five or more days of the week. Children's drinking tends to occur mainly at the weekend.

◆ There is an established trend among teenagers for binge drinking (consuming five or more drinks in one session) and getting seriously drunk.

◆ Boys are more likely to drink than girls. They also consume more than girls. Among boys who drank within the past week, the average consumption was 11.5 units of alcohol, compared with 9.6 units for girls.

◆ Beer, lager and cider are still the most common types of drink consumed by child drinkers. However, alcopops have become increasingly popular, and were consumed by more than two-thirds (68%) of child drinkers in 2002. The proportion of children who drink spirits has also risen considerably over the past decade, whereas fewer now drink wine.

◆ Each year, around 50,000 teenagers are admitted to hospital accident and emergency units with acute alcohol intoxication.

The statistics quoted here derive mainly from government research carried out in England in 2002.

WORRY 6

Might be the victim of crime

32 % of parents worried

∙∙∙

Chances: HIGH   **Consequences: MEDIUM**   **Control: MEDIUM**

Compared with other countries, the UK still has relatively low rates of serious violent crime and murder. Children are very unlikely to be seriously injured or killed in a criminal attack. Fewer than ten children a year are murdered by strangers.

However, the picture is very different when it comes to less serious crime. One in four children claim to have been the victim of some sort of crime within the past year. In recent years there has been a rapid rise in low-level, opportunistic 'street crimes' such as assaults, robberies and muggings. Most street crime (which, despite its name, need not happen on the street) is committed by young males. Most of its victims are also young males. A large proportion of street crime is never reported to the police.

Children who are truanting or excluded from school are more likely to be the victims of street crime. They are also more likely to commit street crime. Therefore, anything that parents can do to prevent their children from truanting or being excluded from school should reduce their risk of suffering from crime, whether as perpetrator or victim.

A big problem with trying to understand trends in crime is the relative lack of solid statistics, especially where child victims are involved. Official police reports provide a reasonably accurate picture of recorded crime. But research suggests that only a small proportion of minor crimes are ever reported, so the official figures can reveal only part of the full picture. Moreover, police statistics fluctuate according to other factors such as changes in how particular crimes are defined and changes in the priorities or methods used by different police forces. An apparent rise or fall in a particular type of crime might therefore have little to do with any change in the real prevalence of that crime.

An alternative approach is to ask large numbers of people about their personal experiences of crime. This method produces a different set of figures, but these are also open to question because they rely on the accuracy and honesty of what people remember and say. Few surveys of crime victims include large numbers of children in their samples. The focus is usually on adults.

The few surveys that have focused on child victims have revealed a disturbingly high frequency of crime. For example, a 2003 survey of young people aged 12–16 found that 1 in 4 claimed to have been a victim of crime within the past year. More than half of these young crime victims said they had been on the receiving end of violence or physical abuse, and half had been the victim of robbery. Seven per cent said they had been bullied and 5 per cent said they had been sexually abused.

Similarly, in 2002 the anti-crime charity Crimestoppers conducted a nationwide survey in which more than 1000 ten- to 15-year-old boys and girls were interviewed about their experiences of crime. The survey found that at least 1 in 5 children had been the victim of some form of crime, with a quarter being attacked by someone their own age. Half the victims knew their assailant, yet less than half had reported the crime to the police. Indeed, nearly half had failed to tell even their parents. Almost 40 per cent said they would be more willing to report a crime if they could do so anonymously and hence avoid the risk of reprisal.

Children are statistically unlikely to be killed or seriously injured in a criminal attack. The UK has relatively low rates of serious violent crime and murder, and many of the violent attacks on children that do occur are committed by their parents, carers or relatives (see Worry 2, page 12).

However, Britain is experiencing a sharp rise in low-level attacks on individuals, especially children. Such attacks, involving mugging or robbery, are generally referred to as 'street crime'. Despite its name, 'street crime' means thefts, muggings, assaults or robberies involving an attack on an individual, regardless of where the incident occurs.

More than half of all street crimes in which the victim is a child occur during the afternoon, when children and young people are making their way home from school or socialising with friends. Incidents typically take place in streets, parks, alleyways, subways, public transport or shopping complexes.

The rise of street crime

While cash is still the most common target in street crime, nearly two-fifths of incidents involve a mobile phone being stolen or demanded. The phone is not always the sole target; sometimes it gets taken along with other items in a child's bag. Even so, more than a quarter of mobile phone robberies occur while the phone is in sight or in use. Children and young people are by far the most likely to have their phones stolen, with under-20s now accounting for more than half of all mobile phone theft victims.

Over the past ten years, street crime has risen in the UK for reasons that are far from clear. Some pundits have suggested that the big rise in street crime has resulted from the spread of mobile phones and other high-value disposable possessions. But this does not work as a full explanation because UK crime rates have outstripped those of other countries where mobile phones are just as readily available. While the UK remains one of the safest countries in the world in terms of murder, it is now one of the worst for robbery.

Although the general picture is one of growing crime, there are large regional differences. Robbery rates in England and Wales are nearly double those of Scotland, where rates have fallen over the last few years. Much of the crime in England is concentrated in two hot spots: London and the West Midlands. Unsurprisingly, urban areas are far more prone to street crime than rural areas.

What is perhaps more worrying than the rise in street crime is the fall in the ages of both victims and offenders. Over the past decade, robbery and street crime have become largely youth crimes. In London, for example, the number of robberies committed against under-20s has tripled, and young people under 20 now make up nearly half of all victims of street crime. The average age of offenders has shown an even more marked decrease: more than three-quarters of all street crime is now committed by young people under the age of 20.

Robbery is very much a male crime. In fact, 9 out of 10 suspects arrested are male. Three out of 4 victims of robbery are also male. In addition, males are more likely to be injured or physically assaulted during a robbery. So, the facts firmly contradict the popular belief that girls are at greater risk than boys from street crime. Parents should be more worried about their sons than about their daughters.

Most robberies against boys are committed by two or more offenders acting together, whereas street crimes against girls tend to be snatch-and-run incidents involving a single offender. Since most victims are young males, it follows that most street crimes (around 70 per cent, in fact) are carried out by two or more offenders, giving rise to media claims that Britain has developed a 'child gang' culture.

Experts continue to debate the reasons why crime is such a predominantly male activity. But understanding why most criminals are male is perhaps easier than understanding why most of their victims are male. One possible explanation is that boys expose themselves to more risk than girls. According to this theory, the typical young male is more confident, spends more time out and about, and is more likely to put himself in harm's way. Another possible factor may be that male criminals somehow see young males as more 'acceptable' targets than young females.

One factor that has a large impact on whether a child will commit or be the victim of crime is whether they are excluded or truanting from school. A quarter of pupils claim to have truanted for at least one day in the last year, and this makes them statistically twice as likely to have committed a crime.

Exclusion from school makes things even worse. While a quarter of mainstream pupils claim to have committed a crime in the last year, nearly 70 per cent of excluded pupils say they turned to crime. And once they start, they seem to find it hard to stop. The average number of offences committed by a convicted teenage male is 16, whereas for a male excluded from school it is 44. Making sure that children attend school regularly may be one of the most effective ways of reducing the risk that they will commit or be the victims of a crime.

What can you do?

◆ *Arrange for your child to travel with someone.*

Try to ensure that your child travels to and from school with an adult or with friends. Lone children are more likely to be targeted than groups.

◆ *Tell your child not to display valuable items.*

Advise your child not to display their wallet, money, mobile phone, jewellery or other desirable items in public places. Young people are more likely to be attacked if they are seen carrying valuable items. If your child must use a mobile phone in public, tell him or her to use it discreetly and in a place where there are plenty of people around.

◆ *Be especially concerned about boys.*

If you have a son, point out to him that boys are at greater risk from street crime than girls. Boys should not have a false sense of security, even if they feel strong and confident. Knowing the facts might make them more vigilant.

◆ *Try to ensure that your child attends school every day.*

Do your best to stop your child truanting or being excluded from school. Apart from the obvious educational disadvantages, exclusion and truanting increase a child's chances of becoming a victim or a perpetrator of crime. If in doubt, check with the school about their attendance record. Occasional absences might not have been reported to you.

◆ *Tell your child to put their personal safety first.*

One golden rule you should drum into your child is that their personal safety always takes priority over money and possessions. If in any doubt about what to do in a confrontation, they should hand over their money, wallet or mobile phone rather than risk being injured. Boys, in particular, should be told to resist any macho instinct to fight. It is far better to run away than to end up being injured.

◆ *Talk to your child about crime before it happens.*

Make it clear that if they ever were to become the victim of a crime, you would not blame or criticise them. A natural reaction of someone who has been a victim is to feel humiliated and not want to tell anyone. As a parent, you should aim to reduce the risk of not being told. As in so many other areas, the key lies in establishing good communication with your child. Keep a rough track of their possessions, as a sudden 'loss' of a high value item might be a clue that something has happened.

◆ *Talk to the experts.*

Find out if your school arranges any special classes or talks on personal security. These are often provided by the local police through schools and cover issues such as situational awareness and being street-wise. The police should be able to point out the highest risk areas in your local region. ▶

◆ *Don't teach your child to fight back.*

We have some doubts about sending children to martial arts classes purely as a way of improving their self-defence. Martial arts such as karate, judo and kick-boxing have many benefits, and they can make excellent hobbies if properly taught. But martial arts should be learned for their own sake. Encouraging a young child to regard a martial art purely as a weapon to use against would-be criminals could give them a false sense of security and might even encourage them to seek out conflict. It is better for young people to avoid risky situations in the first place than to try fighting their way out. Their assailant may be bigger, stronger, armed with a knife, or part of a gang.

Further advice

Crimestoppers
Freephone: 0800 555111 (Anonymity guaranteed)
www.crimestoppers-uk.org
Offers support to young victims of crime, as well as resources to help prevent children becoming involved in criminal activity.

Childline
Helpline: 0800 1111
www.childline.org.uk
Telephone counselling service for children.

Related worries

2. Might be abducted or murdered
10. Might be the victim of physical violence
19. Is reckless and not sufficiently aware of dangers
28. Is being bullied
37. Is not safe on public transport
38. Might get into trouble with the authorities or commit a crime

WORRY 7

Eats too much junk food or convenience food

31% of parents worried

....

Chances: HIGH   **Consequences: HIGH**   **Control: HIGH**

Ever-increasing quantities of convenience food, fast food and junk food are being eaten in the UK. Their high fat, sugar and salt content make them especially attractive to children, who also respond well to their consistency and predictability. Advertising adds even further to their appeal.

The main hazard to any child (or adult) who eats too much of this type of food is obesity, which has reached epidemic proportions. Obese children are at risk from life-threatening illnesses such as diabetes and heart disease. Research shows that young people who consume large amounts of fast food tend to have a larger calorie (total energy) intake and weigh more.

Even if your child is not overweight, eating lots of junk food will reduce their likelihood of having a diet containing a healthy balance of vitamins, minerals, fibre, antioxidants and other nutrients. Only 1 in 7 children in the UK eats the recommended five portions a day of fruit and vegetables.

Another concern is salt, which is present in large quantities in many convenience foods. Excessive salt intake is a risk factor for high blood pressure and heart disease. British children consume far more than the recommended intake, and most of it comes from processed food.

The British diet – never the envy of other nations – has changed markedly over the past 30 years, and not entirely for the better. One of the biggest transformations has been the huge rise in the consumption of convenience foods and fast food.

Since the 1970s the traditional 'three meals a day' have progressively been replaced by ready-made meals, snacks, pub grub, restaurant meals and fast food. More than a third of all the food consumed in the UK is now eaten outside the home, with 1 person in 3 eating a ready-made meal more than once a week, compared with only 1 in 6 people in France. The rate of growth has been remarkable, with the demand for instant meals growing by 44 per cent between 1998 and 2002 alone.

The amount of food bought from fast food outlets has grown by more than a fifth over the past decade. The first McDonalds in the UK opened in Woolwich, south east London, in 1974; now there are more than 1200 McDonalds and more than a quarter of a million other food outlets in the UK. And when we Brits are not feasting on fast food or takeaways, we are eating snacks and convenience foods at home. Research shows that the foods eaten most often by young people are white bread, savoury snacks, potato chips, biscuits, potatoes and chocolate.

Does this matter? Some of the ready-made meals and convenience foods sold in supermarkets are of good nutritional quality and do not differ greatly from home-cooked food (other than perhaps in expense). But some types of convenience food and fast food are of dubious nutritional quality and can pose a long-term threat to children's health if eaten in excessive quantities.

Junk food is typically high in energy (calories), saturated fat, salt and/or sugar, while providing relatively modest amounts of vitamins, minerals, antioxidants and fibre. A fast-food meal comprising a large cheeseburger, regular fries, large milkshake and an ice cream dessert can contain more than 60 grams of fat and 1500 Calories [2] of energy, which is 80–90 per cent of the *total* daily energy requirement for the average 7- to 10-year-old.

Government guidelines recommend that no more than 35 per cent of our total energy intake should come from fat, as opposed to carbohydrates or protein. However, if you eat some types of fast food, more than half the energy you take in will come in the form of fat, accompanied by a hefty dose of salt. Some frozen burgers contain meat that is 50 per cent fat; a single portion can contain 6 teaspoons of fat even after it has been grilled. Children's packed lunches can also be a problem, as many of the products that supermarkets sell specifically for children's lunch boxes, such as processed cheese, crisps, chocolate and soft drinks, contain large amounts of fat, salt and/or sugar.

There are good reasons for believing that this growth in the consumption of junk food and fast food has been a major contributor to the current epidemic of childhood obesity. For example, scientists have found that young people who eat a lot of fast food also tend to have a larger total energy intake and weigh more than those who eat moderate quantities. One study found that adolescent girls who ate fast food at least four times a week had an average energy intake that was between 185 and 260 Calories a day more than girls who ate less fast food. That equates to five or six Mars bars a week. Research has also shown that children tend to consume more calories when they eat a restaurant meal than when they eat at home, mainly because restaurant food is more calorific and comes in larger portions.

The risks of obesity and other hazards

Obesity can result from many factors, including lack of physical activity and genetic predispositions. But eating too much fatty or sugary food is a key factor. If you consume more food energy than your body expends, then the surplus will be stored as body fat. Ultimately, the only certain way for

[2] 1 Calorie (with a big C) = 1000 calories (with a small c) = 4200 joules = 4.2 kJ.

children to avoid becoming overweight is to be physically active and not over-eat. Sadly, it appears that many children are doing neither.

The proportion of children in the UK and other countries who are overweight or obese started to rise sharply in the 1980s and continues to grow at an alarming rate. At least 1 in 5 children in the UK are overweight and at least 1 in 10 are clinically obese. Moreover, the fattest children have become proportionally even fatter. Fat children tend to become fat adults, and obesity is now a global health problem.

Obesity is bad news in many ways. Fat people are more likely to develop high blood pressure and coronary heart disease. Someone who is overweight in childhood is twice as likely to die of heart disease in adulthood. Childhood obesity has also fuelled a large rise in diabetes, which was once rare among adolescents. Other consequences of childhood obesity can include sleep disorders and psychological problems: today's image-obsessed society has a strongly negative view of obesity, so a fat child may be teased, suffer from low self-esteem and find it harder to make friends.

As if that were not enough, high-fat diets and obesity also increase the risks of certain sorts of cancer, including cancers of the colon, rectum and breast. The evidence suggests that diet plays a role in about a third of all cancers, and some experts regard obesity as second only to smoking as a cause of cancer.

Of course, not every child who regularly eats junk food is obese, and obesity is not the only hazard. Another cause for concern is excessive salt (sodium chloride), which is found in high quantities in most fast and processed foods. Too much salt in the diet can lead to raised blood pressure, which is a risk factor for heart disease and strokes. Most of us eat far more salt than we need. The average British adult consumes 9 grams a day, which is considerably more than the amount needed. Government guidelines recommend that adults should reduce their salt intake by a third, to no more than 6 grams a day.

Excessive salt intake is an even bigger problem for children, who need less than adults. The recommended maximum intake is 2 grams a day for children aged 1–6 years, and 5 grams a day for children aged 7–14 years. Most children eat about twice as much salt as the recommended level, and more than half of it comes from processed food.

Researchers have found that children who add salt to their food tend to have higher blood pressure. You don't need to add salt to your food in order to consume too much, however. Much of our salt intake is hidden in everyday foods like bread, baked beans and tinned soup. Some products that are aimed specifically at children contain surprisingly large amounts of salt; for example, a single serving of tinned pasta or a takeaway burger meal can give a young child more than the recommended daily intake of salt.

To make matters worse, some products have become saltier over the past 25 years, as manufacturers have tried to make them taste more attractive. For instance, the salt content of crisps has almost doubled, rising from an average of 0.54 grams of salt per 100 grams in 1978 to 1.05 grams per 100 grams in 2003. Baked beans also contain more salt now than in 1978. The Food Standards Agency and the Department of Health have been trying to persuade food manufacturers and retailers to reduce the salt contents of processed foods.

So, eating too much fast food, processed food and convenience food can make children fat and give them too much salt. But it is undesirable for other reasons too. A child who routinely fills up on burgers, chips, fried chicken, pizza, biscuits and fizzy drinks is unlikely to be eating lots of fruit and vegetables as well. This is a general national problem. Despite a growing awareness of the need for healthy food, we British still eat relatively little fruit, vegetables and fish compared with people in other countries.

The World Health Organisation (WHO) and British government guidelines strongly recommend that we should all be eating at least five portions of fruit and vegetables a day. In reality, many of us eat far less than this, and children eat even less than adults. The average English child consumes 2.7 portions of fruit and vegetables a day, which is just over half the recommended minimum. Only 1 in 7 children eat the recommended five or more portions a day, while about the same proportion of children eat less than one portion a day. Many children and young people would undoubtedly benefit from eating more fruit and vegetables and less food that is high in calories and saturated fatty acids.

Incidentally, people are sometimes surprised at the sorts of things that can count as one of their five portions a day of fruit and vegetables. Examples include a glass of fruit juice, a portion of baked beans and one heaped tablespoon of dried fruit. So, if you're a parent who finds it hard to persuade your child to eat fresh fruit, salad or green vegetables, don't despair at the prospect of feeding them five portions a day.

Why do our children eat so much junk food? In today's Britain, where time is in short supply and the majority of parents work, speed and convenience have become necessities rather than luxuries. Then, of course, there is the taste. Most children prefer food that contains a lot of fat, salt and/or sugar.

Something else that makes fast food appealing to children is its consistency and predictability. Research shows that children positively prefer foods that are familiar. Repeated exposure to a particular type of food, whether healthy or unhealthy, can therefore have a big influence on how much a child will eat.

The trend for larger and larger portions also helps to boost sales – and children's calorie intakes. Fast food outlets and food manufacturers increasingly market their products in super-sized portions or packages. These might offer better value for money, but they also encourage children (and adults) to eat more.

Yet another reason why children eat so much junk food is because of all the clever advertising that is aimed at them by the food and drink industry. The Food Commission has found that for every genuinely healthy food product marketed specifically for children, there are at least ten others that are 'nutritional disasters', because of their high levels of saturated fat, salt or sugar. The Commission has rightly criticised British football clubs, which have a big influence on the nation's children, for promoting fast food products, soft drinks and confectionary as part of lucrative commercial deals.

What can you do?

◆ **Help your child discover the pleasures of fresh food.**

One of the best defences against junk food is enabling children to appreciate how much better fresh food can taste. And a good way of leading younger children to appreciate fresh food is by letting them help you shop for the ingredients, prepare the meal, and cook it. Even very young children can learn to appreciate and enjoy good food. You can create healthier versions of fast food, such as burgers containing less fat and salt, or thick-cut chips that contain less fat than thin-cut or crinkly-cut chips.

◆ **Remember that familiarity tends to breed preference.**

Getting your child hooked on junk food will strengthen their preference for it, while getting them used to fresh food at an early age should have the opposite effect. ▶

◆ *Try your best to ensure your child gets at least five portions a day of fruit and vegetables.*

Remember that a portion can be, for example, a glass of fruit juice or some baked beans.

◆ *Discourage grazing or snacking between meals.*

Grazing or snacking will simply encourage them to eat more of the wrong things. It's bad for their teeth as well.

◆ *Think about what you buy.*

Convenience foods differ greatly in terms of the energy, fat, sugar and salt they contain. Choosing wisely can therefore make a big difference, so it is a good idea to read the labels. Unfortunately, nutritional information is not widely available in fast food outlets. Don't assume that a food product is healthy just because it is aimed at children. Think about the contents of their packed lunches as well: they might be better off, both nutritionally and socially, eating school lunches instead.

◆ *Try to remember a few benchmark figures.*

A typical schoolchild needs roughly 1900 Calories a day, depending on their age and sex and level of physical activity. That equates to about seven Mars bars. If all that energy came in the form of three meals a day, then each meal should contain an average of about 600-700 Calories. If you add in snacks and soft drinks consumed between meals, then the energy content of each meal should obviously be lower. For comparison:

* A standard (330 ml) can of cola drink contains about 140 Calories.

* A modest portion of takeaway chips has about 200 Calories.

* A large burger with cheese can easily contain more than 500 Calories.

◆ *Set a good example.*

Bad habits are catching. Parents who regularly guzzle unhealthy food are encouraging their children to do the same.

◆ *Try to eat some meals together as a family.*

Research shows that the nutritional quality of children's food intake tends to be higher when they eat as part of a family meal. Parents are more likely to cook with fresh ingredients if the whole family is eating together, whereas if everyone eats individually and at different times they are more likely to resort to convenience foods or takeaways.

◆ *Keep an eye on your child's TV-watching habits.*

Spending too long in front of the TV can fuel children's desire for junk food, by exposing them to adverts. They also get less exercise.

Further advice

NHS Direct

Tel: 0845 4647

www.nhsdirect.nhs.uk

Advice on all aspects of health, including the diagnosis, treatment and prevention of conditions caused by poor diet.

Food Standards Agency

Tel: 020 7276 8000

www.foodstandards.gov.uk

Authoritative information concerning children and fast food, salt and healthy eating.

The Food Commission

Tel: 020 7837 2250

www.foodcomm.org.uk

Resources covering children's nutrition and fast food.

British Dietetic Association

Tel: 0121 200 8080

www.bda.uk.com

E-mail: info@bda.uk.com

Pamphlets on children's dietary needs.

Fast Food Nutrition Fact Explorer

www.fatcalories.com

Allows you to calculate the nutritional value of items sold by fast food chains. Also offers recommendations for 'healthy' options in fast food restaurants.

Related worries

3. Eats too much sugar and sweet foods
4. Spends too much time watching TV or playing computer games
12. Will only eat a narrow range of foods/has food fads
32. Does not get enough physical exercise

Worry **8**

Has friends who are or could be a bad influence

28% of parents worried

Chances: HIGH   **Consequences: MEDIUM**   **Control: MEDIUM**

Friends and peers (other children of a comparable age) are an important and influential part of a developing child's life. By the time most children reach secondary school, they are spending more time with their peers than with their parents.

Peer-group influence is not just a matter of friends exerting pressure on a child to behave in certain ways. It is also a matter of the child seeking out friends who fit with his or her own preferences and style – in other words, peer preference as well as peer pressure. Bad behaviour will rarely be the sole and exclusive result of social pressure from friends; it may be more a question of children who are prone to behave badly being drawn to each other's company.

Beyond deciding where to live and what kind of school their child will attend, parents can exert relatively little control over who their child will choose as friends. They can, however, make a big difference to how much their child will be influenced by those peers. Children who have strong relation-ships with their parents are less likely to succumb to undesirable peer influences.

Parents obviously have profound and long-term influences on their children's development. Not only do they have a direct impact through their daily interactions with their children, they also have a big indirect influence in many different ways. Parents, for example, are normally the ones who determine where a family lives, how affluent it is, which school their child will attend and hence the sorts of other children their child will encounter. However, a child's peers also have a big influence. For example, a child's spoken accent will tend to reflect the accent of their peers rather than their parents. Children of secondary school age spend roughly twice as much time with their peers as with their parents or other adults.

Children go through different stages of friendship. While the timing varies considerably between individuals, the general pattern is for friends to play an increasingly prominent role as children get older. During the first couple of years of life, children are much more interested in themselves than in other children. Between the ages of about two and seven they socialise with children of both sexes. During the later years of primary school their friendships tend to be more with children of the same sex. Once they reach adolescence, the picture becomes more mixed as sexual attraction starts to intrude.

The peak period for peer influence seems to be between the ages of about 11 and 13, when adolescents are going through marked hormonal and physical changes and are becoming more independent. This is also the time when they start secondary school and establish new friends in a new environment. By the time a young person is in their late teens, their fundamental life choices tend once again to reflect the influence of their parents, as family background exerts a prominent role in big decisions about education and careers.

The desire to belong and affiliate with a group is a normal part of growing up; it supports children's growing independence from their parents and helps them to define their personality. During the early teen years the group will have as much, or more, influence on a child than will individual best friends or the school, especially in the case of girls.

Parents sometimes worry about the suitability of the friends their children are mixing with. Of course, they want their children to have friends – but they don't always like the particular friends their children have chosen. Unfortunately, some parents are too ready to judge their children's friends by superficial criteria such as the way they dress and talk. But the truth is that a polite, well-presented child can still be a malign influence, while a youth with body piercing and unconventional hair might in fact be a decent and supportive friend.

Friends can have a major bearing on a child's self-esteem and social status at school. This is especially true for girls. They can also provide valuable support to a child during times of instability at home, such as when parents are divorcing, or there is a death in the family.

But while the influence of peers is largely positive for most children, this is not always the case. Mixing with a group of young people who regularly engage in anti-social or self-destructive behaviour can make other members of the group more likely to exhibit similar behaviour. If the majority of a group smoke, take illicit drugs, drink alcohol, commit crimes or have promiscuous sex, then other members of that group are more likely to behave in the same way.

The traditional explanation for this type of peer-group influence is that young people are pressurised by their peers into adopting the same bad habits, and there is some evidence to show that this can happen. For example, in one study, the majority of children who called a cocaine helpline claimed that they had been pressurised by their friends into taking the drug. But then, they would say that, wouldn't they? More solid evidence suggests that the notion of 'peer pressure' is often an over-simplified view of how children are influenced by their peers. The reality is as much to do with peer *preference* as peer *pressure*. In other words, children tend to choose friends who think and behave in similar ways.

Children naturally gravitate towards a peer

group in which they feel comfortable and accepted, especially if they have been rejected by another group. In most cases, peer groups do not simply impose new desires or new ways of behaving on an otherwise unwilling child, but, more often, create a social environment in which the child's own inclinations will be reinforced and expressed. Peer groups can undoubtedly be a malign influence, but they rarely conjure up bad behaviour out of thin air. For a peer group to exert pressure on a child there must usually be some degree of fit between that child and the group in the first place.

To take one example, research has shown that children who choose to socialise with smokers are themselves more likely to smoke. Much the same applies to drinking, taking drugs and committing crime. However, the key factor seems to be the process of choosing those friends in the first place, as opposed to simply being passively influenced by them. The child who has some inclination to smoke ends up in the smokers' group, rather than being pressured into smoking after befriending them. To blame the child's smoking entirely on the group would be to miss the point.

Risk-taking provides another example. Some children enjoy trying new and potentially dangerous activities, whereas others prefer safety and predictability. Children whose personality makes them natural risk-takers and excitement-seekers tend to be attracted to groups of people who also enjoy risk-taking and excitement.

The idea of peer preference is perhaps more obvious when it comes to fashion. Adolescents typically adopt the particular look of their group, choosing exactly the right styles, colours and brand names. They actively want to be identified with a distinctive style and group that symbolise the type of person they wish to be. For many kids, the most important thing is to be 'cool' (or, at least, to avoid being 'uncool').

Some children are more susceptible than others to peer-group influences. One of the most important factors affecting the extent to which a child is influenced by peers is the child's parents. A strong parent–child relationship can limit the impact of social pressures from peer groups. Because children tend to seek out peers with whom they feel comfortable, children who are in conflict with their parents may seek out peers who reinforce this conflict. These are the sorts of peers that many parents would regard as bad influences. Hence, authoritarian parents who try to control their child's every move often end up with children who want to rebel and who socialise with other rebellious children.

Responding to the risk

Parents who have little contact with, or apparent interest in, their children's lives also tend to reinforce the influence of peers. Researchers have found that children who spend a lot of unstructured time with peers, and whose parents do not monitor their behaviour much, are more likely to abuse drugs and alcohol.

One implication for parents is that they should try to strike a balance between having enough contact with their child's social life to make the child feel loved and monitored, but not so much that he or she feels distrusted and controlled. Research has found that teenagers who feel their parents are highly involved in their lives are roughly half as likely to smoke or drink as those who feel their parents are not involved.

A good starting point can be simply talking to children from an early age about the risks and social pressures they are likely to face as they get older. Drugs education researchers found that children who were talked to about drugs every week by their form teacher at the age of nine had more negative attitudes towards drugs, were more resistant to perceived peer pressure, and were less likely to have smoked cigarettes or used illegal drugs when they were 13–14 years of age.

A child's self-confidence and knowledge will also have an important bearing on their susceptibility to peer pressure. Peers are less likely to be a bad influence on children who have the self-confidence and conviction to make the right choices for themselves. Anti-drug campaigns of the past that simply told children to 'just say no' were generally ineffectual. Research has shown that better outcomes are achieved by building up children's self-confidence and understanding, as well as teaching them how to refuse drugs. Children are better able to resist temptation and social pressure if they understand why they should say no and have the self-confidence to do it.

Thinking about choices, assessing their consequences, and making decisions, are general life skills that all children need to develop. And like most skills, they are better developed through practice. Schools and parents can contribute by getting children to think about relatively neutral issues, such as who to invite to a party. Similar thought processes can be helpful to the child in more serious contexts such as refusing drugs.

What can you do?

◆ **Don't try to control your child's choice of friends.**

Ultimately, only your child can decide who he or she wants to have as friends. You cannot impose your own choices. It may be OK to say what you think of your child's friends, provided you do this diplomatically, but don't tell your child what to think.

◆ **Try to avoid being too judgemental.**

Try not to jump to conclusions about your child's friends based on superficial trappings such as dress, hairstyle or accent. Try to look beyond the veneer to more fundamental things such as attitudes, personality and behaviour.

◆ **The three Ws: Who, Where, When**

Show an interest in your child's social life and be aware of how they spend their time. Try to limit the amount of unstructured time when they are simply out and roaming with their peers, since that is when they are most likely to get into trouble. Always aim to know *who* they are with, *where* they are and *when* they'll be back.

◆ **Talk to the parents of your child's friends.**

Other parents can often be a valuable source of information and can help you build up a fuller picture of what your child is getting up to when they're away from you. But be careful not to be too intrusive. Older children will probably be furious if they think their parents have been checking up on them with their friends' parents.

◆ **Talk to your child about the big risks.**

Talk about the hazards of early sex, drinking, smoking and drugs before these become a live issue. Generally these topics should be tackled well before the start of secondary school. By the time a child reaches the age of peak risk (around 11–13) it may already be too late to change their attitudes. It is better to have an embarrassing conversation at an early stage than to wait until things get out of hand.

◆ **Practise what you preach.**

Try not to display double standards in your own behaviour about issues like sex, smoking, alcohol and drugs.

◆ **Try to make your child feel unconditionally loved.**

Children are less likely to fall into bad company and bad ways if they feel secure in who they are and have high self-esteem. ▶

You can make a big difference by providing a secure home environment in which they feel loved unconditionally for who they are, not what they do. If you only ever praise them for behaving in certain ways, they will learn that your approval is conditional and depends on their doing certain things. If they apply this same belief towards peer groups then it will encourage them to seek their peers' approval by behaving in certain ways. A child who feels secure and confident is better equipped to resist 'bad influences'.

◆ *Talk to the school.*

If you are worried about your child's peer group, talk to the school. The school should know if there are problems such as truancy or bullying.

◆ *Don't just talk at your child: listen.*

Listen before you start lecturing them. For example, if you want to tackle the subject of drugs, you will probably be better off asking them first what they know about the subject (which may be quite a lot) before launching into a lecture. Discover the gaps in their knowledge before telling them what to do.

Further advice

Kidscape

Tel: 020 7730 3300

www.kidscape.org.uk

Advice to parents and children about bullying and friends.

Action on Smoking Health, ASH

Tel: 020 7739 5902

www.ash.org.uk

The website has an anti-smoking section for young people.

Drinkline

Tel: 0800 917 8282

Government sponsored helpline for alcohol-related issues.

National Drugs Helpline

Tel: 0800 776600

www.talktofrank.com

Information and advice about drug abuse.

Related worries

16. Doesn't tell me what he/she is really thinking or feeling
19. Is reckless and not sufficiently aware of dangers
24. Won't listen to me/is disobedient
28. Is being bullied
38. Might get into trouble with the authorities or commit a crime

Smoking

- 1 in 10 (10%) of school children aged 11–15 are regular smokers (defined as smoking at least one cigarette a week).

- 1 in 6 (16%) of children aged 11–15 have smoked within the past week.

- By the age of 16, two-thirds of children will have experimented with smoking.

- Children are three times more likely to smoke if both their parents smoke.

- The likelihood that a child will smoke rises sharply with age. Among 11-year-olds, only 1 in 100 (1%) are regular smokers, but nearly a quarter (23%) of 15-year-olds are regular smokers.

- Girls are more likely to smoke than boys, and have been since the early 1980s. However, among those who do smoke, boys tend to be the heavier smokers.

- The number of cigarettes smoked each week by children who smoke regularly has remained fairly level since the early 1980s.

- There is a firm statistical association between smoking and using cannabis.

- Children who smoke regularly are more likely than non-smokers to have truanted or to have been excluded from school.

- It is illegal to sell any tobacco product to anyone below the age of 16. However, a 1996 study found that the UK government received £108 million in taxation from the illegal sale of cigarettes to children.

- More than two-thirds (69%) of children who regularly smoke usually buy their cigarettes from a newsagent. Occasional smokers are usually given their cigarettes by friends.

- Tobacco is the only legally available consumer product that kills people when used entirely as intended.

- The death toll from smoking in the UK is about 330 people a day. Tobacco kills around six times more people in the UK than road traffic accidents, other accidents, poisoning and overdose, murder and manslaughter, suicide and HIV combined. Half of all regular cigarette smokers will die from their habit.

- Children tend to smoke the brands that are promoted most heavily. A study in the late 1990s found that boys whose favourite sport was motor racing were twice as likely to become a regular smoker than those who were uninterested in the sport.

The statistics quoted here derive mainly from government research carried out in England in 2002.

WORRY 9

Might get a serious illness

28% of parents worried

....

Chances: MEDIUM   **Consequences: HIGH**   **Control: MEDIUM**

School-aged children are generally much less likely to die from illness (or other causes) than their parents. For example, the average middle-aged father is at least 30 times more likely to die within the next year than his primary school-aged son. In fact, the average person in the UK is less likely to die from any cause between the ages of five and 14 than at any other stage in life.

A child is far more likely to die during its first year than between the ages of one and 16. Many of these early deaths are birth-related or the result of congenital abnormalities. The chances that an average British school-age child will die from illness in a given year are less than 1 in 10,000.

Among the few school-aged girls who do die, the most common cause of death is cancer, which accounts for just under a quarter of all female deaths among five to 15-year-olds. For school-aged boys, the most common cause of death is accidents, with cancer second. Children are much more likely now to survive cancer than they were 15–20 years ago.

Up to 1 in 5 children will suffer from a chronic medical condition at some point in their childhood. The most common of these is asthma, which affects 10–15 per cent of school children.

Statistically, the chances of a child in the UK dying before reaching adulthood are comfortingly small. By far the riskiest time in a child's life is its first year, when birth defects and birth-related problems are a significant cause of death. The death rate in the UK among infants under the age of one is more than 40 times higher than the death rate among children aged 5–15. Relatively few school-aged children die, and even fewer die as a result of illness. The chances of an average British school-child dying from a serious illness in a given year are less than 1 in 10,000.

The risk of a child dying depends on its sex as well as age. Males are more likely to die than females at any age in their lifespan. Among infants aged 0–1 years, the death rate for males is 20 per cent higher than for females. The sex difference in mortality becomes even starker later in life. For instance, the death rate for young men in their late teens is more than double the death rate for young women of the same age.

Serious illness, in the form of cancer, is the most common single cause of death among school-aged girls. Cancer accounts for 23 per cent of all deaths among school-aged girls. However, a boy is more likely to die in an accident than from cancer: 27 per cent of all deaths among school-aged boys result from accidents. Cancer is the second most common cause for boys, accounting for 24 per cent of all deaths. The three most common types of child-hood cancer are leukaemia, brain tumours and lymphomas (tumours of the lymph nodes).

Cancer might be the leading medical cause of death among school-aged children, but it is still not very common. One child in 650 develops cancer before the age of 15. However, many of them survive. And thanks to advances in medical science, children with cancer are more likely to survive now than they were even a few years ago. The mortality rates from childhood cancer fell by a third between 1985 and 2000, despite little change in the actual incidence of the disease. More than 7 out of 10 children with cancer survive for at least five years.

Many other childhood illnesses are long-lasting rather than life-threatening. An illness is described as 'chronic' if it lasts more than three months and is severe enough to interfere to some extent with the child's normal activities. Some 10–20 per cent of all children experience a chronic illness at some stage during childhood. The most common are asthma, epilepsy, congenital heart disease (i.e., abnormalities in the heart at birth), diabetes and arthritis.

The most common chronic illness of childhood is asthma, which affects 10–15 per cent of school-aged children. It has become considerably more common over the past 30 years. The second most common chronic childhood illness is epilepsy, which affects around 5 out of every 1000 school-aged children in the UK. Third is congenital heart disease; 7 or 8 out of every 1000 babies are born with significant malformations of the heart. The fourth most common chronic condition is diabetes, which has been steadily increasing over the past 20 years and now affects around 2 out of every 1000 school-aged children. The most common condition for which children have prolonged absence from school is chronic fatigue syndrome.

Then, of course, there are mental illnesses, some of which can be seriously debilitating, and in extreme cases can lead to suicide. A national study found that 1 in 10 school-aged children in the UK have some form of mental health problem. Children with mental health problems are at greater risk of, among other things, accidents, prolonged absences from school, being excluded from school, abusing drugs or alcohol, and committing suicide. Although suicide is rare among young children, it is becoming increasingly common among teenagers. It is estimated that around 1 in 100 school-aged children suffers from depression. Even toddlers can be depressed, but their condition is often hard for adults to recognise. A depressed toddler can just appear to be unresponsive and withdrawn.

Thanks to improvements in living conditions, sanitation, nutrition and medical care – notably antibiotics and national immunisation programmes

– life-threatening infectious diseases, such as smallpox, diphtheria, polio, pneumonia and measles, have become much less common over the past 50 years. Nowadays, a schoolchild in the UK is more likely to die in an accident or from cancer than from an infectious disease. Nonetheless, serious infectious diseases have certainly not disappeared altogether and some, such as tuberculosis (TB), have been staging a comeback. The number of TB cases in the UK has been increasing in recent years.

Certain other infectious illnesses, while relatively rare among children in the UK, can pose a significant threat to life. The most serious are meningitis, meningococcal septicaemia (a form of blood poisoning), pneumonia, HIV, and assorted other viral infections.

Meningitis – an inflammation of the membranes enclosing the brain and spinal cord – can result from either bacterial or viral infection, and is the most common infectious disease that causes death among children and young people in the UK. Viral meningitis tends to resolve itself, but bacterial meningitis can be life-threatening, with a mortality rate of 5–10 per cent. Since 1999, babies born in the UK have been vaccinated against meningitis C, the form of the disease that causes most deaths. As part of a catch-up process, children and young people in the age groups at highest risk (initially 15- to 17-year-olds) have also been receiving the meningitis C vaccine. Since 1992, babies have also been immunised against Haemophilus influenzae (Hib), a bacterial infection that causes a number of serious diseases including meningitis and septicaemia.

Parents often feel powerless to prevent their children getting a serious illness, and in some senses they are. Ultimately, there is nothing a parent can do to guarantee that their child will never be one of the unfortunate few who do develop cancer or contract meningitis.

Worrying about relatively small risks can be stressful for both parent and child. Parents communicate their fears to their children, even if they don't mean to. And making children paranoid about their health will probably do them more harm than good. Apart from causing needless anxiety it may, paradoxically, *increase* the child's chances of becoming ill. Prolonged psychological stress and anxiety can lower a person's immune defences and thereby make them more susceptible to a range of diseases, including bacterial and viral infections. There is a real need here for a balanced and calm perspective based on evidence.

Responding to the risk

That said, parents can do various things to lower the risk of their child becoming seriously ill. The simplest and most effective way of protecting your child's health – and the health of other people too – is to get them vaccinated. Thanks to childhood vaccination, life-threatening infectious diseases have largely been eradicated from the UK, saving many thousands of lives a year. But these killer diseases could easily return if enough parents fail to get their children vaccinated. Moreover, the risk of exposure to life-threatening infectious diseases is growing as more and more people travel abroad.

Despite scare stories in the media, the vaccines that are given to children in the UK are essentially safe. No vaccine can be guaranteed 100 per cent risk-free, and some adverse side-effects do occasionally occur, but they are rare. Most children show no adverse reaction to vaccination and very few suffer any significant problems. A child is far more likely to become seriously ill or die as a consequence of *not* being vaccinated than from being vaccinated.

Even the controversial MMR vaccine, which protects children against measles, mumps and rubella (German measles), has been given a clean bill of health by the vast majority of scientists and medical experts in the UK and other countries, after extensive investigations into its potential side effects.

Before the MMR vaccine was introduced in the UK in 1988, about 90 children a year (nearly two a week) died from measles, and many more suffered brain damage and other serious complications from this highly infectious and serious disease. Mumps used to cause deafness and was the commonest cause of viral meningitis in children, while rubella used to cause serious damage to unborn babies. Even if the scare stories were true, it would still be safer to vaccinate children than not, given the all-too-real risks of being killed or permanently damaged by measles, mumps or rubella.

Another way of reducing children's chances of becoming ill is to ensure that their diet is balanced and healthy. Diet has a significant impact on health, both in childhood and later in life. Nutritional factors are thought to account for about a third of cancers in Western nations, making diet second only to smoking as a potentially preventable cause of cancer.

Not eating enough fruit and vegetables increases the risk of developing cancer of the bowel, while obesity and eating too much saturated fat increase the risk of diabetes, coronary heart disease and several types of cancer, including cancers of the oesophagus, bowel, rectum and breast. Early diet also has an influence on allergies: the evidence shows that children are less likely to develop allergies if they are exclusively breastfed.

Which brings us to breastfeeding – another good way of improving a child's long-term prospects. Children who are breastfed for the first several months of life enjoy better physical health in later life and are less susceptible to many illnesses than bottle-fed children. The biggest benefits accrue to babies who are exclusively breastfed for at least the first six months.

Breast milk is perfectly tailored to the developing baby's changing nutritional requirements. Research has shown that breastfed babies are less likely to become obese in childhood. They are also less likely to get infections of the respiratory tract, middle ear or bowel, and less likely to develop diabetes in childhood. In addition, the evidence suggests that breastfeeding a baby for more than six months reduces its risk of later developing two of the most common forms of childhood cancer – namely, leukaemia and lymphomas. Adults who were breastfed as babies are found to have lower than average levels of blood cholesterol, implying that breastfeeding might reduce the long-term risk of cardiovascular disease.

As if that were not enough, breastfeeding seems to make children smarter. Other things being equal, breastfed children score higher on intelligence tests than children who were bottle-fed. Breastfeeding even confers health benefits on the mother, such as reducing her risk of developing certain types of breast and ovarian cancer. Breast is certainly best.

Taking a longer-term view, one of the biggest contributions any parent can make to their child's chances of enjoying a long and healthy life is to discourage them from becoming a smoker.

Smoking significantly increases the likelihood of developing coronary heart disease, lung cancer, bronchitis and emphysema. It is the riskiest thing that many people will ever do in their lives. Six times as many people die each year in the UK from smoking than from the combined effects of road and other accidents, poisoning, overdose, murder, manslaughter, suicide and HIV infection.

Around 1 in 10 children aged 11–15 smoke at least one cigarette a week, with girls now outnumbering boys (see Smoking, page 48). If these young people continue to smoke into adulthood, 1 in 4 of them will die before they reach the age of 70, having shortened their lives by an average of 23 years. Admittedly, stopping children from smoking is easier said than done. Nonetheless, parents can start by not smoking themselves, since the evidence clearly shows that children are more likely to smoke if their parents do.

What can you do?

◆ *Encourage a healthy lifestyle.*

Try to ensure that your child receives a healthy, balanced diet, both at home and elsewhere, and takes plenty of exercise. Physical activity and exercise are crucial to long-term health. Lack of exercise is one of the main factors behind the current epidemic of childhood obesity. Couch potatoes die younger.

◆ *Keep an eye on your child's weight.*

If your child starts to become seriously overweight for his or her age, the sooner you know about it the better. Conversely, a sudden and unexplained drop in weight can also be a sign that something might be wrong. Try not to encourage an obsession with thinness and dieting, however, as this can lead to unhappiness and eating disorders.

◆ *Seriously discourage smoking.*

If you want your child to survive past middle age, do your very best to discourage him or her from taking up smoking. Set a good example by not smoking yourself.

◆ *Breastfeed.*

Mothers are strongly recommended to breastfeed their babies exclusively for at least the first six months. Breastfeeding provides an excellent foundation for better health in childhood and later life.

◆ *Make sure your child gets all the recommended vaccinations.*

Some vaccinations carry small risks of side-effects. But those risks are worth taking, because the risks of *not* being vaccinated are much bigger and could even result in your child dying.

◆ *Be aware of your family's health history.*

The health histories of parents and other close relatives are certainly not firm predictors of a child's health. But they can sometimes provide useful indications of potential risk factors such as an inherited tendency to develop coronary heart disease, diabetes or some forms of mental illness. If in doubt, consult your GP.

◆ *Keep health risks in perspective.*

You and your children will not benefit from becoming excessively anxious about relatively unlikely events. Scare stories in the media sometimes turn out to have been based on flawed or misinterpreted evidence. Aim to base your worries and your actions on reliable evidence from authoritative and independent sources.

Further advice

NHS Direct

Tel: 0845 4647 (24 hours)

www.nhsdirect.nhs.uk

The encyclopaedia section of the website contains accessible information on a wide range of illnesses, explaining causes, symptoms, diagnosis and treatment.

Department of Health Immunisation Programme

www.immunisation.org.uk

Guidance for parents about immunisation.

Association for Children with Life–threatening or Terminal Conditions and their Family (ACT)

Helpline: 0117 922 1556

www.act.org.uk

Campaigns to raise awareness about children with life-threatening conditions and their families.

Related worries

1. Might be knocked over by a vehicle
3. Eats too much sugar and sweet foods
7. Eats too much junk food or convenience food
32. Does not get enough physical exercise
35. Doesn't get enough vitamins from his/her normal diet

WORRY **10**

Might be the victim of physical violence

27% of parents worried

Chances: HIGH   Consequences: HIGH   Control: HIGH

Fewer than 100 children are murdered each year in the UK. The majority of those murders are committed by the victims' parents, not by strangers. However, many children are subjected to violence at some stage in their lives. According to one estimate, 7 per cent of children are on the receiving end of serious physical violence at some point during their childhood.

Around 80 per cent of all violence against children is committed in the home by adults known to the victim – mostly parents, relatives and carers. Each year, around 8000 children are judged to be at sufficient risk of being physically abused that their names are added to a child protection register for close monitoring.

Another common source of violence against children, albeit usually less severe, is bullying in or around school. Almost two-thirds of all young people claim to have been physically bullied at some point during their school years. Although the level of physical violence involved in most bullying is relatively minor, there has been a worrying trend in recent years for increasingly severe violence among girls.

One or two children are murdered each week in the UK, but the great majority of these crimes are committed by the victim's parents, carers or relatives (see Worry 2, page 12). A similar picture applies to other acts of violence against children: nearly all incidents resulting in serious injury involve an adult known to the child. The second biggest threat comes from violent bullying or muggings by other children or young people. Violence against children by adult strangers is relatively rare in the UK.

Accurate figures on the extent of childhood violence are hard to obtain, as many incidents go unreported, but research shows that about one-third of all 12- to 15-year-olds claim to have been assaulted in some way during the previous year, though only 1 in 20 of these cases are serious enough to be classified as a crime.

Other evidence comes from surveys that ask individuals to recall their experiences of violence in childhood. These retrospective surveys tend to produce higher estimates than formal crime statistics, although they suffer from having to rely on people's faulty memories and truthfulness. Around 7 per cent of young adults claim to have endured serious and persistent violence during childhood, and a further 14 per cent say they suffered less severe physical abuse. When British parents were asked, 1 in 20 admitted that they had been physically abusive to their child within the past year and 1 in 10 admitted having been physically abusive at some point in the child's life. Overall levels of violence against children appear to be static, with no significant increase over the past decade.

Violence against children is obviously not a new phenomenon. In the UK, public debate about the rights of children bloomed during the Victorian era. This led to the establishment in 1884 of the National Society for the Prevention of Cruelty to Children (NSPCC). The NSPCC lobbied Parliament, and in 1889 the first legislation for the prevention of cruelty to children, popularly known as the Children's Charter, was passed. However, almost another century elapsed before local author-ities began to take an active role in the prevention of violence against children. In 1974 the government issued guidelines to all local authorities on the management of 'non-accidental injury to children'.

Contrary to what many parents believe, placing a child on a child protection register does not mean that he or she will automatically be taken into care. Registration signifies that the child's future will be regularly monitored because he or she has been deemed to be at risk. It also signifies that there should be a plan to reduce the risk, including the provision of any additional support that may be needed. The great majority of children who are on a child protection register remain in the care of their immediate families, but they are monitored by social services and their development and progress are assessed regularly.

At any one time approximately 35,000 children are on a child protection register in the UK, of whom around a quarter have been referred because of concerns about physical abuse. More than 3 out of 4 children remain on a register for less than a year. Overall, there are more boys than girls on a register, but girls form the majority among the over-12s. Girls are also more likely to sustain more serious injuries.

The majority of physically abused children who come to the notice of child protection services are moderately, rather than severely, injured. Severe physical abuse is judged to have occurred when the injuries last longer than a day. While child protection registers pick up most of the more serious cases, some experts believe that the true extent of violence against children is greater, with many cases going unreported.

It is not against the law for a parent to smack or hit a child, provided the parent can demonstrate that the violence was 'reasonable chastisement' (see Smacking, page 133). One obviously difficulty here is defining what is meant by 'reasonable'. Some older parents may have grown up in an environment where corporal punishment was regarded as a normal and acceptable way of disciplining children.

Few parents deliberately set out to harm their child, so what causes them to go too far? A parent who would normally never hit their child might do so out of fear and relief – say, because their young child has just run across the road. But when it comes to more frequent or more serious violence, a common cause is stress. Statistics show that parents are more likely to harm their children if they are unemployed, have a low income, are younger, or have a large family. An increased risk of violence is also associated with non-traditional family structures such as single-parent families and families with a step-parent. Only a third of physically abused children live with their natural mother and father, while a similar proportion live with a step-parent. Fathers, stepfathers and father substitutes are twice as likely as natural mothers to be implicated in abuse. That said, violence to children occurs in all types of families and all strata of society, from the richest to the poorest, and the overwhelming majority of single parents and step-parents never abuse their children.

Violence between adults poses a further threat to children. In half of all cases of domestic adult-on-adult violence, a child ends up getting injured as well. Another source of low-level violence in the home is violence between siblings (see Worry 23, page 123).

Unsurprisingly, physical violence can cause serious long-term problems for the victim. Follow-up studies of physically abused children have found poorer physical and intellectual development, more problematic and aggressive behaviour, poorer relations with peers, and more arrests for juvenile and adult crimes, particularly violent crimes.

Violence against children can create a vicious cycle. Individuals who are abused in childhood are more likely to become abusive parents themselves, although this is far from inevitable. Research suggests that an abused individual who becomes a parent has a 30 per cent chance of abusing their own children in turn. If the only model of behaviour they have experienced in early life is one where physical violence is a normal way of solving problems or imposing discipline, then it is hardly surprising that some of these children turn into violent adults themselves. Being in a stable marriage substantially reduces the risk that a victim of abuse will later abuse their own children.

Outside the home, one of the biggest physical threats to children comes from violent bullying by other children or young people (see Worry 28, page 151). Children often put up with bullying for weeks or months without feeling able to report it to their parents or teacher.

While most bullying is verbal or emotional rather than physical, surveys have found that 3 out of 4 men and 3 out of 5 women claim to have been physically bullied at some point during their childhood. Much of this self-reported bullying involves minor incidents, such as pushing or shoving, though some incidents are more severe and include beatings. One survey found that the bullying usually started between the ages of seven and 13 and peaked at 11 or 12, around the time of entering secondary school.

A recent and worrying development has been a rise in violent girl-on-girl bullying, which has grown considerably in the past few years. Previously, while verbal bullying was common in both sexes, physically violent bullying was largely restricted to boys. This is no longer the case.

What can you do?

♦ *Talk, don't hit.*

Teach your child from the earliest age to resolve conflicts using discussion and negotiation rather than violence. Make it clear that physical violence is simply not acceptable.

♦ *Set a good example.*

Avoid resorting to physical violence or the threat of violence. Even the implied threat of violence by their parents can signal to children that aggression is an acceptable means of solving problems. Fathers, in particular, can be good role models by behaving assertively rather than aggressively – in other words, being firm but not violent.

♦ *Remind your child of the differences between real life and TV.*

Point out to your child that most violence on TV and in films is not a true reflection of real life. Just because the characters in their favourite soap routinely shout, swear and hit each other does not make it acceptable or desirable for real people to do the same. Nor is it a realistic portrayal of life for the vast majority of people.

♦ *Think about your approach to discipline.*

Try to have a clear idea about the methods you will, and will not, use to maintain discipline with your children. If you have a well thought-through and non-violent system, you are less likely to resort to physical force if your emotions get the better of you. For example, many parents use a 'time out' rule to discipline younger children. 'Time out' will not instantly dispel your own frustration, but it will at least give both of you some breathing space to calm down.

A non-violent system of discipline will expose your child to the idea that conflicts can, and should, be resolved by talking rather than hitting. Make sure that anyone who is left to look after your child understands your rules regarding physical discipline. If you never smack your child, and believe it is wrong to do so, you should not permit anyone caring for your child to smack them in your absence.

♦ *Try never to involve your child in rows with your partner or spouse.*

While minor tiffs are a standard feature of marriage, parents should try to shield children from serious conflict, let alone violence. Seeing a parent engaged in verbal or physical aggression can be traumatic. Remember that in half the cases of domestic violence, children end up getting hurt as well.

♦ *Keep an eye on aggression between siblings.*

Some rough-and-tumble between siblings is normal and probably unavoidable. But be prepared to intervene and clamp down firmly if it starts to escalate into more serious violence. It should be no more acceptable for your son to hit his younger brother than for you to hit either of them.

♦ *Break the abuse cycle.*

If you were physically abused as a child, and worry that you might do the same to your child, you can ask your GP or social services to refer you to one of the counselling services that help people to learn other ways of managing their anger and controlling their aggression. ▶

◆ *Teach your child to be street-wise.*
Much of the physical bullying that children experience happens on the way to or from school. Ideally, they should walk to school with friends and use routes where there are other people about. (For more specific advice about bullying, see Worry 28, page 151.)

◆ *Go to the police.*
If your child has been attacked by another child, and the assault involved theft or physical injury, then a crime has been committed and it should be reported to the police. If your child is reluctant to report it, point out to them that they presumably wouldn't want the same thing to happen to another child. You should also talk to your child's teacher or head teacher if someone from their school was involved. Local education authorities and schools should have formal policies and procedures for dealing with bullying. The charity Crimestoppers offers an anonymous freephone number for young victims who do not want to go to the police, either because they fear reprisal or because they have heard that giving a statement to the police can be a harrowing experience.

Further advice

NSPCC
Helpline: 0808 800 5000
www.nspcc.org.uk
A range of support and advice for those worried about cruelty and violence towards children. The NSPCC also has statutory powers that enable it to take action to safeguard children at risk of abuse.

Women's Aid Federation of England
Domestic violence 24-hour helpline:
08457 023 468
www.womensaid.org.uk
Support, legal advice and refuge for women and children affected by violence.

Children are Unbeatable!
Tel: 020 7713 0569
E-mail: info@endcorporalpunishment.org
www.childrenareunbeatable.org.uk
Advice to help parents use positive, non-violent discipline.

Crimestoppers
Freephone: 0800 555111 (anonymity guaranteed)
www.crimestoppers-uk.org
Offers support to young victims of crime, as well as advice to prevent children becoming involved in criminal activity.

Kidscape
Tel: 020 7730 3300
www.kidscape.org.uk
A range of advice for parents and children, including how to deal with bullying.

Related worries
2. Might be abducted or murdered
6. Might be the victim of crime
11. Might be abused by an adult
28. Is being bullied
37. Is not safe on public transport

WORRY **11**

Might be abused by an adult

27% of parents worried

....

Chances: HIGH   **Consequences: HIGH**   **Control: MEDIUM**

More than 3000 children are placed on a child protection register in the UK each year because of actual or suspected sexual abuse. Even so, sexual abuse accounts for only 1 in 8 of all child protection cases. Emotional abuse, physical abuse and neglect are far more common. The reported incidence of child sexual abuse has shown no clear increase in the UK in recent years.

The vast majority of child sexual abuse is carried out by someone known to the victim, such as a parent, relative, family friend or minder. Sexual abuse by strangers is rare. Up to a third of all child sexual abuse is committed by young people, mainly adolescent males. Most sexual abusers were themselves victims of sexual abuse in childhood.

At any one time, about 30,000 children in the UK are on a child protection register because they are at risk in some way. Only about 1 in 8 of these cases involve actual or suspected sexual abuse. Far more children are at risk from physical abuse, emotional abuse or neglect than from sexual abuse.

Emotional abuse can include persistent verbal abuse and denigration, refusing to talk to the child, denying them warmth and affection, or shutting them up in their bedroom (or even a cupboard). It can cause deep and lasting psychological damage, leading to difficulties in forming lasting relationships, severe depression and even suicide.

Sexual abuse occurs when someone persuades or forces a child into sexual acts. These may range from showing the child sexual images to sexual touching, masturbation, oral sex or full intercourse. People who are sexually attracted to children (paedophiles) often 'groom' their victims by gradually introducing them into a sexually abusive relationship through small increments.

How common is child abuse? Reliable figures are hard to find. Only a proportion of cases ever result in criminal proceedings, and many others are never reported to the police or social services. Crime statistics therefore tend to underestimate the true extent of the problem. Another reason why abuse is under-reported is the common belief that any child who is placed on a child protection register will automatically be taken away from its parents and placed in care. But that is not the case. Social services and family courts have a range of protective and supportive measures to draw upon, most of which do not involve separating the child from his or her family.

The lack of really solid statistics is a particular problem when it comes to sexual abuse. Different researchers use different definitions of sexual abuse and different methods to measure it, making comparisons difficult. Some researchers ask children to describe their own experience, some ask parents about their children, and some ask adults to recall what happened to them when they were children.

Not surprisingly, statistics based on self-report surveys tend to be much higher than official crime figures. For example, one large study found that 3 out of every 100 young adults said they had been the victims of child sexual abuse (which was defined as sexual acts to which they had not consented when aged 12 or less). However, human memory is highly fallible, so statistics based on adults recalling their childhood experiences can be unreliable.

Media reporting can sometimes give the impression that there has been a huge increase in child sexual abuse in the UK in recent years. However, the evidence for this is not clear-cut. Neither criminal statistics nor child protection statistics have shown any systematic increase in the scale of child sexual abuse in recent years. However, there has been an increase in the number of criminal cases involving the taking, making or possession of indecent images of children. This presumably reflects both the extra opportunities that the Internet provides for committing such crimes, and greater public awareness following extensive media publicity about paedophile pornography.

Recognising sexual abuse

How can a parent tell if their child is being sexually abused? The victims of child sexual abuse often feel under pressure to keep it secret for a variety of reasons, including fear of punishment by the abuser, embarrassment, guilt, fear of being removed from home or fear that the abuser (often a close relative) might be sent to prison. Even so, the problem may reveal itself indirectly.

Children who are being sexually abused may become depressed and withdrawn or unusually clingy. They may suddenly start doing badly at school, become aggressive, sleep badly, or start wetting the bed. They may display sexually precocious behaviour or language that is out of character, or become fearful of a particular adult or social activity. They may hint at their problem indirectly – perhaps referring to keeping a 'secret' or to a relative getting into trouble. Of course, most children who behave in these ways are not being sexually abused. Nonetheless, a pattern of symptoms like these might prompt parents to consider the possibility.

Common signs of physical abuse, emotional abuse or neglect include frequent 'accidents', unexplained injuries, withdrawn or suddenly changed behaviour, loss of weight or serious failure to thrive.

Who is responsible for child abuse? In the great majority of cases, the abuser is well known to the victim – often a relative or friend of the victim's parents or the parents themselves. For example, of the several thousand children and young people who call the charity Childline each year to report sexual or physical abuse, 95 per cent say they know their abuser. Sexual or physical abuse of children by strangers is rare, although these cases are the ones that tend to hit the headlines.

In the case of sexual abuse, the abuser may be the victim's parent, step parent, live-in partner of a parent, grandparent, brother, sister, uncle, aunt, teacher, neighbour or family friend. Child sexual abusers come from a wide range of social classes, age groups, ethnic origins, educational backgrounds and professions. They may act alone or organise themselves into groups. They may be professionals holding responsible positions in society, they may be religious, and they often appear respectable. Sexual abusers tend to be good at getting on well with children and are often perceived to be nice, friendly people.

Despite this great variety of backgrounds, child sexual abusers do tend to have one characteristic in common: they are much more likely than the average person to have been sexually abused themselves when they were children. Up to 8 out of 10 abusers were victims of sexual abuse in childhood. However, this does *not* mean that most child sex abuse victims will go on to become abusers. The majority do not. One long-term study of men who had been the victims of sexual abuse in childhood found that only about 12 per cent of them subsequently committed sexual offences. To put it

another way, 88 per cent did *not* go on to commit sexual offences.

Most sexual abusers of children are male, although some women and girls do sexually abuse children. Of the several thousand people who are convicted of sexual offences each year in England and Wales, only 1–2 per cent are women. Female abusers are more likely to be the parent or close relative of the victim, and they often co-offend with one or more men. Female sexual abusers, like male sexual abusers, are likely to have been sexually abused themselves as children. They are also more likely than the average person to have had a traumatic childhood and to use alcohol or drugs.

Reducing the risk

Not all sexual abusers are adults. Some experts estimate that as much as a third of all child sexual abuse is committed by other children or young people, mainly adolescent males. Sexual abuse by a brother or sister may also be more common than is often supposed. The evidence suggests that sexual abuse of children by siblings is rarely reported. One survey found that 10 per cent of men and 15 per cent of women said they had had some form of sexual experience with a sibling when younger. However, not all sexual behaviour between siblings is abusive: innocent sex play sometimes occurs between siblings who are young and close together in age.

One form of child abuse that has received a lot of attention from the media is sexual abuse involving the Internet, and there has been much publicity about the danger the Internet poses to children. Some paedophiles are known to target and 'groom' their potential victims by engaging them in discussion in Internet chat rooms. The Internet has certainly made it easier for paedophiles to gratify their desires, although by the same token it has also created new ways for the police to identify them.

The dangers posed by the Internet are real, but they should be kept in perspective. Some simple precautions can greatly reduce the risks (see What can you do? on page 63). Children should be taught about basic Internet security so that it becomes as natural to them as real-world security precautions such as locking the front door when they leave the house and not talking to strangers they meet in the street.

Public concern and media publicity about paedophiles have probably helped to prevent or uncover many dreadful cases of abuse. However, the intense focus on child sexual abuse can have a downside too. Some parents have become so sensitised to this issue that they feel worried about displaying physical affection towards their own children in case their behaviour is misinterpreted. Some men, in particular, are hesitant about kissing, cuddling or bathing their children. For similar reasons, many adults (and especially men) have become more hesitant about intervening if they encounter an unknown child who looks lost or in distress. Their natural wish to help the child is tempered by a fear that their motives might be misinterpreted.

Two simple points are worth remembering here. First, it is absolutely normal, healthy and desirable for parents to display physical warmth and affection towards their children, and that includes kissing, cuddling and hugging them. Affectionate physical contact is an important part of making children feel secure and loved. The second point is that the vast majority of men (and women) are not child abusers.

Child sexual abuse is an appalling crime with long-term effects, and it often goes undetected. For that reason, any hint or allegation that a child makes about sexual abuse should be taken seriously. No child with a real problem should be made to feel that there is no one they can talk to or that they are not being taken seriously. However, it is also an uncomfortable fact that some allegations of sexual abuse turn out to be untrue, either because a child has lied in order to get an adult into trouble or because a child has been led into saying things that are exaggerated or untrue.

False allegations have become a real source of anxiety for teachers, who face immediate suspension and a lengthy investigation if they are accused of sexually abusing a child. Deciding the truth sometimes comes down to weighing the teacher's word against the accuser's. More than 1500 teachers in the UK have faced investigation because of alleged sexual abuse over the past decade, but the great majority of them have been exonerated. Some falsely accused teachers have had their careers, their personal relationships and their mental health ruined, and a few have ended up committing suicide. Another unfortunate consequence is that most teachers no longer feel able to put a comforting arm around a child in distress, for fear of their action being misinterpreted.

What can you do?

◆ *Communicate.*

Make time to talk to your child and keep the communication channels open. If you have a warm, open and trusting relationship, your child will be more likely to let you know if he or she is worried or in trouble. Encourage them to tell you straight away if anything is making them anxious.

◆ *Think about who has access to your child.*

By far the biggest risk of sexual abuse comes from individuals who know your child. Be aware of who they are or might be. It is worth thinking about anyone who has unsupervised access to your child, such as an over-friendly uncle or football coach. Are you confident about them?

◆ **Apply the three Ws: Where, Who and When.**

Make sure you know *where* they are, *who* they are with and *when* they will be back. Also make sure they know where *you* are and how to contact you at all times.

◆ **Keep an eye on your child's Internet behaviour.**

Without being too intrusive, build up a picture of your child's Internet usage. Pay particular attention if they seem to be spending a lot of time in online chat rooms. Ask them what they have been doing and make sure they understand the dangers. One basic rule is never to reveal personal details to strangers they encounter in chat rooms or online discussion groups. In particular, children should never reveal their home address or phone number, the name or location of their school, or any other personal information from which they could be identified. (Needless to say, they should not give out their parents' credit card details either.) They should also be advised not to open e-mails from strangers.

◆ **Make sure your child knows enough to recognise sexual abuse.**

Help your child to develop a clear understanding of the boundaries between acceptable and unacceptable sexual behaviour – for example, the difference between normal physical contact and inappropriate sexual touching. Children should understand from an early age that when two people engage in sexual behaviour, neither person should feel under compulsion from the other.

◆ **Don't stop cuddling your child.**

Try not to let an awareness of child sexual abuse inhibit the normal physical affection that all parents feel for their children. Don't stop cuddling, hugging or kissing your children just because you are worried that someone might misinterpret your motives.

◆ **Get help if you think there is a problem.**

If you do suspect that a child is being, or has been, abused, you should get immediate professional advice. You should do this before attempting to confront the suspected abuser. Contact your local social services, your doctor, health visitor, the police, or the NSPCC Child Protection helpline. Doing this will not automatically result in police involvement, or in the child being removed from the home.

Further advice

Kidscape
Tel: 020 7730 3300
www.kidscape.org.uk
Extensive advice about the nature of abuse and how to keep children safe.

Childwatch
01482 325 552
e-mail: info@childwatch.org.uk
www.childwatch.org.uk

Confidential counselling for child and adult victims of abuse. The website contains an information section for parents.

Childline
Helpline: 0800 1111
www.childline.org.uk
Provides comfort, support and advice to children who feel that they are in danger. The website also offers information and advice for parents.

NSPCC

Tel 020 7825 2500

Helpline: 0808 800 5000

www.nspcc.org.uk

Offers a range of support and advice about abuse.

The Internet

www.wiseuptothenet.co.uk

www.childnet-int.org

For advice on safe use of the Internet by children.

Related worries

2. Might be abducted or murdered

6. Might be the victim of crime

10. Might be the victim of physical violence

16. Doesn't tell me what he/she is really thinking or feeling

28. Is being bullied

WORRY 12

Will only eat a narrow range of food/has food fads

Chances: HIGH   **Consequences: LOW**   **Control: MEDIUM**

Food fads are common in children, especially when younger. Two out of 3 children go through a stage of refusing to eat certain foods and 1 in 20 may reject most of what is set before them.

The most frequently rejected foods tend to be those with a bitter or unusual taste or texture. Two-thirds of under-10s regularly refuse fresh fruit and vegetables and 1 in 5 refuses anything green. Brussel sprouts, cabbage and tomatoes are the most disliked items.

One obvious reason why many children reject these foods is because of their taste. Children have a natural preference for sweet things and are far more sensitive to bitter tastes than adults. The vast majority of children grow out of these fads as their sense of taste develops.

Even with restricted diets, the vast majority of children still meet their necessary calorie intake and few children in the UK end up seriously malnourished.

Food fads are very common in children, especially amongst the under-tens. For the vast majority, such fads do little harm and they usually grow out of it in a year or less. Food fads are very different from serious eating disorders such as anorexia or bulimia, which are very rare in children under ten. Anorexia and bulimia tend to afflict older girls, and even then they are uncommon, affecting less than 1person in 3000. Food fads are often relatively short lived and, unlike eating disorders, they rarely have long-term negative implications.

Most children go through a period of fussy eating at least once in their childhood. This is in many respects a normal part of a child's growing independence and choice. For many children they are simply beginning to show preference for certain foods above others. As adults, we all prefer certain foods yet we may consider it strange when children start to exhibit their own choices.

Food fads are marked by the child consistently choosing to eat a very narrow range of food over an extended period. They can start and stop without apparent reason and tend to occur most often in children between the ages of two and ten. Food fads can be divided into four main types:

- *Selective eating.* Will only eat a narrow range of foods such as biscuits, fish fingers and chips. Refuses whole categories of food such as fruit and vegetables. Often claims to feel sick if asked to eat anything outside their chosen range.

- *Restrictive eating.* Seems not to eat much at all. Eats a range of foods but in very small amounts. Seems uninterested in food and often grazes rather than eating full meals.

- *Food refusal.* Eats normally some of the time but refuses to eat in certain situations or with certain people; for example, at school.

- *Inappropriate texture of food for age.* Will not eat certain textures; for example, still wants puréed or mashed food and won't eat lumps or crunchy items.

Why do some children adopt these patterns of eating? Young children can find food an arena for expressing their emotions, as it is one of the few issues where they are in control. Food refusal can be a response to anger, anxiety, or perceived lack of attention – by refusing to eat, the child gains the control in a relationship. Beginning to dictate food choices is also a simple way of a child expressing his or her growing independence and personality. Such behaviour is often unconscious rather than deliberate.

An additional factor is children's natural suspicion of novel flavours or textures. Research has found that the average child takes five or more presentations of a new food before he or she willingly accepts it. This is true even with favourites such as fruit and biscuits. Rather than just being picky, the child might be seen as playing it safe. The gastro-intestinal tract of a child is not as mature as that of an adult and pickiness may be an instinctive protective mechanism.

Mild intolerance to a food may be another explanation. Long before they can explain why, some children know that certain foods, such as dairy or wheat products, disagree with them. The child is not allergic as such: an allergy would cause physical symptoms such as a rash, vomiting or respiratory problems. Rather, they just find that the food does not 'agree' with them terribly well. For example, it may make them feel bloated or give them a slight stomach ache. Such a reaction can be amplified if a parent responds too strongly. Many parents have become so anxious about certain types of food that they unconsciously communicate their worries or superstitions to their children.

Probably the most important factor behind food fads is the most obvious one – taste. Clearly, taste is the primary reason for enjoying food at any age, but its influence is especially heightened during pregnancy and childhood. Children tend to like sweet tastes and dislike bitter tastes. These preferences can be seen in babies as young as a day old.

The conventional explanation is that sweetness signals that the food is a good source of calories, whereas bitterness signals possible danger. Breast milk contains both sugar and fat, making it taste sweet, whereas the alkaloids and other toxins found in plant foods tend to have a bitter taste. Hence young children appear to be predisposed to prefer sweet foods over bitter foods such as green vegetables. Foods containing fat, sugar or both are commonly described as palatable by children and adults alike. Women have a more negative reaction to bitterness than men, while infants have five times the concentration of taste buds than adults, and larger and more abundant receptors on the tongue. This makes them more sensitive to bitter tastes.

Responding to fussy eating

Despite all this, even fussy eaters nearly always manage to meet their basic nutritional needs – a fact that surprises some anxious parents. One reason is that a fussy eater's diet may not be quite as narrow as their parents think. Worried parents often overlook the fact that their child is regularly consuming, for example, milk or fruit juice, which will provide at least some of their requirements.

A second reason is that parents sometimes underestimate the adequacy of diets that might appear to be very narrow. The basic requirements for growth and development can be provided by a surprisingly restricted diet. Indeed the historic feeding patterns of people in many parts of the world demonstrate the ability of humans to survive and thrive on what appear to be remarkably restricted diets.

Fussy eating is often more upsetting for the parents than for the child. Preparing food for the family can be a rewarding task, even if it only involves heating up some baked beans and fish fingers – it reassures us that we are caring and providing for our children, and their appreciation can be very fulfilling. When a child rejects our efforts, we may take it personally and find the experience upsetting. Children are good observers and can sense the parent's feeling of rejection, which might encourage them to do it even more.

It has been suggested that parents can be grouped into one of four broad categories in terms of how they deal with their children's food fads: coaxers, detectives, diplomats or dictators. Younger parents tend to be either coaxers or detectives. Coaxers understand why good nutrition is important and try to persuade their child to eat more healthily, but they do not insist if the child still refuses. Detectives try to discover why their child dislikes a rejected food and are more anxious to provide foods packed with nutrients. Older parents tend to either be diplomats or dictators. Diplomats make no comment when their child refuses to eat something, but simply avoid serving the rejected food in future. Dictators order their child to eat and refuse to take no for an answer. Dictators are the ones most likely to report that their child's refusal to eat is a major cause of mealtime misery.

Most parents do not fall neatly into one of these four categories, but use a combination of two or more of the strategies. Experience suggests that this flexibility is a good idea. While it is highly desirable to establish healthy eating habits in childhood, research suggests that parents should not make food into a battleground. They should try not to give children lots of attention when they refuse to eat, as young children are more likely to continue with behaviour that has this effect. A better strategy is to praise them when they do show an interest in food, but to make no comment otherwise.

The evidence also shows that parents are better off not punishing, bribing, forcing or rewarding young children for eating certain things. Eating and discipline should be kept apart as two different areas in a child's life. If you promise your child a chocolate bar as long as she finishes her lunch, she may regard lunch as a punishment to be endured, with chocolate as a reward at the end. She may then place more value on the chocolate and less on the meal. A more effective strategy is to encourage your child to eat freely from whatever food you have prepared. If she is not hungry, however, make it clear that there will be nothing else until the next snack or mealtime, and stick to your guns.

What can you do?

◆ *Try not to over-react.*

However unreasonable your child's eating habits might seem, try to respond calmly. The bigger the drama you make out of a food fad, the longer it's likely to last. If your child refuses his meal, don't make a big fuss, but leave the meal in front of him and carry on eating yourself. He will soon realise that refusing food is less fun when he doesn't get the attention he is looking for. For the same reason, it may help if you do not invest too much time and effort in creating elaborate meals, as you may be even more frustrated if your child refuses to eat your creation.

◆ *Buy what you want your child to eat.*

Try to buy mainly the foods that you want your child to eat. This sounds very obvious, but too often we fill our cupboards with biscuits and then wonder why our children grow up wanting them. When they are hungry, most children will end up eating what is readily available.

◆ *Don't bribe your child to eat healthy foods.*

Children who are trained to regard, say, vegetables as something to be endured in order to win a reward (such as chocolate) are unlikely to develop a taste for vegetables.

◆ *Encourage your child to help with preparing food.*

Ask your child to help with planning and preparing meals and perhaps even with cooking. Children who help to make their own food are more likely to eat it.

◆ *Consider trying to conceal unpopular foods.*

You might try tricks such as blending vegetables into a sauce and putting it over pasta. As one food writer has pointed out, 'What children can't see, they can't pick out.' Similarly, you can often conceal unpleasant tastes; adding a little honey to a vegetable sauce, for example, will take the bitter edge off it. Obviously, tricks like these are easier to pull off with younger children. Teenagers are not easily fooled.

◆ *Limit snacks between meals.*

Children will have less appetite at mealtimes if they have been snacking. Try to limit food to mealtimes rather than allowing them to graze throughout the day.

◆ *Pick the right time to introduce new foods.*

It may be better not to introduce a new type of food when a young child is tired or really hungry, as they are more likely to reject it. Instead, pick a day when they are happy and rested, and introduce one new taste at a time. Combining a new taste with an old favourite is always a good tactic.

◆ *Try new foods yourself.*

Children are good observers. If you are a fussy eater your children will pick up on this and may follow your example.

◆ *Try to eat as many meals together as you can.*

Children are more likely to eat something if they see you eating the same food. Following the same principle, think about asking their friends over for lunch or tea. Many parents find that their child will eat more when other people are present.

Further advice

British Nutrition Foundation
Tel: 020 7404 6504.
www.nutrition.org.uk
Information on the nutritional needs of children and adolescents.

The Food Commission
Tel: 020 7837 2250
www.foodcomm.org.uk
Independent advice and information about healthy eating, including tips on getting children to eat well.

Scottish Healthy Eating Campaign
Tel: 0845 278 8878
www.healthyliving.gov.uk
Specific advice on how to tackle fussy eating.

Related worries

3. Eats too much sugar and sweet foods.
7. Eats too much junk food or convenience food.
25. Doesn't eat enough.
35. Doesn't get enough vitamins from his/her normal diet.

WORRY **13**

Has difficulty concentrating/ paying attention

23% of parents worried

....

Chances: HIGH   **Consequences: MEDIUM**   **Control: MEDIUM**

Most pre-school and primary school-aged children appear to have poor concentration and short attention spans in some situations, especially if they are doing something that does not interest them. That does not mean there is something wrong with them. Children are by nature active, inquisitive and somewhat impulsive.

Children may have difficulties concentrating for many different reasons. They may be disengaged at school because the work is too hard or too easy for them. They may have poor language skills, poor listening skills, or problems with their hearing or vision. They may be depressed. A small minority of children may be diagnosed as having Attention Deficit/Hyperactivity Disorder (ADHD) if their attention problems are severe and interfere with normal daily life.

Parents and teachers can use various behavioural tactics to help focus children's attention. These tactics can be helpful with 'normally overactive' children, as well as children with ADHD.

All normal young children are active and exploratory. They are also to some degree distractible and impulsive, and will often attend to a particular task or activity for only a relatively short period of time. Their ability to focus their attention depends a great deal on what they are doing – a young child will usually be able to concentrate for far longer if watching a favourite television programme than if they are trying to read a boring story.

Children actually have considerable powers of concentration from a very early age. Many adults would envy the capacity of a baby just a few days old to concentrate on feeding from the breast or bottle. But as babies grow into toddlers, and then into young children, adults expect them to be able to concentrate on an ever-widening range of activities and for longer periods of time. Some parents have unrealistically high expectations about the ability of a normal four- or five-year-old to sit still and focus on one task for a long time, especially if that task is not something the child finds remotely interesting.

Children's powers of concentration continue to improve during childhood, although they are always greater when a child is really interested in a task. All the same, individual children differ considerably in how long they can concentrate on tasks such as drawing, following a parent around a supermarket, sitting in class listening to a story, or getting on with school work on their own. Some children can persist with demanding tasks in the classroom, while others just do not have the patience.

A child's ability to concentrate depends partly on their temperament. It also depends on their upbringing – for example, whether they have been consistently praised or rewarded for concentrating, and the degree to which their parents have laid down clear boundaries between acceptable and unacceptable behaviour.

It is normal, then, for pre-school or primary school-aged children to have difficulty concentrating under certain circumstances. However, some children have more difficulty than others, and a small minority have severe and persistent problems. A school-aged child who finds it unusually hard to concentrate may also find it difficult to cope with the demands of everyday life, especially in the classroom. They may appear to be lazy or defiant, their learning may suffer, and their behaviour will often annoy their teachers and parents.

There are many different reasons why a child may have greater than normal difficulties with concentrating. One possible explanation may be that the child has unrecognised problems with their hearing or vision. A child who cannot see or hear properly may well become frustrated and fidgety, especially in the classroom. And they may be unaware that they have a problem. It's often the teacher or parent who first realises that a child cannot see or hear properly.

Restlessness in school can sometimes be a sign that a child has become disengaged because the tasks they are being asked to perform are not well matched to their level of achievement. If the work is too hard, or too easy, the child may just switch off.

Lack of concentration might also reflect some other issue, such as a personality clash between the child and a particular teacher. Indeed, concentration difficulties can often result from something as trivial as the seating arrangements: put two chatty friends together in the classroom and both may have problems attending to the teacher. However, problems such as these are likely to be specific to the classroom, and should not show up to the same extent at home and elsewhere.

Many school-age children have occasional problems concentrating because they are not getting enough sleep and therefore feel sleepy during the day (see Worry 15, page 81). Tired children, like tired adults, can find it very hard to pay attention, especially when asked to perform long, boring tasks. General difficulties in concentrating can also result from poorly developed language skills or poorly developed listening skills.

In a few cases, depression may lie at the root of the problem. Depression is thought to affect around

1 in 100 children and a larger proportion of teenagers, but it is often difficult to spot among younger children. A depressed school-age child may find it hard to concentrate and lose interest in school or social activities.

Looking at ADHD

A small minority of children are not able to focus on anything for more than a few moments. As well as showing poor concentration, these children are generally impulsive, overactive, distractible and unusually uninhibited with people they don't know very well. In school, they are unable to sit in their seats for more than a few moments and they frequently disrupt the work of others. These children may be diagnosed as having Attention Deficit/Hyperactivity Disorder (ADHD). Some children are more likely than others to develop ADHD. As in many other areas of life, boys are at greater risk than girls; in fact, boys are at least three times more likely than girls to be diagnosed with the condition.

There is no sharp division between children who are thought to have ADHD and children who are just unusually active and distractible. So it's not surprising that doctors and psychologists sometimes differ in their opinions about whether a child is affected in this way or not. To make things even more confusing, there are two official definitions of ADHD: one American and one accepted by the World Health Organisation (WHO). The American definition of ADHD is broader than the WHO definition, and doctors who use it find that about 1 in 20 children are affected. However, using the stricter WHO definition, only about 1 in 50 children are reckoned to have ADHD. This is because the WHO definition of ADHD requires children to be affected in their daily lives to a greater extent and to exhibit their problems in all aspects of their lives, in school as well as at home. In the UK, the WHO definition is generally preferred.

Some doctors (both psychiatrists and paediatricians), psychologists and teachers do not like making the ADHD diagnosis at all. They point to the fact that some children diagnosed as ADHD behave perfectly well in some situations, if not in others. What these children need, they argue, is not a diagnosis and medication, but suitable upbringing and care. They feel the world ought to accept that there are differences between children and make allowances accordingly, tailoring the environment to the child rather than trying to mould the child into a pattern of behaviour that does not come naturally.

However, while many experts think the ADHD diagnosis is applied too liberally, most accept that there are some children who are badly affected by their concentration problems, and that these children would have difficulties no matter how much other people tried to make allowances for them. Of course, we're not talking here about children who are simply more active and 'into things' than their parents would like them to be. We are also not talking about the 'normally overactive' children who are more active than most, and whose parents find them wearing, but who do not fit the criteria for ADHD.

Most children with ADHD have an inherited vulnerability to develop the problem. They have been born with a propensity to be unusually active and lacking in concentration. Some ADHD children are born to parents who have difficulty in setting clear limits to what is permitted. Some have parents who are not very good at noticing when their children want attention, perhaps because they are preoccupied with their own problems. A combination of predisposition and unsuitable environment is likely to lead to a child developing ADHD. However, some ADHD children are so genetically vulnerable that they would probably develop the problem no matter how marvellous their parents were.

Children with ADHD have a greater risk of experiencing educational and other behavioural problems as well as social difficulties. Their language development may be delayed and they may have difficulty learning to read. One of the biggest risks arises when the disorder leads to the development of anti-social behaviour in childhood and adolescence. Obviously, the outlook worsens considerably if this happens – children with disruptive behaviour are less likely to do well in the standard school system.

The good news is that many children with ADHD go on to do well in later life. They may choose jobs that suit their restlessness. Most will be able to lead normal lives, although they may have more than their fair share of ups and downs in their personal relationships. Children who are 'normally hyperactive' (as opposed to having ADHD) may not experience any unusual difficulties later in life.

Responding to ADHD

Whatever a child's level of concentration problems, parents can do a great deal to try to improve the situation (see What can you do? below). However, for the small minority of children with ADHD, professional help will also be needed. The official government National Institute for Clinical Excellence (NICE) guidelines suggest that all children who are significantly impaired by ADHD-type symptoms should have a specialist assessment.

If a specialist assessment confirms a diagnosis of 'WHO-type' ADHD, then the first step will be some form of behavioural intervention. This generally involves advising the child's parents about the need for consistency, a calm environment, avoidance of over-stimulation, rewards for small improvements in behaviour, and so on. This type of intervention often brings about improvement in the child's behaviour, but if it fails to make things better, then a course of stimulant drugs will usually be offered, perhaps at a specialist clinic run by a psychiatrist or paediatrician.

Of course, whether or not their child receives medication is a matter for parents to decide. They can refuse. However, most doctors in the UK only offer medication where it is really thought to be necessary. Methylphenidate (better known under its trade name of Ritalin) is still the drug of first choice, although there are others that can be tried if this does not work.

Stimulant drugs such as Ritalin have been in use since 1939. Dozens of trials comparing their effectiveness to dummy tablets have shown that they work. All children, including normal children without ADHD, will show some improvements in their concentration if they take these drugs. However, professionals agree that they should be given only to children whose lives are significantly affected at home and at school by ADHD. The drugs do not cure the condition, they just improve it. But sometimes the improvement is quite large.

The drugs used to treat ADHD can have various side-effects, including weight loss, irritability, sleep disturbances, headaches and stomach aches, and the child's growth may also be affected. Some children do not experience any of these problems, but quite a few have one or two. As with all drugs, the side effects must be balanced against any positive effects. If the drug makes the crucial difference to the child's ability to attend a normal school or to make friends, then some side effects may be regarded as acceptable. Some children cannot tolerate Ritalin or do not benefit from it. If so, there are other similar drugs that can be tried.

The number of children taking drugs for ADHD has risen markedly over the past decade. Moreover, a growing number of teenagers and young adults in the USA and UK are choosing to take Ritalin as a performance enhancer, because it improves their ability to concentrate at work or when studying for exams. Most of these individuals do not suffer from ADHD. No case of addiction has been reported among children who have been properly prescribed this medication, but the drugs do have a street value and might cause addiction if they fell into the wrong hands.

Unfortunately ADHD is usually a long-lasting problem. Although the level of hyperactivity usually declines with age, difficulties with attention may persist into adolescence and adulthood. Some people find that they continue to benefit from medication and carry on taking it until they are adults.

What can you do?

◆ **Don't expect too much of your child.**

Try to be realistic about your child's ability to concentrate on single tasks for long periods, especially if they do not find those tasks particularly interesting.

◆ **Find out if your child's problem is specific to one situation or more general.**

If your child shows concentration difficulties at home, talk to their teacher to find out if the same difficulties are also apparent in school.

◆ **Make sure your child's hearing and vision are OK.**

A child who cannot hear or see properly in the classroom may become bored, frustrated and disengaged.

◆ **Make sure your child is getting enough sleep.**

Many school-aged children do not get enough sleep during the week and consequently feel sleepy during the day (see Worry 15, page 81). Sleepy people cannot easily concentrate or pay attention for long.

◆ **Be clear and consistent when you ask your child to do things.**

Give clear, simple instructions and try not to be vague or long-winded. Divide up tasks into small, easily achievable steps. Make sure your child has everything they need to complete a task before they start it. (This is especially helpful in the classroom.)

◆ **Reward success.**

Praise your child for concentrating just a bit longer than he or she can normally manage.

◆ **Try not to over-stimulate your child.**

Let your child have only one toy or one book at a time, or only one friend round to play. In the classroom, they might do better if they sit next to a child who is good at concentrating, rather than their best friend who wants to chat all the time.

◆ **Encourage your child to get plenty of physical exercise.**

Take your child to the park, let them run around the garden or encourage them to play football.

Further advice

NHS Direct
Tel: 0845 4647
www.nhsdirect.nhs.uk
Information about ADHD, and problems with hearing or sight.

ADDers
www.adders.org
Information, support and practical help to ADHD sufferers and their families.

Mental Health Foundation
Tel: 020 7802 0300
E-mail: mhf@mhf.org.uk
www.mhf.org.uk
Information and advice on ADHD.

Related worries

15. Does not get enough sleep
27. Is bored or under-stimulated at school
29. Is disorganised/loses things

WORRY 14

Will not be successful in adult life if he/she does not do well at school

23% of parents worried

Chances: MEDIUM   **Consequences: MEDIUM**   **Control: MEDIUM**

Education is about developing as a person and acquiring skills in the broadest sense. It should be as much about developing social skills, life skills, self-confidence, independence, maturity, physical fitness and happiness as it is about gaining qualifications. Yet some parents choose to measure their child's success at school mainly on the basis of grades.

Children are gaining more qualifications and staying on in education longer than ever before. Around half of all children in England and Wales get five or more A–C grade GCSEs and 7 out of 10 stay on after 16 for some sort of further or higher education. Less than 1 in 20 leave school with no GCSEs.

Qualifications definitely help children. They open up more options and career paths. The higher the qualifications a person has, the more they are likely to earn and the less likely they are to be unemployed. People with higher qualifications are also more likely to enjoy their work, to live longer and be healthier.

Academic success is not everything. Once in a job, an individual's motivation, persistence and experience will have a stronger influence on their future success than their school grades. And for certain roles, such as sales or entrepreneurship, formal qualifications may be of limited help.

Parents can have a big influence on how well their children do at school. Generally speaking, the greater the importance parents place on education, and the more they communicate this to their children, the better their children are likely to do in life.

There is little doubt that doing well at school and achieving good qualifications are very important. If nothing else, they will give a child a wider range of options in life.

Young people are gaining more qualifications and staying in education longer. Today, more than two million are in higher education and 1 in 3 children go to university; in the early 1960s it was 1 in 20. The number of women in higher education has also soared. In 1970 only a third of students in higher education were female, whereas today it is half.

Why have academic qualifications become so important? Fifty years ago the majority of jobs in Britain were manual or skilled labour. Today, the majority are in service- or knowledge-based industries and this trend is only likely to accelerate. For some jobs such as medicine, law and accountancy, high-level qualifications have always been a requirement, but the list of careers requiring further education is growing.

Qualifications not only open doors, they also allow people to earn more and help them to find their job more fulfilling. Someone with qualifications is four times less likely to end up unemployed than someone who has left school without qualifications.

However, some parents have perhaps become overly concerned with such statistics. The UK currently has a low and stable rate of unemployment, and most children will go on to get a job, form happy relationships and earn a reasonable living whether or not they have good qualifications. The government has set a target of getting half of all young people into higher education, and more than a third of children now get two or more A-levels. Nonetheless, 1 in 20 children leave school with no qualifications and just under a third of children in England and Wales still leave school at 16. One in 6 of the current work force still have no qualifications.

Parents can be very demanding of their children when it comes to passing exams. It is easy to fall into the trap of comparing your child against the best in their class rather than checking what is the average. Generally speaking, children will end up in roughly the same earning band as their parents. Social mobility (moving from one social or economic class to another) has not increased since the 1950s.

Qualifications versus education

Several factors are worth bearing in mind here. One is that not all qualifications do much to improve the earning potential of a child. Getting two or more A-level passes significantly increases earning potential, but getting only one A-level pass makes only a marginal difference compared with getting five or more good GCSEs.

Also, students now have to consider the short-term financial hit they are likely to take by staying on in education. Obviously, they are forgoing earning while studying. But most also leave higher education with debts of up to £20,000. Many may therefore be worse off financially for perhaps several years after leaving education than those with fewer qualifications. Indeed, some could remain worse off in the longer term too, depending on the career path they choose.

On average, graduates earn significantly more

than non-graduates – around £400,000 over their working lifetime. But this is an *average* figure, which is skewed by a relatively small number of high earners. In fact, many graduates earn little or no more than many non-graduates. Those who go into careers such as teaching, academia, scientific research or charitable work end up earning little more than many non-graduates. For example, at the time of writing, a university lecturer or newly qualified teacher will probably start on a salary of under £20,000. By comparison, police officers who require no higher education can start on as much as £26,000.

Although entry to many jobs does require academic qualifications, there are other spheres where this is not the case, such as sales and entre-preneurship. Those making it to sales manager level are just as likely to have no degree, and being a graduate offers no real financial advantage for sales people. For them, success is more to do with motivation and immediate results. A survey of Britain's top 500 entrepreneurs found that only half had a degree and many had left school at 16. Classic examples are people such as Jamie Oliver and Richard Branson. Both found school extremely tough, but used their drive, passion and risk-taking skills to achieve huge success.

Gaining qualifications and a higher income will not necessarily make your child happier either. Research shows that people in industrialised coun-tries are not generally becoming happier over time, despite much greater prosperity. We assume that getting qualifications, and hence earning more money, will make us happier. But all the evidence points to a different conclusion.

Money does matter, and being very poor is cer-tainly associated with unhappiness, but earning more and more money may not make your children happier. The evidence suggests that there is a ceiling beyond which more money hardly increases personal happiness. An individual's ability to create and maintain successful relationships with other people has a much bigger influence on their happiness than their income.

So, acquiring lots of qualifications is not the be-all and end-all that some parents believe it to be. However, qualifications and education are two dif-ferent things. Education and the life experience of being at school or university provide far more than just formal qualifications. They give individuals the opportunity to develop the other skills and personal qualities that will be crucial to their success and happiness, including the ability to relate successfully with other people.

What can parents do to help their children succeed at school? Obviously a child's basic intel-lectual abilities will have an influence on how well they do. So, too, will simply attending school: less than a quarter of persistent truants and those excluded from school stay on in full-time education at 16 and more than a quarter are out of work.

Another important factor is a parent's own edu-cation level. Generally speaking, the higher the level of a parent's education, the more likely their child is to do well at school. Eight out of 10 children with parents in professional jobs achieve five GCSEs, compared with only 3 out of 10 children whose parents have routine occupations. Children of professional parents are almost four times more likely to progress to higher education.

Signalling to children that learning is both valuable and satisfying can have a huge impact. This is not to say that parents should push or 'hothouse' their children. Indeed, it has been shown that what children need to develop is intrinsic (or self-driven) rather than extrinsic or external motivation. If parents focus too much on grades or gold stars, children learn to be moti-vated only when an external prize or reward is offered. This can undermine their ability to value learning for its own sake, which in the long run could reduce their potential more than receiving a B grade rather than an A. School is about learning to learn.

Qualifications may gain a child entry to their chosen career, but their attitude and personality will be the biggest factors in determining how well they do in it. Perhaps surprisingly, an individual's likeability seems to have little influence on their success. Instead, research shows that one of the most important personality traits appears to be conscientiousness, which means having the internal drive and motivation to see a task through to completion, even when faced with obstacles and frustrations.

Emotional intelligence plays a huge role in people's career success – a fact that is now widely recognised. Being emotionally intelligent means knowing your emotions (having self-awareness), managing them, motivating yourself, recognising emotions in others (empathy) and handling relationships. Not only do these skills aid children in later life, but they also appear to boost academic performance. Emotionally intelligent children tend to be better motivated and better organised, enabling them to perform better in exams.

What can you do?

◆ **Make sure your child attends school regularly.**

Your child will stand little chance of doing well if he or she is truanting. If you suspect your child might be truanting, talk to the school immediately and develop a joint plan of action. Your child might be experiencing trouble at school, such as bullying, or they might have become disillusioned. Whatever the reason, truancy can usually be sorted out if tackled promptly.

◆ **Don't rely too much on bribery.**

Rewards and incentives have their place. But if bribery is over-used, it can encourage an attitude that the only reason for working is to receive a reward, and that learning must therefore not be worthwhile in its own right. A child who is routinely bribed to do school work may end up thinking that it cannot be satisfying or otherwise rewarding.

◆ **Try to understand what your child is learning at school.**

You can find this out from their form teacher, or perhaps from the Department for Education and Skills website. Try to think of experiences or outings that will help to bring subjects to life for your child.

◆ **Make it clear that education is something you value.**

One of the best ways to do this is to get involved in your child's school. Helping out at sports day, or with classroom reading practice, signals to your child that you think school is important.

◆ **Lead by example.**

Consider enrolling in an adult education course or taking up something you can do with your child, such as learning a new musical instrument. This shows your child that learning should continue throughout life, not just until a test is passed.

◆ **Encourage your child to stick with things.**

Remember that people can do well in their careers even if they did not do well academically, provided they are conscientious, focused and persistent. Before your child takes up a new hobby, explain to them that they will have to stick with this new interest for a while, and not just drop it straight away if they find it hard going.

▸

◆ *Choose your child's school carefully.*

Although a school that does best academically might be the most appealing to you, your child might actually do better in a less pressured environment. Find out what emphasis the school gives to personal as well as academic development. Most importantly, find out how much your child likes the school and wants to be part of it.

Further advice

The Parent Centre

Tel: 0870 000 22 88 (Department for Education and Skills)

www.parentcentre.gov.uk

Comprehensive guide to the education system for parents, with links to other organisations and online discussion forums.

Department for Education and Skills, Aim Higher website

www.dfes.gov.uk/aimhigher/

Website for young people encouraging them to go into higher education, along with information for parents.

The National Curriculum Online

www.nc.uk.net

Details of all subjects covered in schools and the standards expected of children at different stages.

Related worries

13. Has difficulty concentrating/paying attention.

26. Isn't reading or writing as well as he/she should.

27. Is bored or under-stimulated at school.

36. Won't do his/her homework.

39. Isn't as good at maths as he/she should be.

WORRY 15

Does not get enough sleep

23% of parents worried

....

Chances: HIGH   **Consequences: MEDIUM**   **Control: HIGH**

Children differ considerably in their individual requirements for sleep. Some need more than others. However, many school-aged children do not get sleep of sufficient quantity and quality, especially on weekday nights during the school term, and as a consequence their mental and physical well-being can suffer. Lack of sleep can seriously impair a child's ability to concentrate and perform in the classroom, as well as having other undesirable effects.

The problem of insufficient sleep tends to get worse during adolescence, when children go to bed later but still have to get up early for school. Adolescents and teenagers generally need more sleep than adults.

Possible solutions include giving sleep a higher priority in the family lifestyle, sticking to a regular sleep schedule, and keeping TVs, computers and other forms of entertainment out of the bedroom.

We all spend a good third of our lives asleep. Sleep is an absolute biological necessity, but one that is often neglected in our busy 24/7 society. We live in a culture where many people regard sleep as unproductive down-time which would be better spent working or being entertained.

Research in several countries has shown that a substantial proportion of children, young people and adults routinely get less sleep than they need to function on peak form. Parents are therefore right to be concerned about this issue.

There is no one-size-fits-all answer to the question 'How much sleep does a child need?' Like adults, children differ considerably in their sleep requirements. If a child is bright, cheerful and wide-awake all day, every day, then he or she is probably getting enough sleep. But if a child often seems sleepy during the day and frequently complains of feeling tired, there may be a problem. As a very crude rule of thumb, the gold standard of eight hours a night is probably not far off the mark for most people.

The most obvious sign that someone is not getting sleep of sufficient quantity or quality is that they feel sleepy during the day and find it hard to concentrate. Research has revealed that a surprisingly high percentage of school-age children suffer from daytime sleepiness. According to some experts, up to a quarter of children are affected, and even the more cautious estimates put the figure at 5-10 per cent. When children are asked about their own sleep, as many as half of them say they are not getting enough and that they find it difficult to stay awake during the day.

In most schools it is not unusual to see children who are having obvious difficulty staying alert in the classroom. Some even fall asleep during lessons. (It is probably no coincidence that these same sleepy pupils can often describe late-night TV programmes they have watched the night before.) Lack of sleep is certainly not unique to British children; for example, researchers in China have found that 1 in 10 Chinese primary-school children sometimes fall asleep at school.

Does it really matter if a child is not getting enough sleep to meet their needs? The answer is a definite yes. The occasional late night is no disaster, but consistently failing to get enough sleep over long periods can be altogether more serious. Sleep of sufficient quantity and quality is essential for mental and physical well-being. We can survive longer without food than we can without sleep.

Lack of sleep has wide-ranging effects on the body, mind, behaviour and emotions, and nearly all of them are bad. Sleep deprivation impairs people's attention, memory, decision-making, communication skills and creativity. Sleep-deprived adults and children perform worse on most mental tasks. Mood and emotions are also affected: tired people usually feel low, their social skills are impaired and they often appear irritable. Research has found that children with persistent sleep problems tend to have poorer relationships with their parents and with other children.

Insufficient sleep can have a big impact on children's behaviour and performance in school. About a fifth of primary school children who have sleep problems also experience academic problems at school. Similarly, teenagers who regularly get less than seven hours' sleep a night are found to be more likely to struggle or fail in school, other things being equal. Conversely, researchers have found that children who sleep well tend to have higher self-esteem and to be more motivated at school, more receptive to their teachers, less bored and better able to control their aggression.

Sleep deprivation has a particularly big impact on the higher mental faculties such as abstract thinking and creativity, whereas its effect on a person's ability to perform routine tasks is often milder. Therefore, tired children can often still go through the motions at school, making it harder to spot that they are sleep-deprived. However, their fatigue makes them unable to realise their full potential.

Lack of sleep can have even more serious consequences in the longer term. Adolescents and teenagers who sleep badly are statistically more likely to suffer from depression, anxiety and emotional instability. They are also more likely to have accidents and more likely to use tobacco, alcohol and illicit drugs. As if that were not enough, sleep problems are associated with various physical symptoms, including headaches, backaches, stomach upsets and a general perception of being in poor health.

Consequences of sleep deprivation

More and more evidence has been emerging in recent years that sleep disorders may be contributing to the rising tide of behavioural and emotional problems among children. Numerous scientific studies have uncovered links between sleep problems and behaviour problems in pre-school and school-aged children. In particular, several studies have found evidence of connections between sleep problems and Attention Deficit/Hyperactivity Disorder (ADHD) – see Worry 13, page 71.

ADHD is characterised by severe lack of concentration, impulsiveness, hyperactivity, or some combination of the three, but lack of sleep can sometimes produce similar symptoms in children. Tiredness affects children differently from adults. Whereas tired adults lack energy and become less active, tired children often do the reverse, becoming fidgety, irritable, inattentive, disruptive, impulsive and generally bad company. A very tired child can sometimes behave like a child with symptoms of ADHD. A significant proportion of children diagnosed with ADHD suffer from sleep problems which result in irregular sleep patterns, less sleep and poorer quality sleep.

Part of the explanation for the association between daytime behaviour problems and sleep problems seems to lie with a sleep-related breathing disorder known as sleep apnoea, which involves repeated interruptions in breathing during sleep. Some children display a marked improvement in behaviour when their sleep apnoea is treated.

Why do so many children and teenagers get insufficient sleep, and what can be done about it? One big barrier to good sleep is lifestyle. As children enter adolescence they tend to go to bed later and later. Nonetheless, on weekdays they still have to get up early for school. The net result is less sleep.

Many adolescents end up with barely seven hours of sleep on weekday nights, when they probably need eight or nine. They build up a sleep deficit during the week, which they pay off by sleeping more at the weekends. Most children and teenagers get substantially less sleep on school nights than they do at weekends and on holiday. It is not unusual for teenagers to wake two or three hours later at weekends, if given the chance.

Another reason why some children get insufficient sleep is because they have a sleep problem which curtails or disrupts their sleep, such as insomnia, recurrent nightmares or sleep apnoea. Some younger children have disrupted sleep because they frequently wet the bed. Blind and visually impaired children are especially prone to sleep problems.

Insomnia, which means difficulty going to sleep or staying asleep, is a surprisingly common problem among children and teenagers. And a common cause of insomnia is anxiety. Worries about school, exams, friendships or relationships with the opposite sex can make it hard to fall asleep. Caffeine from coffee, tea or soft drinks will also make it harder to fall asleep.

Lack of sleep can be infectious, in the sense that children who sleep badly may disrupt the sleep of other family members. This can be a particular problem if they share a bedroom with a brother or sister.

What can you do?

◆ **Give sleep a high priority in your family's life.**

It is in children's interests for parents to be fairly strict about bedtime and not allow them regularly to stay up late for trivial reasons such as watching TV. Conversely, children should not be made to feel guilty about having a nap or catching up on their sleep at weekends (within reason). Sending your child to bed is not the same thing as ensuring that he or she gets sufficient sleep, especially during adolescence. Check that they have actually gone to bed and turned the light out.

◆ **Do not assume your child must be getting enough sleep.**

Some adolescents deprive themselves of sleep during the week without even realising it. You can judge whether they are getting enough by whether they remain bright and alert during the day. If your child awakes spontaneously each morning full of beans, and feels wide awake all day, they are probably getting enough sleep. However, if they often feel sleepy during the day and find it hard to concentrate or stay awake, they may not be getting enough.

◆ **Aim for a regular sleep schedule.**

In an ideal world, children (and adults too) should go to bed and get up at about the same times every day, including at weekends. Sticking to a regular sleep schedule will usually help to improve both the quantity and quality of sleep. In reality, busy people tend to short-change their sleep during the week and catch up by sleeping in at the weekends, so a regular sleep schedule can be hard to achieve.

◆ **Set a good example.**

Demonstrate through your own behaviour that you value sleep.

◆ **Encourage your child to wind down before going to bed.**

Many children (and adults) find it harder to get to sleep if they have been doing something mentally stimulating during the hour or so before bedtime, such as playing an exciting computer game, watching an action-packed movie, talking to a friend on the phone, or rushing to finish an important piece of work. It may be helpful for your child to have a 'winding down' period immediately before they go to bed.

◆ **Keep TVs out of bedrooms.**

Ideally, children should not have TVs or computers in their bedrooms, since these compete with sleep. Bedrooms should be places of rest, not activity and stimulation.

◆ **Warn your child about caffeine.**

Caffeine makes it harder to fall asleep, so discourage your child from consuming too much during the day. Remember that many young people get most of their caffeine from soft drinks, not tea or coffee.

◆ **Do not ignore heavy and persistent snoring.**

If your child snores heavily every night and is sleepy during the day, you should consider the possibility that he or she might be suffering from a sleep-related breathing disorder known as sleep apnoea. If you suspect that your child might have sleep apnoea, or some other sleep problem, ask your GP for advice. If appropriate, your GP may refer your child to a specialist sleep clinic.

Further advice

British Sleep Society

www.british-sleep-society.org.uk

Charity that aims to improve public health by promoting education and research into sleep and its disorders.

British Snoring and Sleep Apnoea Association

www.britishsnoring.com

Products and advice to help with snoring and sleep apnoea.

Related worries

13. Has difficulty concentrating/paying attention
17. Won't go to bed
21. Won't get up, get dressed and get ready in the mornings

Doesn't tell me what he/she is really thinking or feeling

22% of parents worried

Chances: HIGH   **Consequences: MEDIUM**   **Control: MEDIUM**

As children grow up and become more independent they may begin to withhold information from their parents. Children do not need to, and won't, tell their parents everything they are thinking and feeling. Parents should nonetheless feel that their children will talk if they are worried or need help.

Almost half of all teenagers feel unable to discuss their problems with their parents. The most common time for encountering communication problems is from the age of about 12 or 13. Boys typically find it harder than girls to talk to their parents. Children of all ages tend to talk more to their mother than to their father.

Practical constraints such as parents not being around, the TV being on, or siblings listening in, can impede communication between parents and children. The biggest barrier, however, seems to be some parents' inability simply to listen. Parents are often too ready to lecture or dictate rather than stop and listen.

Trying to open a conversation with a stroppy adolescent can sometimes feel like talking to a brick wall. 'How was school?' 'Fine.' 'What did you do today?' 'Nothing.' Such conversations can leave parents feeling rejected and unaware of what is going on in their child's world. More importantly, teaching children good communication skills and establishing good communication with them are vital to their development and long-term happiness.

As many parents have discovered, good communication with children does not always happen automatically or easily. Indeed, poor communication between parents and children is one of the most common reasons for tension in families. Research shows that the desire to talk comes from both sides, with fathers, mothers and children regarding taking time to communicate as equally essential. Yet 3 out of 5 parents believe that communication with their school-aged children is getting worse, and nearly half of all teenagers feel they cannot discuss their problems with their parents. The problem seems to be not so much a lack of desire to communicate, but more a lack of practical knowledge of how to overcome the many obstacles to good communication.

Children who are good communicators tend to form stronger bonds with their own parents and other adult figures in their life. They are able to express their own needs clearly, and to interpret and read accurately the signals communicated by those around them. Research shows that good communicators tend to be accepted more easily by their peers, do better at school and are less likely to fall into drug or alcohol abuse. They go on to be more successful in their careers and are less likely to experience depression or other mental health problems.

For all these reasons, helping children to be good communicators, both with their parents and with other people, is clearly worth the effort. So, how can they be helped?

Children begin to acquire and develop complex communication skills from a very early age. From birth onwards their relationship and communica-tion with their main caregiver can have a profound influence on their willingness to share their feelings. Just like adults, infants learn to communicate partly as a means of getting another person to do something: they might, for example, want a drink, to be held, or simply to be acknowledged with a smile. Psychologists believe that when infants communicate in this way they are judging both the dependability and responsiveness of their carer. If a carer reliably responds to their communication, the infant is more likely to learn that communicating is an effective way of getting what they want. Conversely, if their cries and chatter are ignored, they become less likely to initiate interactions in future.

Children who develop a strong relationship with at least one carer in their early years tend to become better communicators who are more willing to talk openly to parents and others later in life. One sign of a good relationship is the amount of non-verbal communication that passes between two people. Sometimes, a facial expression or silence can convey more than words. A parent who develops an ability to read the individual signs from their child early on stands a better chance of understanding their feelings as they develop.

In the early childhood years, poor communication between parent and child can result from limited language development. Research has shown that by three to four years of age, children are able to recognise their own internal emotional states and to make general comments about their feelings. However, until they are a few years older (around the age of eight) children have a limited vocabulary to describe their emotions in detail or depth, and so they may find it hard to express how or why they do things. Even the average ten-year-old is unable to exploit the full vocabulary that an adult would use to express their emotions. Finding their verbal abilities limited, many children choose to express their emotions through their behaviour instead.

The barriers to good communication change as children get older. As their confidence and independence develop, and their own views and opinions are shaped, children may simply be less *willing* to talk to their parents. Boys generally have more of a problem in this regard than girls.

If there is a key age for change, it seems to be around 13. According to one study, only half of 13-year-olds feel they can talk to their parents, compared with 70 per cent of 12-year-olds. This timing might tie in with changes at school. The first year of secondary school can be a testing time for many children, during which they rely heavily on their parents for support. By their second year, however, most of them have become more comfortable, and are getting more of their support from peers.

A few simple principles can help to keep communication open during the testing years of adolescence. The first is simply to keep talking, however banal the topic may seem. Families where communication between parent and child is judged to be good by both sides are found to spend more time talking about mundane aspects of domestic life, such as TV, bedtime, household chores, homework, and personal possessions. It appears that simply by being there, and keeping the channels of communication open, parents can encourage children to talk to them when something troubling or significant happens. Talking has become a habit.

Three out of 4 parents who believe that communication with their children is getting worse blame TV and computer games. And they are probably right. TV can be a real obstacle to good communication. By switching on the TV, a parent may be indicating that their desire to watch TV is greater than their desire to interact with their child.

Having a TV on in the room makes it difficult to have any meaningful discussion, yet in many families the TV remains on from when children return home from school until bedtime. Six out of 10 families with children eat their evening meal in front of the TV, killing any chance of quality communication. It is not surprising, therefore, that children who watch the most TV tend to have poorer and fewer social interactions, both with their family and with others.

If we want our children to talk to us, we must sometimes pick a time and a topic of interest to them. Grilling a child on what they did at school that day is unlikely to result in a free-flowing discussion. Many children are tired by the time they get home and simply want to relax. Moreover, describing in detail what they did in school is simply not that interesting for them. The early evening, when parents have perhaps just returned home from work, may be a convenient time for them to talk about their child's day, but it probably won't be a good time from the child's point of view. Six out of 10 parents blame their longer working hours for their unsatisfactory communication with their children.

However, the one thing that seems to make the biggest difference to parent–child communication is whether parents know how to listen. Many adults are much better at talking than they are at truly listening. One of the most common reasons that teenagers give for unsatisfactory communication with older members of their family is that they are not listened to. Indeed, 3 out of 4 11- to 16-year-olds say that being listened to is the key determinant of the quality of their relationship with their parents.

Good communication depends on each person's ability to consider and understand the other's point of view. Children need to have their feelings respected, even if their parents do not agree with them. A parent can acknowledge a child's feelings without necessarily accepting their behaviour – it should be acceptable for a child to feel angry, for example, but not to hit. If a child's feelings are ignored, they may deduce that there is little point trying to explain anything to their parents.

Obviously, few parents set out deliberately to ignore their child's views or feelings. More often it is just that listening can be difficult to do. Parents may already be wedded to a particular outcome, or believe that offering advice is the most helpful thing to do, when often the last thing a child needs is more advice. They just want to be listened to.

What can you do?

◆ **Don't just talk – listen.**

A fundamental principle of good communication is that it must be two-way. Being an adult should not mean dominating every exchange. The aim should be to listen as much as you talk. Obviously, children sometimes do need clear advice and guidance, but try not to give it before you have listened to them. Hear them out first, and try not to interrupt or inject your opinions until they have had their say.

◆ **Be attentive.**

Listening requires attentiveness. Paying attention and putting aside what you are doing, even if that is not very convenient, shows that you intend to listen. A harder part of being attentive may be putting aside your opinions, thoughts and conclusions until you have heard what your child is trying to say. You may not agree with what they're saying, but at least be willing to listen.

◆ **Check understanding.**

You need to know whether you have understood what your child really means. Listening requires both hearing words and sensing feelings. Check out your interpretation of the messages you are getting by asking appropriate questions such as, 'Do you mean ...?' 'Are you saying ...?'

◆ **Don't feel you always have to give an answer.**

Listening requires a validating response, but not necessarily an answer. 'Tell me more about that' or 'How long have you felt that way?' are examples of responses that at least let the other person know you are ready to hear more.

◆ **Make it personal.**

Use 'I' language to express your own feelings. For example, instead of saying 'You made me angry when ...' say 'I felt angry when ...'. Couching criticisms in terms of your own feelings may make your child feel less blamed and more likely to talk.

◆ **Ask open questions.**

Open questions encourage more discussion, whereas closed ones simply invite a one-word answer (usually 'no'). For example, instead of asking 'Do you like school?' ask 'What are the things you like about school and what are the things you don't like?'

◆ **Criticise the behaviour not the child.**

Try to make it clear to your child at all times that you love them and will support them, even if their actions are unacceptable. It is better to criticise the specific behaviour you disliked rather than making a more general criticism of them as a person. For example, it would be better to say 'That was careless to drop the glass' than to say 'You stupid child'.

◆ **Put yourself in the other person's shoes.**

Try to understand your child's perspective. This shows that you respect his or her point of view, even though you may not agree with it.

◆ **Be available.**

You cannot dictate when your child will feel like talking. What you can do, as far as possible, is to make yourself available and willing to talk when they choose to. ▶

◆ *Remember.*

Make a real effort to remember the names and backgrounds of key friends in your child's life. Your child is more likely to talk to you about being bullied by Sarah if you remember who Sarah is.

◆ *If you have more than one child, spend time alone with each.*

If you have more than one child, it is a good idea to spend time with each of them individually, even if only for ten minutes before bedtime. One common reason for children not talking is that they do not want their siblings to hear.

Further advice

Parentline Plus
Free helpline: 0808 800 2222
www.parentlineplus.org.uk
Advice on all aspects of parenting, including specifics tips on communicating with children.

Parentalk
Tel: 020 7450 9072/3
www.parentalk.co.uk
Tips and practical advice for parents.

National Family and Parenting Institute (NFPI)
Tel: 020 7424 3460
E-mail: info@nfpi.org
www.nfpi.org
Extensive information and advice on parent-child relationships.

Related worries

24. Won't listen to me/is disobedient

Working parents

- The majority of mothers and fathers in the UK work. The proportion of families in which both parents work has been increasing for many years.

- Nearly two-thirds (65%) of women with dependent children are in work. The majority of them work part-time, but a fifth (20%) work full-time. 89 per cent of men with dependent children are in work.

- More than half (53%) of all mothers with children under the age of five work.

- More than half (54%) of all single parents work. The government currently has a target to increase this to 70% by 2010.

- More than a third (36%) of all working adults have at least one dependent child.

- 70% of women in the UK work – one of the highest female employment rates in Europe and well above the EU average of 54%.

- Working fathers and mothers in the UK work the longest hours in Europe. Fathers with children under the age of 11 work an average of 48 hours a week. Women are more likely than men to have flexible working patterns.

- More than half of all parents who work full-time are concerned about having too little time to spend with their families. Working parents who feel they have more control over their work/life balance tend to feel happier and less stressed; they also tend to have better relationships with their children.

- Research suggests that children whose mothers work full-time during the first five years after birth are more likely to have lower educational achievement, be unemployed in early adulthood and experience psychological distress in early adulthood, compared to children of mothers who do not work. Part-time working during the pre-school years is found to have fewer adverse effects than full-time working.

- Research also suggests that boys tend to suffer more negative consequences than girls from having a full-time working mother.

- Since 2003, employers have had a legal obligation to *consider* applications for flexible working from workers who are parents of young or disabled children.

WORRY **17**

Won't go to bed

21% of parents worried

....

Chances: HIGH **Consequences: MEDIUM** **Control: HIGH**

A consistent reluctance to go to bed at a reasonably early hour ('bedtime resistance') is common among young children, adolescents and teenagers. Three lifestyle factors that contribute to bedtime resistance are inconsistent bedtimes, TV and caffeine. In an ideal (but possibly boring) world, children would go to bed and get up at roughly the same times every day, not watch too much TV in the evening, and avoid caffeine from lunchtime onwards.

In addition to lifestyle factors, bedtime resistance and later bedtimes are to some extent a natural reflection of the growing child's biology. Children's biological clocks shift during adolescence towards a later (more 'owl'-like) setting, which makes them feel like going to bed and getting up later than when they were younger. Going to bed later can also be a way of asserting independence.

Many young children regularly refuse to go to bed, or to stay in their bedroom, when their parents want them to. Others reluctantly go to their bedroom, but drag out the process of actually going to sleep with endless delay, fuss and protest. This type of behaviour is referred to as bedtime resistance and it is surprisingly common in pre-adolescents.

Bedtime resistance is one of the most widely reported behavioural issues in childhood, and it is the one that parents complain of the most. Between 15 and 25 per cent of pre-school children and 10 per cent of primary school children display marked bedtime resistance. Apart from the aggravation they cause to their parents, these children also tend to wake later and get less sleep.

Children and teenagers may be reluctant to go to bed for many different reasons. Environment and lifestyle are obviously important, but so, too, is parental behaviour. Furthermore, wanting to go to bed later is a normal characteristic of growing up.

Research has shown that two of the main lifestyle factors associated with bedtime resistance in younger children are having an inconsistent bedtime and falling asleep somewhere other than in bed – for example, in front of the TV.

Parents must obviously shoulder much of the responsibility if their children are going to bed at irregular times. Some parents understandably want to spend time with their offspring after getting home from work, even if that means delaying their child's bedtime. And many give in to children's requests to stay up late to watch TV or play computer games. Either way, children end up going to bed later and getting less sleep.

Television can be a real problem when it comes to children's sleep. Researchers have found that younger children who watch a lot of TV are more likely to display bedtime resistance, take longer to fall asleep and get less sleep on average than children who watch less TV. The effect is even greater for children whose bedroom contains a TV, as most of them now do.

Children's bedrooms have increasingly become places of entertainment rather than rest. A 2001 survey found that more than half of all children in Britain had a TV in their bedroom. A bedroom equipped with a TV, video recorder, computer games, Internet access and phone may provide a child with endless stimulation and excitement, but it is hardly the ideal environment for sleeping. Watching a gripping film or playing violent computer games before bed can leave a child feeling over-stimulated or anxious, making it harder to get to sleep when they do eventually go to bed.

Another very common reason why children and teenagers don't feel like going to bed is because they have been taking stimulant drugs, the most popular of which is caffeine.

Caffeine is the most widely consumed psychoactive drug in the world, and the only one that children are actively encouraged to consume. It is present in coffee, tea, fizzy drinks, chocolate and many medicines. About three quarters of the world's population (and 9 out of 10 Americans) habitually consume caffeine in one form or another. On average, boys consume significantly more than girls.

Caffeine is a stimulant. It makes us feel more lively and awake during the day, but the downside is that it interferes with sleep. As well as delaying the onset of sleep, caffeine also disrupts sleep and reduces its quality. The more caffeine you have in your bloodstream when you go to bed, the longer it will take you to fall asleep and the more your sleep will be disrupted. Children have smaller bodies than adults, so a given dose of caffeine will have a bigger effect on them.

A typical cup of instant coffee contains about 65 milligrams of caffeine, while real (ground) coffee contains about twice as much. Tea has slightly less caffeine than coffee, averaging around 50 milligrams a cup. However, children and young people consume most of their caffeine in the form of soft drinks. A standard (330 ml) can of cola drink contains more than 30 milligrams of caffeine, equivalent to about half a cup of coffee. The sugar-free 'diet' version contains even more caffeine than the standard variety.

Research has shown that teenagers who consume more fizzy drinks containing caffeine tend to take longer to fall asleep, are more likely to wake up again during the night, and get less sleep. They also tend to be sleepier during the day than those who consume less fizzy drinks. This link between caffeine intake, disrupted sleep and subsequent daytime tiredness can produce a vicious cycle, in which the person drinks more caffeine-containing drinks to combat their tiredness, but ends up feeling even worse because the caffeine then disrupts their sleep.

Chocolate also contains small quantities of caffeine, along with larger quantities of a related (but milder) stimulant called theobromine. An average bar of milk chocolate contains several milligrams of caffeine, equivalent to about one eighth of a cup of instant coffee. Plain chocolate contains considerably more caffeine, typically around 25 milligrams per bar.

Nicotine is another stimulant drug, which means that smoking also disrupts sleep. Studies have found that adolescents and teenagers who smoke cigarettes also tend to go to bed later, have more problems getting to sleep, spend less time asleep, have sleep of poorer quality, and suffer from more daytime sleepiness than non-smokers. The more someone smokes, the more likely they are to experience frequent and long-lasting sleep problems. Of course, there are far more compelling reasons for not wanting your child to smoke, such as the fact that it will shorten their life. But here is a less well-known hazard to add to the list.

Regardless of lifestyle, a desire to go to bed later is a natural part of growing up. Children and adolescents may be reluctant to go to bed when their parents want them to because they are asserting their maturity and independence. Bedtime is one of the most frequent battlegrounds between parents and children: the later children stay up, the more grown-up they feel.

Parents often unwittingly encourage this conflict. Being sent to bed is traditionally seen as a punishment, not a reward, and some children absorb the lesson that their parents have unconsciously taught them – namely, that staying up late is a desirable aspect of adult life and going to bed early is bad. Parents who send their children to bed early as a punishment are therefore sending out the wrong message. Ironically, many overworked and exhausted parents would regard going to bed early themselves as a big treat.

Parents who respond to bedtime tantrums by getting stressed may be reinforcing the problem. Removing the emotion from the situation can help, although this is easier said than done. One useful tactic is to establish a relaxing bedtime routine (see What can you do? below). As well as taking the conflict out of bedtime, this will also help the child to wind down at the end of the day.

Research has uncovered links between Attention Deficit/Hyperactivity Disorder (ADHD) and bedtime resistance. Parents of ADHD children are much more likely than average to have problems getting their children to bed and to sleep. Even among children who are not diagnosed with ADHD, bedtime resistance is still associated with a higher incidence of behaviour problems during the day.

Some children are unenthusiastic about going to bed because they have genuine difficulty getting to sleep. Insomnia affects between 6 per cent and 11 per cent of primary school-age children. The desire to go to bed later also has a biological basis. During adolescence, children's biological clocks (or circadian rhythms) shift towards a later, more 'owl'-like, setting. Consequently, most adolescents genuinely feel like going to bed later and getting up later than they did when they were younger. Unfortunately, on school days they can't stay in bed longer to compensate for the later nights, so their sleep tends to get squeezed. Consequently, many adolescents and teenagers end up getting insufficient sleep and feeling tired during the day (see Worry 15, page 81).

Over and above this general shift towards later bedtimes, individuals differ considerably in the timing of their sleep cycle. Some people are natural 'owls' who consistently prefer to stay up late and get up late, while others are 'larks' who feel happier rising early and going to bed early. A few people suffer from an extreme disturbance of their body clock setting, producing a problem known as Delayed Sleep Phase Syndrome. They go to sleep later and later each night, until eventually they are staying awake until the small hours of the morning.

Older siblings can be a problem if they keep their younger siblings up later. Not surprisingly, being part of a large family tends to make matters worse, because children are more likely to share a bedroom. Research has found that the more siblings a child has, the later on average they go to bed and the less time they spend in bed.

What can you do?

◆ *Take sleep seriously.*

Remember that your child's mental and physical well-being will suffer if they regularly get insufficient sleep because of going to bed late. Routinely letting your child stay up late to watch TV will not do them any favours, though it won't do any harm as an occasional treat. Explain to your child that sleep is important, and that they will feel worse the next day if they do not get enough.

◆ *Be firm and consistent.*

Set out some basic ground rules about good sleep habits and stick to them. Young children should be told that it is unacceptable to disturb other people who are trying to sleep. With older children it is often better not to be too rigid about bedtimes: negotiate and agree an approximate bedtime (e.g., between 9.30 p.m. and 10.00 p.m.) rather than a precise deadline, to leave yourself some room for manoeuvre. This should help to reduce the amount of unnecessary conflict. However, once you have made an agreement you should try to stick to it.

◆ *Develop a relaxing pre-bedtime routine.*

Develop a consistent, predictable and pleasant bedtime routine for your child. This might include, for example, having a bath, talking about the day and (depending on their age) giving them a milky drink and reading them a story. The aim should be to make the process enjoyable and relaxing for both of you. Consistency is the key, so stick to the ritual. Once the pre-bed routine is completed, check that they are OK, say goodnight and do not return to their bedroom until morning (except in an emergency). If they come into your bedroom during the night, make it clear that you are not pleased and send them back immediately.

◆ *Keep an eye on the caffeine.*

Discourage your child from drinking coffee, tea or caffeinated fizzy drinks in the afternoon and evening, because the caffeine will interfere with their sleep. If they do drink a lot of caffeinated fizzy drinks during the day, try to persuade them to cut down (for the sake of their waistline and teeth as well as their sleep).

◆ *Make your child's bedroom more restful.*

Children (and adults) would be better off not having a TV or computer in their bedroom. If your child does have a TV or computer in their room, you should negotiate additional rules about using them ▶

after bedtime, possibly backed up by the threat that you will remove the TV or computer if those rules are broken. If the bedroom curtains do not block out the light, your child may be more reluctant to go to bed on light summer nights. If so, use thicker curtains.

◆ *Avoid reinforcing bad behaviour.*

The simplest and most effective strategy for dealing with young children who persistently make a fuss about going to bed is to put them to bed and then firmly ignore their tantrums (the so-called 'extinction' method). The idea is never to reward their bad behaviour by responding, which is what they want you to do. A gentler version of the extinction strategy involves leaving them to make a fuss for progressively longer each night until eventually they stop doing it (the 'graduated extinction' method). Either

way, the key thing is never to relent. If you do give in to their tantrums, even once in a while, the problem will persist and your efforts will have been wasted.

◆ *Try shifting your child's bedtime gradually rather than abruptly.*

Another useful strategy for winning the bedtime battle is the 'positive routine' method. Start by putting your child to bed late, at a time when they feel tired and ready for sleep. Combine this with a pleasant bedtime routine to make the whole experience relaxing and enjoyable. Then, each night, systematically shift their bedtime to a slightly earlier time (in steps of say, 20 minutes a night) until eventually they are going to bed at the earlier time of your choice. Obviously, this method only tends to work well with children who are too young to tell the time.

Further advice

The Sleep Council
Insomnia helpline: 020 8994 9874
E-mail: info@sleepcouncil.org.uk
www.sleepcouncil.org.uk
Tips for parents on helping children get a good night's sleep.

Practical Parenting
www.practicalparent.org.uk
Tips on child behaviour, development and family relationships, with specific information about bedtime problems.

Related worries

4. Spends too much time watching TV or playing computer games
13. Has difficulty concentrating/paying attention
15. Does not get enough sleep
21. Won't get up, get dressed and get ready in the mornings

WORRY 18

Is at risk if he/she goes on a school trip

21% of parents worried

....

Chances: LOW   **Consequences: HIGH**   **Control: MEDIUM**

School trips are generally very safe. Just over ten million children attend school and most of them spend about two days a year on trips away from school premises. On average, three children die a year while on school trips, but this must be compared against the 100+ a year who die in accidents in and around their own home. Children are far more likely to die in an accident while in the care of their parents or relatives than when under the supervision of a teacher.

Things are more likely to go wrong on an international trip than a domestic one. Around 60 per cent of school trip deaths have occurred abroad. Within the UK the greatest risks come from activities involving water and while children are being transported.

School trips are closely regulated and, in the vast majority of cases, carefully planned. In maintained schools in England, school trips require written consent from the school, the local education authority and the parents, and can only take place when a risk analysis, insurance and careful teacher supervision are in place. Parents must give written consent for all trips off school premises and have the right to refuse permission.

School trips provide children with valuable experiences they could not have within the conventional school environment, and form an important part of education. Any risks must be weighed against these significant benefits.

Children derive a great deal of benefit and pleasure from taking part in trips or outings with their school. School trips give children opportunities to have experiences that simply are not available in the classroom, and to see things they would not otherwise see. As well as helping to bring the curriculum alive, school trips aid children's social and emotional development. They encourage children to be more independent and self reliant, and it is often during such outings that friendships are formed or strengthened.

The vast majority of school trips take place without incident and the vast majority of teachers demonstrate a very high level of safety awareness. In many respects the degree of care and planning that teachers give to school outings is far greater than most parents would consider necessary when carrying out the same activity with their own children. And the reality is that children are much more likely to die in an accident in their home than on a school trip.

Schools are legally responsible for the safety of children on trips. The Department for Education and Skills (DfES) advises that all schools, whether state maintained or independent, should follow these guidelines:

- All schools should have a written policy on trips, which parents can request to see. The policy should set out what types of visits the school finds acceptable and their broad safety, procedural and behaviour guidelines.
- When a trip is planned, the school must first appoint a lead teacher for the event. This person is ultimately responsible for the safety of the children. Parents should be informed who he or she is.
- A deputy leader and other staff members must then be chosen. The exact number of staff needed on school trips is not fixed by legislation, but most schools follow these guidelines: one adult for every six pupils aged 6–9; one adult for every 10–15 pupils aged 9–11; or one adult for every 15–20 pupils in secondary school. Potentially risky activities or trips abroad should have a higher ratio of staff to pupils.
- School trips are governed by Health and Safety legislation. The trip leader should write a detailed risk analysis, which they submit to the head teacher and (in the case of maintained schools) the local education authority for approval. The risk analysis should set out any likely risks and the measures that have been taken to alleviate them. Parents can ask to see this document.
- The school should check the licences and credentials of any transport suppliers or activity centres being visited and make sure they have all necessary safety plans and insurance in place. These suppliers must clearly state what responsibilities they accept and what they do not.
- Schools must finally seek written permission for the trip from all parents, unless the trip is a standard part of the curriculum for which parents have already consented, such as weekly swimming lessons at a local pool. The consent letter should set out all relevant aspects of the trip, including staff ratios, transport, timings, insurance and costs. Parents should provide an emergency contact number and details of any behavioural or medical conditions their child has which might influence their safety on the trip (for example, an allergy or an inability to swim).

The overwhelming majority of schools follow this process and have successful and safe trips. In the rare instances when something has gone wrong, it has often been because one or more aspects of the safety planning process were not followed. Understandably, these rare but tragic cases tend to receive a lot of publicity.

Statistics show that the highest risks are associated with trips involving water or adventure activities. Because of this, the government stipulated in 1996 that all adventure centres must be inspected and granted a licence for school trips. Over 900 providers currently hold a licence. Caving, climbing, trekking (on foot, horse, cycle, skis, skates or sledges) and water sports all require a licence if they are provided by either a council or commercial centre and if they are used by children under 18 who are unaccompanied by a parent. Voluntary bodies, such as charities, and schools providing their own activities are exempt from needing licences.

Holding a licence means that a provider has been inspected and the licensing authority is satisfied that appropriate safety measures are in place. (Other aspects such as catering and accommodation are not covered by the licensing scheme and should be checked by the school.) At the time of writing, no child has died at an accredited activity centre since the legislation was introduced.

The other potentially risky area for school trips has been transport. Any form of road transport involves some element of risk, and several tragic accidents involving school minibuses have occurred. Again, this has led to legislation. Currently, any minibus that is used to carry a group of three or more school children on an organised school trip must have seat belts fitted throughout the vehicle and all seats must be forward-facing. This legislation ended the so-called three-for-two concession, which permitted three children under the age of 14 to sit in a double seat, and the use of sideways-facing seats.

Some safety organisations believe legislation should go further. They argue that there should be a requirement for teachers who lead school trips to undergo special training. In particular, the Royal Life Saving Society has suggested that specialist training should be mandatory for teachers who supervise swimming on school trips. Currently, no specific training on off-site activities is included in basic teacher training. Some commercial training courses are available, but only a small proportion of teachers have taken one. Moreover, teachers who lead trips are often expected to organise and plan the trips in their own time.

This lack of support and training has left some teachers questioning whether it is worth arranging school trips at all, let alone volunteering to lead one. Many feel they get little thanks or encouragement from parents when things go well, but know they will immediately be criticised if something goes wrong, even if it is not their fault. Indeed, one of the main teachers' unions (the National Association of Schoolmasters Union of Women Teachers) reluctantly concluded that 'until society accepts the notion of a genuine accident, it is advisable for our members not to go on school trips'.

The legal situation is unlikely to calm teachers' concerns. Individual teachers, schools or the local education authority can be sued and found liable for negligence if an accident occurs. If an incident happens, but teachers and the authorities can be shown to have taken 'all reasonable precautions', then it may be judged to have been an accident. However, if the incident resulted from negligence, then compensation can be claimed from the individual or organisation deemed to be at fault.

Several legal cases have occurred in recent years and the compensation bills are rising. It is estimated that school insurance bills have grown by at least 20 per cent in the past few years as a result. Here are some of the most serious examples:

- In 1997 an 11-year-old boy drowned on a day trip at an activity centre in Buckinghamshire. Forty-seven children had been allowed to use a swimming pool without lifeguards. Hounslow council pleaded guilty to negligence and was fined £25,000.

- In 1997 three school children died and 19 others were injured when their minibus plunged down an alpine slope in France. The minibus had no seat belts. The driver, who had never before driven a left-hand drive vehicle, was found guilty of manslaughter by a French court and fined £1200.

- In 2002 the High Court granted £200,000 as an initial compensation payment to the family of a six-year-old boy who suffered severe brain damage after contracting an E.coli infection on a farm visit. The boy's family claimed that the local authority should have checked the farm before agreeing to the trip.

- In September 2003 a geography teacher was sent to prison for a year after the death in 2002 of a ten-year-old boy on a school trip to the Lake District. The teacher was described as 'unbelievably foolhardy and negligent' for allowing the boy to jump into a turbulent mountain pool despite bad weather and warnings from other teachers. He admitted manslaughter, in what is thought to be the first case of a teacher being sent to prison for negligence on a school trip.

Many of the tragic accidents that do occur on school trips could have been prevented if schools and teachers had followed the safety guidelines laid down by the DfES, including a proper risk analysis. If the guidelines are followed, the risks are very small – and almost certainly outweighed by the major benefits to the children. We believe it would be a great shame if school trips were to become a thing of the past.

What can you do?

◆ **Read the school's policy for trips.**

If your child is going on their first school trip with a new school or teacher then you might consider asking to see the school's written policy and the specific plan for the trip.

◆ **Read the consent form before signing it.**

The consent form should set out the details of the trip and should cover aspects such as transport and activities. Look out for higher-risk activities such as those involving water. If you are worried, talk to the lead teacher organising the trip. If the trip involves going abroad, find out whether there will be any special safety guidelines for the countries to be visited.

◆ **Talk to your child about the potential risks before they leave.**

Many children get excited about being out and about on a school day and fail to remember basic safety rules they would normally follow while out with their parents. Obvious ones to remind them of include wearing their seat belt, listening carefully to the teachers and not wandering off on their own.

◆ **Volunteer to be a helper.**

Think about volunteering to go on a school trip as a helper. Teachers are often heavily burdened and may appreciate an extra pair of hands. Obviously, with older children you will want to consider whether your attendance would embarrass them and spoil the experience.

◆ **Think about emotional aspects as well as physical risks.**

Does your child have a friend going on the trip with them? Might your child feel left out or be bullied? Might they be homesick? It may be worth talking through any such concerns that your child might have and devising a plan with them. This could involve taking a mobile phone so they can contact you, or asking their teacher to keep a special eye out.

▶

◆ **Say thank you.**

Make the effort to thank the teachers who take your children on school trips. They are putting themselves out for the benefit of your child, and unless we encourage them school trips could become a thing of the past.

◆ **Be reasonable.**

If something does go wrong, ask yourself whether it could easily have happened under your own care or whether it was real negligence. Some parents demand far higher safety standards from teachers than they ever would from themselves.

Further advice

Royal Society for the Prevention of Accidents (RoSPA)
Tel: 0121 248 2000
www.rospa.com
Guidance about safety on all aspects of school trips.

Adventure Activities Licensing Authority
Tel: 0292 075 5715
www.aala.org
The licensing body for adventure centres used on school trips. You can use the website to find out whether a particular centre has been licensed.

Department for Education and Skills (DfES)
Tel: 0870 000 2288
www.dfes.gov.uk
Guidelines and statistics about school trips.

Related worries

8. Has friends who are or could be a bad influence
19. Is reckless and not sufficiently aware of dangers

WORRY **19**

Is reckless and not sufficiently aware of dangers

20% of parents worried

....

Chances: HIGH   **Consequences: HIGH**   **Control: MEDIUM**

Most children are occasionally reckless, and younger children are seldom sufficiently aware of dangers. More than two million children go to hospital and around 400 die every year as a result of accidents. Younger children and boys are at greatest risk.

Parents often over-estimate children's practical understanding of risk. Young children can learn in abstract terms about hazards such as traffic or drowning, but they are not so good at relating this theoretical knowledge to real situations in their everyday lives. Also, they cannot always be relied upon to think about risks for themselves without prompting from an adult.

Play and exploration are natural and highly beneficial aspects of every child's development. By actively engaging with their world, children acquire crucial skills and experience. One of the main ways in which children learn to make sound judgements about risk is through personal experience. Trying to insulate them from all risks can therefore be counter-productive in the long term. The key is to protect them from the big risks and the pointless risks.

Some individuals have an excitement-seeking personality that draws them towards potentially risky situations.

The most obvious evidence that children are often not sufficiently aware of dangers is the fact that lots of children have accidents. The vast majority are not serious or life-threatening; nonetheless, accidental injury is the biggest single cause of death among British children, outstripping even illness, let alone violent crime.

Each year, about 400 children die from accidental injury or poisoning and more than two million are taken to hospital after having an accident. On top of that, many more children are hurt in less serious accidents that never make it into the official statistics. Fortunately, the numbers have been dropping in recent years. Of the two million accidents that result in a hospital visit, about half occur in the home, and most of these involve children below school age. The most common type of accident is falling.

Accidents outside the home become more common as children get older and spend more time outside. Each year, more than 200,000 children are injured playing football, basketball or other sports, and a further 180,000 are injured in playgrounds. Road accidents are less frequent than falls, but they tend to be more damaging and therefore account for more deaths and serious injuries. Each year about 200 children are killed in, or by, vehicles and a further 4000 are seriously injured.

Accidental injuries are not a modern phenomenon, nor are they unique to humans. Archaeologists have found evidence in ancient human remains of bone fractures and other injuries that appear to have been caused accidentally. Animals of other species also injure themselves accidentally – young monkeys and apes, in particular, occasionally injure themselves while playing. Accidental injury is a normal feature of animal and human life.

Playfulness and exploration might contribute to childhood accidents, but they are also crucial elements in children's development: being playful and testing out your abilities is a normal and healthy part of growing up. Through play, the developing child acquires skills and experiences they need to become fully functioning individuals. Being over-protective of children can therefore do more harm than good, if it deprives them of play and interferes with their physical, social and emotional development. Safety is vital, but so too is play.

Who is most at risk? As you might expect, younger children have more accidents than older children, especially in the home. And boys have more accidents than girls. In fact, boys are roughly twice as likely as girls to have accidents. This is partly because boys tend to expose themselves to more risks and partly because they judge risks as being less serious than girls do.

Children from poorer homes are at greater risk of having a fatal accident than children from more affluent homes, partly because they are more likely to be exposed to hazardous environments. Some children who are neglected by their parents may be at greater risk of accidents because they have very low self-esteem and do not care what happens to them. There is even some evidence that children who watch a lot of TV become more willing to take risks as a result of watching the risky behaviour portrayed in some TV programmes.

Why so many accidents

Both the likelihood and nature of accidents depend greatly on a child's age and experience. Compared with adults, children are especially prone to having accidents for two main reasons. First, developing children are naturally inquisitive and playful, and therefore expose themselves to more risks. They want to explore their world and try new things, and they learn a great deal by doing this. But they are often clumsy and incompetent, especially when trying to do something for the first time.

Secondly, younger children often lack the mental skills and experience to judge whether a particular situation is hazardous. A risk that seems obvious to an adult may not be at all obvious to a six-year-old, even if they have been taught about the various dangers in everyday life.

Young children can usually understand the idea

of a connection between, say, road traffic and danger. However, they are often poor at relating risks to specific situations, such as realising that this particular car is approaching them fast and therefore threatens them. They tend to relate danger to a class of object, such as cars or knives in general, rather than to a specific situation or chain of events. So, for example, a young child might describe a swimming pool as dangerous, regardless of whether they are accompanied by an adult or whether there is a lifeguard on duty. The flipside is that children may be unnecessarily fearful of things that actually pose little risk.

Young children also tend to be bad at consistently recognising or thinking about risks without prompting from an adult. So, even though a child may understand the abstract concept that, say, traffic is dangerous, they may nonetheless pay insufficient attention to traffic if left to their own devices.

The upshot is that simply telling young children about the general nature of risks such as cars, knives, swimming pools or boiling liquids is not enough. Just because they have acquired the relevant knowledge does not mean they will be good at applying it in real-life situations. They also need to practise and learn from their own experience, initially under adult supervision.

Responding to the risk

Personal experience plays an important part in learning to deal with risk. The evidence shows that primary school children who have extensive experience of traffic develop a much better understanding of the dangers posed by it and are more competent at dealing with those risks. This means that driving your children everywhere, because you are worried they might be knocked over, might actually *increase* their risk of being knocked over when they are eventually allowed to walk on their own (see Worry 1, page 7). They are at greater risk if they lack the experience needed to become a competent and safe pedestrian.

Children generally become better at assessing risks by the time they start secondary school. But even then they still do not have the same abilities as adults to identify risks or to understand fully the long-term consequences of their actions. Research has found that in risky situations, adolescents take less account of the available information than adults do. Many adolescents and teenagers also seem to believe they are immortal and that 'it won't happen to me'.

A child's personality has an important bearing on his or her chances of having an accident. Most young children are highly exploratory, but they are also naturally quite self-protective and tend not to take stupid risks. However, a small minority of children (some of whom have Attention Deficit/ Hyperactivity Disorder or ADHD) are impulsive, distractible, restless, disobedient and at higher risk of accidents than other children. These children are more excitement-seeking than most.

An adult with an excitement-seeking or risk-taking personality is more prone to engage in risky activities such as driving at high speeds, skiing or climbing mountains. Excitement-seekers are also more likely to smoke, more likely to abuse drugs or alcohol, and more likely to display antisocial behaviour including criminality, all of which makes them more likely to die younger. On average, men tend to be stronger excitement-seekers than women.

Evidence of a risk-prone or excitement-seeking personality can be found in some children as young as two years of age. Like excitement-seeking adults, these individuals prefer to be in situations where they are exposed to novel and stimulating experiences, and they are less averse to taking physical risks. In fact, the roots of excitement-seeking can even be detected in babies. Researchers have found that babies who are quicker to react to, and reach for, novel toys are more likely to develop into toddlers who are highly exploratory and risk-taking.

What can you do?

◆ *Let your child play and explore.*

It's not a good idea to try to prevent accidents by stopping children from playing and exploring the world around them – provided, of course, they can do this in reasonable safety. All children must eventually learn how to deal with everyday risks such as using a knife, boiling a kettle or crossing a road. Aim to create an environment in which they can express their natural desires to explore and play without getting hurt.

◆ *Teach your child the ground rules and then let them acquire experience under supervision.*

For example, practise walking to the shops and crossing the road before letting them do it alone. Remember that younger children are not very good at recognising potentially dangerous situations, even if they understand in abstract terms about dangers such as traffic, knives or boiling liquids. As well as educating them about risks, you need to heighten their awareness of specific risks in real-life situations – for example, when you are out walking with them or in the kitchen.

◆ *Try to eliminate the big risks and the pointless risks.*

There is of course a huge difference between allowing a child to explore their environment and allowing them to indulge in stupidly dangerous behaviour, such as playing on railway lines, running across the road without looking, experimenting with Class A drugs or committing crime for kicks. Bear down hard on the big risks and the pointless ones. Remove or reduce unnecessary hazards such as those presented by trailing kettle flexes, non-safety glass, scalding water, garden ponds, open windows, medicines, etc. Health Visitors have a home safety checklist that parents of younger children can use.

◆ *Think about whether your child has a risk-prone or excitement-seeking personality.*

Some parents under-estimate children's natural tendency to lark about and seek excitement. Your child's teacher should be able to give a useful perspective on how your child compares in this respect with others of their age. If you do have a highly excitement-seeking child, rejoice in the fact that they are so actively engaged with their world and have the potential to lead a more fulfilling life as a result. However, you will need to pay closer attention to what they do and take even more care to teach them about safety, because they will be more likely to put themselves in harm's way. Think about whether their behaviour might put their brother, sister or friends at risk. Try to channel their desire for excitement in positive ways, such as sport or physical hobbies, rather than allowing it to push them towards self-destructive pursuits.

Further advice

Child Accident Prevention Trust (CAPT)

Tel: 020 7608 3828

E-mail: safe@capt.org.uk

www.capt.org.uk

Extensive advice for parents about preventing accidents to children.

Royal Society for the Prevention of Accidents (RoSPA)

Tel: 0121 248 2000

www.rospa.com

Guidance on all aspects of accident prevention.

Child Alert

Tel: 020 7384 1311

Enquiries: info@childalert.co.uk

www.childalert.co.uk

Web-based resource concerned with child safety and well-being.

Related worries

1. Might be knocked over by a vehicle
2. Might be abducted and/or murdered
8. Has friends who are or could be a bad influence
31. Might have an accident in the home
38. Might get into trouble with the authorities or commit a crime

Drugs

- More than 2 out of 5 (42%) of children aged 11–15 have been offered drugs at some time.

- More than a quarter (26%) of children aged 11–15 have tried one or more illegal drugs at some time, and almost a fifth (18%) have taken drugs within the past year.

- The likelihood that a child has been offered or taken drugs rises sharply with age. Only 3% of 11-year-olds have taken drugs within the past month, compared with 22% of 15-year-olds.

- Nearly two-thirds (65%) of 15-year-olds have been offered drugs, just under half of them (45%) have tried drugs at some time, and more than a third (36%) have taken drugs within the past year.

- Cannabis is by far the most commonly used drug. Almost 1 out of 8 (13%) of children aged 11–15 have taken it within the past year.

- One in 25 (4%) of children aged 11–15 have taken a Class A drug within the past year. Class A drugs include cocaine, crack, ecstasy, heroin, magic mushrooms, methadone and LSD. Cannabis is a Class B drug.

- Boys are slightly more likely than girls to take illicit drugs.

- There is a strong statistical association between cigarette smoking and drug use. Around half the children who have taken cannabis within the last year are regular smokers.

- Research suggests that the most important factors in protecting young people from drug abuse are parental support, good educational attainment, high self-esteem, a healthy lifestyle and early intervention to tackle any problem behaviour.

- There is no clear evidence that lessons on drug abuse reduce children's likelihood of taking Class A drugs.

- Drug abuse is estimated to cost the country between £10 billion and £18 billion a year. There are strong links between drugs and crime.

The statistics quoted here derive mainly from government research in England in 2001 and 2002.

WORRY **20**

Has tantrums

20% of parents worried

··

Chances: MEDIUM   **Consequences: LOW**   **Control: MEDIUM**

Many children go through a stage of throwing tantrums between the ages of roughly two and four. This can involve shouting, screaming, hitting and throwing things. Tantrums at this age often occur because young children lack the verbal and emotional development to deal with their feelings in other ways.

Children generally grow out of this type of behaviour as they learn to understand their emotions and express themselves more clearly. They may continue to have the occasional tantrum, but usually only when they are very tired or seeking attention.

If a child continues to have frequent tantrums (four or five times a week or more) after the age of about five, there may be a more fundamental problem that needs addressing. Tantrums in older children can stem from learning difficulties or behavioural disorders, but the most common cause is ineffective disciplining. Parents who respond to tantrums by shouting or hitting back are more likely to have children who resort to tantrums frequently.

All children sometimes behave badly. This is, unfortunately, very normal. They are finding out what happens when they have a tantrum, hit another child or say rude words. They are experimenting and taking risks. It is part of growing up. Whether consciously or unconsciously, they are testing the boundaries: finding out what they can get away with, and what their parents will draw the line at.

Tantrums can take many forms, but they generally involve kicking, screaming and occasionally holding breath. They typically last minutes, as the child temporarily loses control, and can be quite dramatic. They may then be followed by crying as the child attempts to calm down.

Tantrums are most apparent between the ages of about two and four, when children are becoming increasingly independent. Young children of this age are old enough to have a sense of 'me' and 'my wants', but often too young to know how to satisfy those wants themselves – they must rely on someone else to get the drink, play the game, or whatever. Moreover, their language may not be developed enough to communicate their wants and needs. Sometimes young children get frustrated with these limitations.

A toddler tantrum may also occur because the child has communicated what they want but their parent will not give it. Bedtime and sweets are familiar battlegrounds. At three or four years of age, when children tend to be preoccupied with themselves, they may find it hard to understand why they cannot have their wishes granted instantly. (Perhaps you know one or two adults who fit this description too.)

Tantrums are exceedingly common. Eight out of 10 children in the three-to-four age range have temper tantrums at least occasionally. By the age of five, however, most children stop having full-blown tantrums as their verbal ability improves and they begin to understand concepts such as safety and compromise. Nonetheless, they may occasionally resort to this tactic when very tired or frustrated, or when a major disruption to their routine has occurred.

In older children, traumatic events such as a death in the family, divorce or a school move can trigger a period of disruptive or aggressive behaviour and, just as when they were younger, they find themselves trying to manage emotions that are new to them and which they feel unable to handle. A more physical response may be all they are capable of. During such periods of upset, all the parent may be able to do is to reassure the child and try to provide as much stability and familiarity as possible.

Recognizing a problem

For some older children, however, tantrums are more than an occasional occurrence. A child who 'loses it' on a daily basis, or whose tantrums severely interfere with their normal functioning at school or in the home, may not simply grow out of them. This type of behaviour might signal a more substantial problem.

In some cases the problem revolves around learning. On starting school, some children find themselves slipping behind their peers, perhaps because of a specific learning difficulty or late language development. If the problem goes unrecognised, they can begin to get frustrated and may resort to tantrums and aggression as a means of gaining attention and maintaining their status in the group. For these children, the tantrums will usually occur in or around school. For other children the causes may be closer to home, and they may be picking up their inappropriate behaviour from their parents. Research shows that tantrums are most prevalent among children who experience one of two styles of parenting.

In the first, the parents are disengaged from their children. They may be physically present in the house, but they talk to or touch their children little and ignore many of their requests. When they do interact, there is little two-way dialogue. The parents typically issue instructions rather than discussing or consulting. In such households a child can soon learn to ignore their parents' requests and demands. Why should they listen to their parents if their parents clearly aren't listening to them? If the only time they do get attention is when they misbehave, then their misbehaviour is reinforced and they may start throwing tantrums more often. For most children, even being told off for behaving badly is better than being ignored. Until their parents engage more with them, rather than simply issuing instructions, little progress is likely to be made with reducing tantrums.

In the second problematic style of parenting, the link between tantrums and parental behaviour is even more obvious and a cycle of aggression can be observed. The child throws a tantrum over something that's perhaps quite minor. The parents, who may be tired or stressed, become angry and frustrated by their child's behaviour and in effect respond to the child's tantrum by having a sort of tantrum themselves, which might involve smacking or shouting at the child. Falling into a vicious cycle then becomes all too easy.

By responding to a tantrum with a tantrum, these parents are demonstrating to their children that this form of behaviour is an acceptable way of dealing with their emotions. The child is not being shown a better way to deal with his or her own emotions, and is likely to act out the same cycle again next time. Unless the parent learns to respond in a calmer and more measured way, the child will find it harder to break out of the cycle. In line with this, research shows that many children with behaviour problems come from homes where aggression is common.

Finally, there is a group of children who throw tantrums despite having loving parents and a stable home. In such cases, tantrums are usually accompanied by other disruptive forms of behaviour such as hitting, swearing or breaking things. Some of these children are recognised to be suffering from a behaviour problem of some sort, such as Oppositional Defiant Disorder (ODD), Conduct Disorder (CD) or Attention Deficit/Hyperactivity Disorder (ADHD). These labels may be given to children who have extreme behaviour patterns that occur consistently over an extended period of time. In cases such as this specialist help may be needed. Boys are three times more likely than girls to develop such disorders.

What can you do?

◆ **Try to discover the underlying reason for your child's behaviour.**

Study your child's tantrums. When and where do the tantrums occur? Who is generally involved? What happens before, after, and during a tantrum? Looking for patterns can give clues about the conditions or situations that are bringing on tantrums in your child. What does he or she want but is not getting? It's easy to assume they are just being difficult when actually they are frustrated because they think you do not understand them. Ask why they are misbehaving before jumping to a conclusion.

◆ **Notice, compliment and reward good behaviour.**

Teaching your child to do the right things is more effective, and easier, than repeatedly punishing bad behaviour. Children who receive attention only when they behave badly tend to persist with that behaviour.

◆ **Try to manage your own anger.**

When parents respond out of anger they may over-react, but if they calm down, they can respond more appropriately and present a better example for their child to follow. It's ▶

better to do nothing for a couple of minutes while you calm down than to shout back, let alone hit them.

◆ *Distract or redirect your child's attention.*

When a young child is misbehaving, a calm parent can sometimes re-direct their behaviour. For example, you could suggest that instead of fighting you watch a video together.

◆ *Be prompt and brief with discipline.*

One useful technique is to tell the misbehaving child to leave the room immediately and isolate him or her for a few minutes. This will also give you time to get in control of your own emotions. In rare circumstances, you may find it helpful to hold a young child until he or she calms down.

◆ *Remember to reconnect.*

Never isolate a child for more than a few minutes without checking in on them – the last thing you want is to drive an even bigger wedge between you. Children, especially younger ones, may be alarmed by the strength of their own emotions and often need reassurance once they have calmed down a bit. Give them plenty of opportunity to say sorry and to reunite with you and the rest of the family.

◆ *Be consistent in enforcing rules.*

This is especially important with school-aged children. If they see you give in once, they will probably try the same successful tactic again. Being consistent is often hardest when children throw tantrums in public places, but stick to your guns nonetheless. Try also to ensure that other adults who care for your child don't send out conflicting messages about behaviour. If Gran or Dad give in when Mum doesn't, a child may keep trying the same tactic.

◆ *Teach your child about anger.*

Use different words to describe the varying intensity of angry feelings, such as 'annoyed', 'aggravated', 'irritated', 'frustrated', 'angry', 'furious' and 'enraged'. Children as young as two can learn that anger is a complex emotion with different levels of intensity, and that there are different ways of dealing with it.

◆ *Explain the implications of their actions.*

Teach understanding and empathy by drawing your child's attention to the effects of his or her actions on others. Invite them to see the situation from the other person's point of view. Most children feel some remorse when they do something that hurts another person. Discipline helps them to develop an internal sense of right and wrong.

◆ *Choose your battles carefully.*

Say no to things that are really important, but try to avoid fighting over trivial things. It helps to offer real choices. Don't say 'Would you like to go to bed now?' unless you are prepared to honour your child's choice not to sleep. Instead, try something like 'It's bedtime now'. Be clear and consistent about what they get to choose and what you are prepared to be adamant about.

◆ *Give your child plenty of warning before you end an activity.*

Saying 'We are going to leave the park and go home in a few minutes' or 'I wonder what we can cook for supper when we get home' helps your child get ready for change.

- ◆ **Look after yourself as well.**
  If you allow yourself to take the occasional break to relax or go out, you will probably be in better shape to cope with everything. Get together with other parents and don't be shy to ask for help. Nobody gets it right all the time. It can help to talk things over with family or friends, and they may be able to help in practical ways, too.

Further advice

Parentline Plus

24 hour helpline: 0808 800 2222

www.parentlineplus.org.uk

Advice and support to parents, including information on tantrums and discipline.

Young Minds

Tel: 0800 018 2138

www.youngminds.org.uk

Information and advice about psychological and emotional problems in children and young people.

Related worries

8. Has friends who are or could be a bad influence
24. Won't listen to me/is disobedient
34. Is always asking for things or money
38. Might get into trouble with the authorities or commit a crime

Divorce

◆ More than 1 in 4 children will experience parental divorce by the age of 16.

◆ In the year 2002, a total of 149,000 children in England and Wales were living in families where the parents got divorced; almost a quarter of these children were under the age of five.

◆ Current trends imply that 2 out of 5 marriages will eventually end in divorce.

◆ The UK has one of the highest divorce rates among EU.

◆ 160,000 marriages in the UK ended in divorce in the year 2002.

◆ Individuals are statistically more likely to become divorced if they married at a younger than average age, if they had a baby before marrying, or if they have divorced before.

◆ Experts agree that as far as the children are concerned, parental divorce or separation should be viewed as a long process, not an event. The process starts before the actual divorce and continues long afterwards.

◆ Interviews have revealed that most children of divorce did not want their parents to separate and hoped they would get back together.

◆ As far as the law is concerned, divorced parents continue to have parental responsibility for their children: it is not lost on divorce. A parent can never lose parental responsibility unless their child is adopted.

◆ Any will that a parent has made ceases to be valid when they divorce.

◆ Extensive research has been carried out into the effects of divorce on children. The results are complex and not clear-cut. Most children experience unhappiness and distress at the start of the divorce process, but most will eventually settle back into a normal pattern of development. Lasting damage is by no means inevitable.

◆ However, there is consistent evidence that children of divorce face a heightened risk of behaviour problems, depression, difficulties in school, low educational achievement, low income, health problems, becoming a parent at an early age, and their own marriage ending in divorce.

◆ The impact that parental divorce may have on an individual child will depend upon many different factors, including the amount of family conflict before, during and after the separation, loss of high-quality contact with one parent, financial hardship, and the parents' own ability to adjust.

Won't get up, get dressed and get ready in the mornings

20% of parents worried

....

Chances: HIGH   **Consequences: LOW**   **Control: HIGH**

A reluctance to get up in the mornings is not at all unusual among children. It tends to get worse in adolescence, partly because children's biological clocks naturally shift towards a later, more 'owl'-like, setting. Children (like adults) find it even harder to wake early during the dark winter months.

Adolescents go to bed later than young children. But they still have to get up, perhaps even earlier, to go to school. They therefore get less sleep during the week and may need to sleep in at weekends and during holidays to catch up. Getting up later at weekends and on holidays, within reason, is not necessarily a bad thing.

Two obstacles to early rising that can be avoided are staying up late to watch TV and consuming too much caffeine.

Ask any parent to describe a typical teenager and the chances are that one of the characteristics they will mention is the reluctance to get out of bed in the mornings. Adolescents and teenagers are notorious for wanting to go to bed late and then wanting stay there for as long as possible. There is good evidence that teenagers tend to wake later than young adults in their 20s. To be fair to teenagers, though, many adults also have trouble getting up in the mornings, especially on weekdays. After all, 3 out of 4 people use an alarm clock – and the only reason for using an alarm clock is being unable to rely on waking up unaided.

Quite a few younger children are sleepyheads too. According to one study, 1 in 6 children in the 5–12 age range have problems waking in the mornings (at least, according to their parents). Where younger children are concerned, the biggest problem is often their reluctance to get dressed within a reasonable time rather than getting out of bed as such.

Many children and teenagers are unenthusiastic about getting up early, but some are far worse than others. One reason is that individuals differ naturally in the timing of their biological cycle of waking and sleeping (otherwise known as their circadian rhythm). From an early age, people can be divided into two broad types. Some individuals are 'owls' (or evening types) who consistently prefer to go to bed relatively late and get up late. Others are 'larks' (or morning types) who feel happier going to bed relatively early and rising early. Children and adults who dislike going to bed early in the evening also tend to dislike getting up early in the morning. We all lie somewhere along a spectrum, ranging from extreme larks to extreme owls, with most people somewhere in the middle range.

Unfortunately for the owls, scientists have found that they typically get less sleep during the week than larks, making them more inclined to sleep longer at weekends in order to catch up. What is more, owls have less regular sleep patterns and poorer quality sleep. Owls therefore tend to complain more of feeling sleepy during the day and consume more caffeine than larks. If you could choose between being an owl or a lark, the sensible choice would probably be a lark. However, you cannot choose: it is difficult for someone with strong owl-like characteristics to become a lark, or vice versa.

Over and above these individual differences between larks and owls, children's circadian rhythms tend to shift towards a later, more owl-like, setting during adolescence. Hence, the typical adolescent feels like going to bed later and getting up later than the typical five-year-old. This general shift towards a later sleep cycle during adolescence is linked to biology rather than social influences. (Incidentally, our biological clocks generally shift back to a more lark-like setting during middle and old age, which is one reason why elderly people tend to wake early.)

The effect of school schedules

So, thanks partly to changes in their biological rhythms, most adolescents go to bed and fall asleep later than young children. The problem is that they still have to get up early the next morning to go to school. The net result is that they get less sleep and therefore feel sleepier during the day. Research has confirmed that the amount of sleep that adolescents and teenagers get is closely tied to their school schedules. They sleep substantially less in term time than during holidays, largely as a result of having to get up earlier.

To make matters worse, many adolescents must get out of bed even earlier than younger children after they start secondary school at the age of 11 or 12. Many secondary schools start earlier in the mornings than primary schools. In addition, the typical journey between home and school can be considerably longer for secondary-school children. The average school journey for primary school children is 1.4 miles; this doubles when they move to secondary school, where the average commute is 2.9 miles.

Research in several countries has shown that

the transition to secondary school is accompanied by a distinct drop in the amount of sleep. For example, the average American high school student gets about 45 minutes less sleep each night from the age of 13 onwards, largely because their school starts even earlier in the morning. This sharp reduction in sleep is mirrored by a rise in daytime sleepiness.

To find out whether a later school start time would relieve the problem, American researchers allowed teenagers in one school district to start school an hour later than normal. As predicted, the students' average sleep duration rose by about 45 minutes a night. More importantly, they felt less sleepy during the day, were less likely to arrive late, and had fewer days off school for sickness. Their teachers felt better too.

Similar findings have emerged from other countries, especially those where children start school at a much earlier time than in the UK. For instance, when scientists monitored Israeli school children, they found that those who started school at about 7 a.m. at least twice a week got significantly less sleep than those who normally started school at the more civilised hour of 8 a.m. As well as sleeping less, the early risers complained more of daytime sleepiness and found it harder to concentrate at school. Evidence like this implies that starting school too early in the morning can cause real problems, in the form of sleep deprivation and daytime fatigue.

And other reasons...

Of course, there are many other reasons why children can fail to get enough sleep and consequently find it hard to get up in the mornings. (We looked at some of these in Worry 15, page 81.) One of the main culprits is staying up late to watch TV or play computer games. Another is consuming too much caffeine, usually in the form of fizzy drinks. If your child regularly goes to bed late at night, with their brain fizzing from the combined effects of caffeine and violent computer games, it should come as no surprise if they fail to spring out of bed first thing the following morning.

Another well-known characteristic of adolescents is their remarkable capacity for indulging in long lie-ins at weekends and during school holidays. When given the opportunity, adolescents typically wake between one and three hours later at weekends and during holidays than in term time. The reason is simple: they are catching up on their sleep after failing to get enough on school days.

The fact that weekend lie-ins help to compensate for inadequate sleep during the week means that parents should think twice before prising their slumbering offspring out of bed at the crack of dawn on Saturday mornings. Depriving them of the opportunity to catch up on their sleep could make them even more sleep-deprived, and this, in turn, would make them less able to concentrate or perform well in school. Indeed, severe lack of sleep can lead to behavioural problems. For some children, at least, staying in bed a bit longer when they don't have to get up for school can be a good thing.

Not all reluctance to get up in the mornings results from tiredness or shifting biological rhythms. For some children, it can signify a form of defiance or oppositional behaviour: refusing to get out of bed or get dressed in the mornings is one way for a child to exert control and assert independence. On the other hand, a regular refusal to be up and ready on school days might be symptomatic of a problem with school.

Getting out of bed in the mornings often becomes more difficult in the winter months. This happens because human sleep patterns vary somewhat according to the time of year. Children are no exception. Like adults, they tend to wake slightly later and sleep slightly longer during the winter months when the days are shorter. These seasonal changes in sleep patterns are usually small in comparison to the differences between weekdays and weekends, or between term time and holidays. However, a few unfortunate individuals experience a much more severe response to the dark days of winter, in the form of Seasonal

Affective Disorder, or SAD. When winter arrives and the days become shorter, SAD-sufferers' sleeping and eating patterns undergo marked changes, and they feel like staying in bed and sleeping longer. During the day they feel sleepy, apathetic and lacking in energy, their appetite increases – especially for carbohydrates and sweet foods – and they put on weight. And their mood declines – in severe cases, plunging them into misery and depression. The symptoms disappear in the spring as the days lengthen again.

SAD is caused by biochemical changes in the body, resulting from the shorter daylight hours and lack of sunlight in winter. In its more severe forms it can be a serious and disabling condition. It usually develops in early adulthood, but it has also been observed in children and adolescents. According to one estimate, up to 4 per cent of children may be affected by the condition. A milder version, sometimes referred to as 'the winter blues', is surprisingly common.

Even though the vast majority of children do not suffer from SAD or the winter blues, the fact remains that many *do* feel like sleeping more during the winter months, making them even more reluctant to get out of bed in the mornings.

What can you do?

◆ *Give sleep a high priority in your family's lifestyle.*

Sleep is very important, for the reasons outlined in Worry 15. Getting sleep of sufficient quantity and quality, and at the right times, is essential for everyone's mental and physical well-being. Don't routinely allow sleep to take second place to other activities such as watching TV.

◆ *Encourage your child to go to bed earlier and cut down on the caffeine.*

Try to ensure that your child goes to bed at a reasonable time and gets enough sleep. They might then be readier to get up in the mornings. Letting them deprive themselves of sleep – say, by watching late-night TV and consuming large amounts of caffeine – will only make the problem worse.

◆ *Be reasonable about weekends and holidays.*

In an ideal world, children (and adults) would go to bed and get up at the same times every day, including weekends and holidays, because regular sleep schedules lead to better quality sleep. However, this is rarely feasible for busy adolescents and teenagers who have to rise early for school. Getting sufficient sleep is the most important thing, even if this means having to sleep for an extra hour or two at the weekends. Remember, it is natural for children to want to go to bed later and rise later as they get older, partly because of a shift in their biological rhythms towards a more owl-like setting.

◆ *Give yourself more time in the mornings.*

Mornings can be stressful if everyone is in a tearing hurry to get ready for work or school. For some children, refusing to get out of bed can be a form of defiance, and the effect is heightened if everyone is rushing. Therefore aim to give everyone, including yourself, enough time to do things calmly. Allowing an extra half-hour should make the mornings less fraught. The morning rush can also be eased by encouraging children to do as much preparation as possible the night before; for example, by sorting out their school ▶

clothes, packing their school bag and collecting their games kit. However, an earlier start should not be at the expense of getting less sleep. If you do get up earlier you should probably go to bed earlier as well.

◆ *Ease your child's re-entry into the day.*

Most people find it easier to get out of bed in the mornings if their bedroom is heated to a comfortable temperature during the winter months. Exposing them to a good blast of daylight (if there is any) soon after they wake up should also help to get them going.

Further advice

The Sleep Council
Tel: 01756 791089
E-mail: info@sleepcouncil.org.uk
www.sleepcouncil.org.uk
Tips for parents on helping their children get a good night's sleep.

Seasonal Affective Disorder Association (SADA)
www.sada.org.uk
Support and advice for those affected by SAD.

Related worries

4. Spends too much time watching TV or playing computer games
15. Does not get enough sleep
17. Won't go to bed
24. Won't listen to me/is disobedient

WORRY **22**

Is shy/lacks confidence

20% of parents worried

···

Chances: HIGH   **Consequences: MEDIUM**   **Control: MEDIUM**

Shyness has no precise definition and is hard to measure. There is no absolute scale of shyness. Generally, though, the term refers to people who find social situations and interactions difficult or stressful. In some children shyness might be the result of inadequate social skills. Other children lack basic self-confidence, causing them to take excessive notice of what other people think of them.

Shyness can be spotted as early as two months of age and appears to have at least in part an inherited component. Shy parents are more likely to have shy children. However, shyness can be alleviated to quite a large degree by parents' and teachers' efforts to build up the child's inner confidence and social skills.

Most people claim to be 'shy' to some degree and everyone finds certain social situations difficult, but 1 in 10 people find that their level of shyness adversely affects their everyday lives.

Chronically shy children do just as well at school, but on average they tend to marry later, be less content overall and less successful in their jobs.

Parents and teachers typically refer to a child as shy if the child is quieter than average, primarily plays on his or her own or has few friends. In the Western world we generally perceive these attributes to be negative and feel better if a child is extrovert and the centre of attention. This is a subjective judgement, however. In some other parts of the world, quiet children are seen as clever and thoughtful, while being too brash is frowned on.

Being a quieter child, or one who prefers to play alone, is not necessarily a cause for concern. The first question a parent should ask is whether social situations are causing their child anxiety or stress. A child who is happy and confident but simply prefers their own company is no cause for worry, but a child who finds social situations very difficult, and gets upset as a result, is showing signs of shyness that may need to be addressed.

Estimating the numbers of children (or adults) who suffer from shyness is difficult, not least because external appearances can be deceptive. A child might outwardly be going through the motions of socialising but inwardly be finding the experience very uncomfortable.

Most statistics come from asking people about their experience, rather than observing their behaviour. Research has found that about 40 per cent of adults report feeling shy on a regular basis, 40 per cent once considered themselves shy but no longer, and 15 per cent admit to being shy in some situations. Only about 5 per cent of adults believe they were never shy. If such figures are to be believed – and of course they depend greatly on how you define shyness – then most of us feel shy to some degree at least some of the time. However, around 1 in 10 adults say they suffer more seriously from their shyness, to the extent that it has a negative impact on their functioning in everyday life.

A different way of assessing shyness is to look at the physical and behavioural responses that social situations elicit in a person. Many of us find new social situations tricky, but for some people the anxiety has a measurable effect on their physiology. When faced with a new social situation or person, children who are genuinely fearful of social interactions will typically become anxious, stop moving about, avert their gaze and show a sharp rise in heart rate. As they get older, shy children may develop speech difficulties in social situations, speak extremely quietly or display nervous body gestures such as touching their face, wringing their hands or flicking their hair.

For some children, shyness stems mainly from a lack of well-developed social skills. If a child has had an isolated upbringing, or been exposed to relatively few new people, they might not have had the experience or practice to feel confident in social situations. Children learn how to make friends by observing and trying out different tactics and strategies.

Parents can play a big role here, both as teachers and role models. Children who go on to become chronically shy as adults often remember their parents as being over-protective, lacking in warmth, and highly critical. They also tend to remember being socially quite isolated as children, with few family activities or opportunities to mix with other groups. Such parents may tell their children to socialise while not demonstrating good social skills themselves. The children are shy because they haven't had enough practice in how to interact with others.

In other cases, the problem appears to be tied up with the child's perceptions of him- or herself. Happy, confident children are buoyed up by an inner knowledge that they are 'OK'. They have good self-confidence. While they do take notice of what others think of them, they are driven more by their own views and feelings. However, some shy children lack this basic self-confidence and continually question whether they are accepted by others, taking excessive notice of how other people respond to and evaluate them. As a result, meeting new people and entering new social situations can be stressful because they feel they are on trial or being judged.

Shyness can be spotted very early in life. Research has detected physiological differences between sociable and shy babies from as young as two months of age. Roughly a fifth of newborns are quiet, vigilant and restrained in new situations; a further fifth appear unaffected by novel situations and are at the opposite end of the spectrum, while the remainder (around three-fifths) are somewhere in between. Seeing these differences emerge so young suggests that a predisposition to develop shyness may, to some degree, be inherited. In line with this, shy children are statistically more likely to have shy parents and grandparents.

Some children, then, are born with temperamental and personality traits that make them more likely to develop shyness. But that does not mean that shyness, with all its potentially negative consequences, is inevitable. There is good evidence that positive parenting can go a long way to offset a shy disposition.

Three out of 4 of shy toddlers develop into shy adults, which means that 1 in 4 shy toddlers do not. In these cases it appears to be largely the parents who have given their child the confidence and social skills to break out of the shyness cycle. Positive parents encourage social activities but do not criticise the child's shyness. They communicate to the child that he or she is accepted for who they are, and focus on finding something the child excels at, praising the child during those activities. In short, they work on building the child's self-confidence rather than criticising their shyness or avoiding the subject altogether.

Putting effort into helping a child overcome their shyness is certainly worthwhile, because the consequences of persistent shyness can be troubling and long term. Research evidence shows that, on average, very shy people date less as teenagers, turn to alcohol more frequently, and are more likely to develop eating disorders. (However, they do not appear to do worse in school or receive fewer qualifications.) Shy men are found to marry later and have children later on average than their peers, to have less stable marriages when they do marry, to delay establishing careers, and to achieve and earn less in those careers. Shy people are also statistically more likely to become ill and stay ill. All of these consequences can stem from a basic lack of self-confidence and an inability to interact freely with others.

Conversely, there is considerable evidence that children who are self-confident, even if they are quiet, tend to do better in life. Children's positive self-image at age ten is as good a predictor of their future earnings as their reading and writing ability at that age.

What can you do?

◆ **Try not to criticise shy behaviour.**

Continually pointing out to a child that they are shy will probably just make things worse. Instead, try to be a role model of confident social behaviour yourself, even if you find it difficult. Remember that young children absorb a lot from observing how their parents behave.

◆ **Find an activity that your child is good at.**

Try to find something for your child to do that makes him or her feel successful. It doesn't really matter what it is. Give them plenty of praise for their successes and encourage them to participate further. Socialising can be a by-product of doing the thing they love. A good example is taking part in sport, which can measurably boost a child's self-confidence.

▶

◆ *Expose your child to varied activities and people.*

From an early age, encourage your child to participate in a wide variety of activities with different groups of people. Play groups, scouts or football clubs are all arenas where children can meet different sorts of people and develop their social skills. If your child is reluctant, perhaps agree to go for just a short time. As their confidence grows, outings can be extended.

◆ *Expect some episodes of shyness.*

There may be no need to worry if your child suddenly seems to have entered a shy stage. Many children go through temporary phases of shyness, often in response to something that has happened, such as starting a new school, moving house or starting to wear a bra. They may not be fundamentally shy, just temporarily lacking confidence. In such situations, aim to keep other things in the child's life as stable as possible; there's a good chance they will settle down again as their confidence returns.

◆ *Don't encourage your child to spend too much time on his or her own.*

Try to limit the amount of time your child spends doing things entirely on their own. Independence is good, but spending hours playing computer games or watching TV alone in their bedroom will do little to help. Watching a lot of TV is found to be linked with greater shyness, with one probably feeding off the other.

◆ *Let your child get to know other adults.*

While it is essential for a young child to form a strong attachment to their primary carer, it is also valuable for them to build relationships with other adults as well. If a young child is only ever in the care of their mother, for example, they might develop a view that the world is only safe when she is there. Children who regularly spend some time with other key figures such as grandparents, aunts, uncles or family friends, are less likely to be clingy. (But make sure, of course, that you only ever leave young children alone with people you really trust.)

Further advice

Social Anxiety UK
E-mail: contact@social-anxiety.org.uk
www.social-anxiety.org.uk
Organisation for people with social anxiety problems.

Shy Kids
E-mail: editor@shykids.com
www.shykids.com
Support for parents, children and adolescents affected by shyness.

Practical Parenting
www.practicalparent.org.uk
Advice and information for parents on child behaviour, including specific items on shyness.

Related worries

16. Doesn't tell me what he/she is really thinking or feeling
28. Is being bullied

WORRY **23**

Squabbles with/is too jealous of his/her siblings

20% of parents worried

Chances: HIGH   **Consequences: MEDIUM**   **Control: MEDIUM**

Sibling rivalry is entirely normal in humans and other species. It arises because siblings compete for finite parental resources. A common trigger is the arrival of a new baby – children are highly sensitive from an early age to how they are treated relative to their siblings. Sibling rivalry tends to be more intense in disrupted families and where the age gap between the siblings is small.

Siblings are usually very different from one another. Each child picks its own distinct niche in the family.

Despite their squabbling, most children benefit from having brothers or sisters. Siblings exert powerful and mostly positive influences on each other's development.

A growing proportion of British children have no siblings, as family sizes continue to shrink and only-children become more common.

Most children and young people become jealous or upset if they feel their brother or sister is receiving more of their parents' attention, approval or affection than they are. Sibling rivalry, as this problem is called, manifests itself in all sorts of ways, ranging from mild bickering and put-downs to full-blown physical violence. It is universal.

Many famous examples of sibling rivalry can be found in mythology, legend and fiction. Cinderella's stepsisters were jealous of her beauty and treated her like a servant; Romulus, the co-founder of Rome, killed his twin brother Remus after Remus jeered at his building efforts on the Palatine Hill; Cain became so jealous of his upstanding younger brother Abel that he murdered him; *David Copperfield* is a thinly disguised portrait of the intense jealousy that Charles Dickens felt towards his real-life older sister. And so on.

Sibling rivalry is not unique to humans: it is a fundamental biological phenomenon that occurs in other species as well. An extreme example is the black eagle, which lays a clutch of two eggs. The first chick to hatch usually kills its sibling soon after emerging from the egg, and the parents do nothing to prevent this. Sibling rivalry in mammals tends to be subtler, but it can still be fatal. In species that give birth to several young at a time, such as rats, mice, cats, dogs and pigs, the newborns often have to compete physically for access to one of their mother's teats. In large litters, one or more of the weaker offspring may die because of this competition for limited parental resources.

Even in humans, sibling rivalry can have its serious side when verbal jousting occasionally erupts into physical violence. Indeed, some experts argue that 'sibling abuse' is a surprisingly common form of violence within families. One study, for example, found that more than 8 out of 10 school-aged children reported experiencing some degree of sibling violence within the past year, either as victims or perpetrators.

Violence between siblings can be unpleasant, but it is rarely life-threatening. Although there have been a few documented cases of children deliberately inflicting serious injuries on younger siblings, these children have typically come from seriously disturbed families and have often been the victims of physical abuse themselves.

What causes sibling rivalry? The most fundamental explanation is that the biological interests of siblings are not identical, because they share only half their genes on average. Biology predicts that siblings should both cooperate and compete with each other, with the balance between cooperation and competition varying according to their circumstances. Competition should intensify if vital parental resources are in short supply.

In practical terms, sibling rivalry rears its ugly head when one child perceives – rightly or wrongly – that their brother or sister is receiving more of something from their parents. In its crudest form, sibling rivalry is almost inevitable if parents blatantly favour one child over another, leaving the less-favoured child feeling jealous, cross or inferior. Charles Dickens, for example, was justified in feeling intense rivalry towards his sister Fanny, because she was sent to study at the Royal Academy of Music while Charles was packed off to work in a factory at the age of 12.

A common trigger is the birth of another child. The arrival of a new baby can leave an older child feeling jealous or insecure because they are no longer the sole focus of their parents' attention. And older children have a point: new babies *do* demand a lot of time and effort, and their arrival can strain the relationship between mother and older child. The aggrieved older sibling's feelings may then reveal themselves through attention-seeking, immature behaviour or even outright aggression. Rather than bond with their new brother or sister, the older child may sulk, refuse to share their toys and, as they get older, fight.

Researchers have found that children as young as 14 months are highly sensitive to the arrival of a new baby. Even at that age, they closely monitor their mother's relationship with the new sibling and respond to their changed circumstances by demanding more of her attention. Sibling rivalry also tends to become more intense during adolescence. All being well, it subsides during the later teens, as siblings become more mature, more independent and more secure in their individual identities.

The evidence shows that siblings tend to be more jealous of each other if they are close together in age. Sibling rivalry is usually more intense if the age gap is less than about five years. This makes sense, since the larger the age difference, the less the siblings are competing for exactly the same parental resources. (In some pre-industrial societies, birth intervals of less than five years are associated with greater infant mortality.) The needs and wants of a four-year-old are different from those of a 12-year-old. One downside of a large age gap, however, is that siblings tend to have a less warm and intimate relationship with each other. (On top of which, their parents can end up feeling they have been raising children for a very long time.)

An unsettled or unloving marriage or partnership between the parents will generally increase the likelihood of severe sibling rivalry. Researchers have found that older children are better able to control any jealousy they may feel towards a younger sibling if their parents have a strong, loving marriage. Again, this makes sense, as children in a stable family are less likely to be competing head-on for inadequate parental care. Conversely, intense sibling rivalry is more common in dysfunctional families where the parents are violent to each other and to their children.

One of the most striking things about siblings is how different they can be from one another. Parents who have two or more children are often surprised by just how big the differences can be. Despite being members of the same family, siblings may not act alike, think alike or have the same interests. In fact, research shows that in terms of personality and behaviour, siblings are *less* alike than strangers chosen at random. Twins who are raised together in the same home often turn out to be less similar than twins who are separated early in life and raised separately. How could this be?

One explanation is that successive children growing up together in the same family unconsciously adapt to different niches within that family, with each child seeking out its own personal space and identity. If one child is academic, their brother or sister might be sporty. Rather than compete head-on for the same territory, siblings develop along different pathways and hence become more dissimilar, each child picking a niche for itself on the basis of what its siblings have done. Psychologists have referred to this process as 'niche-picking'. Without it, sibling rivalry would be worse.

Early differences between siblings are often reinforced and amplified by their parents, who respond differently towards them. In its crudest form, this happens when parents label their children according to some distinctive quality or ability. For example, one child might be referred to as the athlete, while the other is the clever one. This labelling is usually done with good intentions, as a way of encouraging each child. But pointing out one child's talents can seem to the other child like implied criticism, intensifying the underlying rivalry. The 'clever one' may feel their physical abilities are being undervalued, while the 'athlete' may think they are just as clever as their supposedly brighter sibling. Celebrating each child's distinctiveness is fine, but not if it is done by crudely comparing one against the other.

Each child's position in the family, or birth order, can have a distinct influence on their behaviour and personality, largely because parents behave differently towards successive children. Parents tend to be more anxious and controlling with their first child than they are with second and subsequent children. The experience of dealing with their first-born usually makes them more relaxed when number two comes along. For example, most parents possess more family photos of their first child than they do of later children. The youngest child is often given special attention because of their special position in the family, whereas middle children can sometimes feel overlooked because they are neither the first nor the last.

Psychological studies have uncovered various patterns linking birth order with children's behaviour and personality. The evidence is not clear-cut, but it generally shows that:

- *First-borns* tend to be more competitive, highly motivated to achieve and interested in careers that involve intellectual skills. They are less likely to be unorthodox or revolutionary in their thinking than later-borns.
- *Middle-borns* tend to be balanced, even-tempered, sociable and cooperative. It is said that they make good leaders and managers, thanks to their ability to negotiate. They are also the most likely to feel they do not belong.
- *Last-borns* tend to be more outgoing, affectionate, creative, rebellious and risk-taking. They tend to possess better social skills and are more likely to choose careers that involve dealing with people, artistic pursuits or working outdoors. It is said that last-borns make good sales people.
- *Only children*, like first-borns, tend to be high-achievers who are drawn to careers involving intellectual skills. They also tend to be attention-seeking loners who prefer the company of adults.

We should stress that these descriptions are based upon statistical correlations and certainly do not apply neatly to every individual. There will be many children who do not fit the descriptions given above.

The fact that siblings are often very different from one another has important practical consequences. It means that no matter how hard parents try to be impartial and treat all their children the same, they can never fully succeed. Each child occupies a distinct niche within the family, and each has a distinct personality. The same words or acts by a parent therefore mean different things to each child. It's not so much what parents say or do, as how their words or actions are interpreted. The strong implication is that parents should try to treat their children *fairly* rather than *identically*.

Sibling rivalry can be an unattractive aspect of family life, but it would be wrong to assume that the picture is entirely negative. On the contrary, siblings can exert powerful and beneficial influences on each other as they develop.

Siblings who are reasonably close in age (less than about five years apart) often provide each other with friendship and practical support, especially during adolescence. They can also help each other in terms of social and emotional development: through their daily interactions with siblings, young children acquire valuable experience in how to control their aggression, how to resolve conflict and how to co-operate with other people. This experience will stand them in good stead for later life, when they will have to manage relationships with partners, work colleagues and strangers.

An older brother or sister can be a confidant, playmate, teacher, protector and role model. A warm relationship with an older sibling can make the younger child's home environment seem even more secure. Having an older sibling of the opposite sex can also help a child to develop a more balanced view of the opposite sex.

Older siblings benefit from the relationship too. Caring for a younger brother or sister can teach them a lot about life. There is even evidence that children who have a younger sibling perform better in IQ tests, possibly because the older child's intellectual development is stimulated by teaching the younger sibling.

Many siblings maintain close and mutually supportive relationships throughout their adult lives. The occasional tiffs or bouts of jealousy during childhood pale in comparison with their life-long bond. Researchers have found that adults who maintain a close relationship with a sibling (especially a sister) are less prone to depression in later life.

A final point is that sibling rivalry is increasingly becoming a thing of the past, because fewer and fewer parents are having two or more children. And without at least two children in a family, there obviously cannot be any sibling rivalry. British families have been getting progressively smaller over the past 30 years. Only 22 per cent of house-holds now contain any sort of family, in the sense of a married or cohabiting couple living with one or more dependent children. And for those couples who do have children, the trend is to have fewer of them. The average number of children per family has fallen from 2.0 in 1971 to 1.8 in 2001. Married couples tend to have slightly more children (an average of 1.9 children) than cohabiting couples (1.6 children) or lone parents (1.7 children). Almost a quarter of all dependent children are now the only child in their family, whereas less than 1 in 20 couples now have three or more children. The last time the typical British family consisted of the proverbial '2.4 children' was in the 1950s.

What can you do?

◆ *Accept that sibling rivalry is a normal part of growing up.*

Resist the urge to intervene every time they start bickering. It's often better to let them work it out for themselves. They will never sort out their differences if you always step in and separate them, and they may end up learning that fighting is a good way of getting your attention. Of course, there will be occasions when you should intervene; for example, if they keep arguing about the same thing over and over again, or if it looks as though there might be serious violence. Otherwise, grit your teeth and stand back. Let them express what they really think about their siblings. If they are feeling cross or jealous towards a sibling, acknowledge that fact and let them know you understand how they feel. There is no point in ordering them not to have those feelings. Acknowledging the problem can go some way towards defusing it.

◆ *Treat each of your children as a unique individual.*

Try to make it clear to your children that you respect each of them as a unique and distinctive individual, which is what they are. Make them feel loved and valued for who they are. Try to respond to their individual needs, rather than acting as though each child should receive the same. Tell them that you do not love one child more than the other, but you do love them differently because each one is unique.

◆ *Spend time with each of your children on their own.*

It is all too easy for busy parents with large families to end up spending nearly all of their time together as a group rather than individually. Try to create opportunities for spending time alone with each of your children. And when you do this, try to avoid talking about the others.

◆ *Aim to treat your children fairly rather than equally.*

There is no point trying to treat siblings absolutely equally, as though they were the same as each other. They are not the same and they will not let you treat them the same. If you allow one child to do something they want, don't feel you must automatically allow their sibling to do the ▶

same; your action will mean something different to each child. No matter how scrupulously you try to treat each child equally, they may still feel they are being treated differently. Aim for *fairness* rather than strict equality.

◆ *Avoid making explicit comparisons between your children, especially if they are listening.*

Attaching labels to siblings can often fuel resentment. If one child has behaved badly, tell them so, but don't tell them they should be a good boy or girl like their brother or sister. That will only make them feel jealous or resentful towards their supposedly superior sibling. The general principle is to criticise the behaviour, not the child. Equally, do not praise one child at the expense of another. If one child has performed well at school, praise their achievement. But do not tell them they are cleverer than their brother or sister.

◆ *Prepare the ground for new arrivals.*

If another baby is on its way, prepare your existing child or children for the arrival of their new brother or sister by talking to them about it. Get them involved with the process – for example, by helping you to prepare the bedroom and choose baby clothes. Leaving a bigger age gap between successive children should reduce the scope for sibling rivalry, other things being equal, but it will also reduce the scope for your children to enjoy close, stimulating and mutually beneficial relationships with each other. There are far stronger reasons for deciding when to have your next child than worries about sibling rivalry.

◆ *Set a good example.*

If children see their parents expressing their own discontent by yelling at each other, they are more likely to use similar tactics themselves.

Further advice

Parentline Plus

24 hour helpline: 0808 800 2222

www.parentlineplus.org.uk

Advice and support to parents, with specific information on family conflicts and new arrivals.

Practical Parenting

www.practicalparent.org.uk

Tips and support on child behaviour, including articles on sibling rivalry.

Related worries

28. Is being bullied

WORRY 24

Won't listen to me/
is disobedient

.19% of parents worried

....

Chances: HIGH   **Consequences: MEDIUM**   **Control: HIGH**

As children grow up and become more independent, they develop views and ways of behaving that differ from those of their parents. A degree of conflict between parents and children is therefore a normal part of family life. Conflict tends to reach its peak in the early adolescent years and is more common in larger families, with boys rather than girls, and with fathers rather than mothers. The most frequent areas of disagreement are social activities and helping around the house.

One of the biggest determinants of how much conflict is present in a family is the style of parenting. Parents who demand a lot of their children but also respond to them (authoritative parents) tend to experience less conflict than those who simply tell a child what to do all the time (authoritarian parents) or those who let their children do whatever they want (indulgent or uninvolved parents).

Good discipline depends on establishing a mutually respectful home environment. Successful disciplinary tactics involve a combination of praising and rewarding good behaviour and penalising bad behaviour.

Physical punishment is a weak long-term strategy for encouraging good behaviour. It is generally less effective than other forms of punishment, and it can encourage reciprocal violence and anger later in life. Physical punishment teaches children to use violence as a way of solving problems.

All parents want their children to grow up to be confident, happy and independent people. Yet it is a child's growing desire to be independent that causes most conflict within a family. Research shows that conflicts occur most often when parents and children have opposing views over everyday issues such as helping around the house (the most common source of conflict by far), homework and studying, appearance and going out. These relatively mundane issues are more frequent causes of conflict than more obvious areas such as drugs and smoking.

Abolishing all conflict from within a family might not be a sensible aim. Families who argue are at least showing they care about each other. Indifference would be worse. If handled well, arguments can teach children useful lessons about decision-making, negotiation, and the consequences of their behaviour. A better aim would be to cut out the pointless, everyday battles and concentrate on teaching children the skills for understanding and dealing with serious disagreements.

As parents, we must decide what we really want to be strict about. We have a duty to impose some boundaries on our children to ensure their safety and well-being. But we do not have a right to try turning them into mini-clones of ourselves. When we complain that our children are not listening, what we often mean is that they are not doing what we want. Obviously, if a child is being careless crossing the road we have a legitimate reason to impose our will on them. However, if we are trying to make them do something because *we* think it would be good, when they clearly don't, then our desire to control may have gone too far.

The amount of disobedience and conflict in a family can be predicted to some extent by looking at the type of relationship that exists between the child and its parents. Psychologists have developed a simple framework that distinguishes between four broad styles of control used by parents. Most parents tend to use one of these patterns more than the others. Their favoured style is established early on and is fairly consistent over time.

The four-way classification is based on two factors: how much the parents demand or attempt to control the child, and how much they respond to the child's own demands and wishes. They are as follows:

- *Authoritarian parents* are demanding and directive, but not responsive. They are focused on obedience and status, and expect their orders to be obeyed without explanation. They often use emotional control over their child when they do not get their way – for example, making the child feel guilty, shaming them or withdrawing love.

- *Authoritative parents* are both demanding and responsive. They monitor their children and impart clear standards for their children's conduct. They are assertive and open about their demands but also listen attentively to the children's views and wishes. They sometimes impose their will, but sometimes let the child have their way too. They rarely use emotional control over the child.

- *Indulgent parents* are undemanding and highly responsive. They accommodate their child's every wish, and impose few and lenient boundaries. They rarely punish. They believe they are being kind to their child.

- *Uninvolved parents* are both undemanding and unresponsive. They can sometimes appear not to care. In extreme cases, this parenting style can encompass rejecting and neglectful parents.

Effective parenting

The authoritative parenting style generally seems to be the most effective, not just in reducing conflict but also in establishing a mutual respect and trust between parent and child. The child will listen because they feel listened to. Children with authoritative parents tend to be measurably more socially competent and are generally doing better at school by as young as five years of age. In contrast, children of authoritarian parents are more likely to become depressed and have lower self-esteem, while those of uninvolved parents do worst of all and are most likely to develop behaviour problems as teenagers.

So, a relationship based on positive two-way interaction between parent and child is the foundation for good behaviour. However, even when this is present, further tools are still needed to handle the inevitable conflicts that crop up in any family.

Research has highlighted the strategies that seem to work best. Most obviously, it confirms that parents must encourage and reward desired behaviour (the most effective strategy of all) and penalise bad behaviour, making it unattractive to the child in the long term. A combination of the two is most effective. Trying to punish bad behaviour tends to be relatively ineffective on its own.

Most children will do what their parents want at least some of the time. The trick is for parents to be attentive and observant enough to spot when good behaviour is occurring, and to reward and reinforce it immediately. The reward could be in the form of spoken praise, a hug, a treat or some form of recognition. Quite simply, children will do more of the things they feel get them attention and recognition. However, there are some types of behaviour that may not appear spontaneously and which parents may therefore need to teach, such as sharing, good manners and good studying habits.

When it comes to discouraging undesirable forms of behaviour, the two most effective punishments seem to be 'time out' or removal of privileges. 'Time out' involves removing the child from an activity or group and forcing them to be on their own for a period. In older children it can be mean 'grounding' them. In pre-school children, 'time out' has been shown to increase compliance with parental wishes by a factor of three. 'Time out' can also be very effective when used appropriately with older children. Removal of privileges means withdrawing a facility or activity that the child values, such as access to the TV or computer. With the majority of children these two simple tactics prove highly effective.

In contrast, two common disciplinary strategies that appear to be rather ineffective are verbally reprimanding the child and smacking. Many parents talk disapprovingly to their child in the hope that this alone will halt the bad behaviour. When used infrequently, and targeted toward specific types of behaviour, a telling-off can be effective in halting or reducing undesirable behaviour. However, if they are used frequently and indiscriminately, reprimands lose their effectiveness. Indeed, they tend to have the opposite effect because they provide the child with attention.

Smacking is also a dubious way of trying to control children's behaviour. Whether you agree with it or not, smacking has been shown to be a relatively ineffective form of punishment and one that has worrying long-term implications (see Smacking, page 133). The shock of being hit will often stop a child's bad behaviour in the short term, but research shows that the intensity and frequency of physical punishment may have to be increased over time to elicit the same response. Children become increasingly resistant to physical punishment and parents may therefore have to act in more extreme ways to produce the same effect. Obviously, there will also come a time when a child is simply too big and strong to be physically punished, and parents who have relied on this strategy up to then are left with no other means of control.

Perhaps more worrying are the longer term effects of smacking. There is good evidence that children who experience their parents resorting to physical violence to impose their will are more likely to become violent teenagers and adults themselves. They are more likely to go on to hit their own children or partner, and more likely to turn to crime when they grow up.

To summarise, three key elements help to encourage good behaviour and discipline:

- a positive and mutually respectful relationship between child and parent
- a reward system for reinforcing good behaviour
- time out or removal of privileges for bad behaviour

What can you do?

- **Pick your battles.**

  There is little point being in continual conflict with your child, especially over trivial issues. Decide the areas you really feel strongly about and deal with those firmly and consistently. When it comes to minor issues, try to avoid putting yourself in a position where your bluff might be called.

- **Be consistent.**

  If you allow a child get away with something one day but not the next, they may become confused and try to extend the boundaries. Try as far as possible to be consistent with your partner's behaviour as well. It will not help if Mum always lets them do something but Dad does not.

- **Explain your behaviour.**

  Get in the habit of explaining why you are making your decisions or requests, even with very young children. If a child understands why they are not allowed to do something they are more likely to accept the ruling. Explaining is also a good way of checking whether you are being reasonable. If your only reason is 'because I say so' then perhaps you should think about your decision.

- **Mean what you say.**

  Don't threaten to punish your child unless you are really willing to do it. Threats quickly lose their power if they are shown to be empty.

- **Act swiftly.**

  If you are going to punish your child for bad behaviour, or enforce some sanction, do it quickly. Your actions will have a greater impact on your child's behaviour if there is an immediate and obvious link between what they have just done and the consequences. Delay muddies the waters.

- **Be reasonable.**

  Discipline becomes less effective if it is too strict or applied indiscriminately. Children soon learn if it is impossible to please their parents, and may just give up trying. Why should they try to be good if they are going to be told off anyway? Try to ensure that punishments are reasonable, just, and proportionate.

- **Be aware of your own emotions.**

  If you find yourself in a confrontation with your child, try to remain aware of your own emotional state. If you are so angry that you might do something you will later regret, such as hitting your child, then it's probably best to step back for a few minutes until you have calmed down.

- **Reward good behaviour.**

  Keep an eye out for good behaviour and reward it, if only by letting your child know that you have noticed. It is easier to spot bad behaviour and criticise it.

- **Listen.**

  Children usually misbehave for a reason, even if that reason is unclear. Ultimately, the biggest risk to your relationship with your child is a breakdown in communication. Even if they appear to be taking no notice of you, try to listen to them. At least then the communication channels will remain open, allowing you to re-establish better relations later.

Further advice

Parentline Plus
Free helpline: 0808 800 2222
www.parentlineplus.org.uk
Advice for parents and children on all aspects of parenting, including tips on discipline and communication.

National Family and Parenting Institute (NFPI)
Tel: 020 7424 3460
E-mail: info@nfpi.org
www.nfpi.org

Information on the parent-child relationship, with specific material on the smacking debate.

Related worries

16. Doesn't tell me what he/she is really thinking or feeling
20. Has tantrums
33. Won't help with household chores
36. Won't do his/her homework
38. Might get into trouble with the authorities or commit a crime

---

FACE THE FACTS 7

Smacking

◆ At the time of writing, it is *not* against the law in the UK for parents to smack their children.

◆ It *is* against the law for one person to assault another person. But if the 'assault' involves a parent smacking their child, then the parent can argue a legal defence of 'reasonable chastisement'.

◆ 'Reasonable chastisement' has no precise definition in law, and the judgement of what is 'reasonable' would depend on the circumstances of the case. However, if a parent uses a cane, belt or other implement to smack the child, or if the smacking is so severe that it leaves marks on the child then it is unlikely to be regarded as 'reasonable', in which case the parent could be charged with assault.

◆ In most other European countries children have the same legal rights as adults to legal protection from assault, and there is no defence of 'reasonable chastisement'. Sweden banned all forms of corporal punishment in 1979, and many other countries have since done the same, including Germany, Italy, Denmark and Austria.

◆ It is *not* against the law for someone who is privately employed by a parent – for example, a nanny or babysitter – to smack a child, provided they have the parent's agreement.

▶

FACE THE FACTS SMACKING

- It *is* against the law for a teacher, nursery worker or childcare worker to smack, hit or shake a child. Smacking and caning are illegal in all schools. However, a teacher might be permitted to physically restrain a school pupil under certain tightly defined circumstances – for example, if that child is about to cause injury to themselves or another person.

- A recent national study found that only 1 in 10 British parents regard physical punishment as 'always acceptable', 40% of parents regard it as never acceptable to smack a child, and virtually all parents reject severe forms of punishment like hitting with an implement. One in 7 parents have used physical punishment in the past year despite not approving of it in principle.

- Parents who describe their relationship with their child as less warm and involved, or more hostile or critical, are much more likely to use physical punishment.

- Parents with unsupportive partners are significantly more likely than other parents to use physical punishment.

- Most experts (and most parents) do not believe that smacking is a good way of disciplining children or of teaching them the difference between right and wrong. Children who have been physically punished are in fact more likely to respond by escalating into even worse behaviour or becoming aggressive.

- Research evidence indicates that hitting children increases the risk that they will behave aggressively or criminally in adult life.

WORRY 25

Doesn't eat enough

19% of parents worried

Chances: MEDIUM   Consequences: HIGH   Control: MEDIUM

The vast majority of children clearly do eat enough, and many children eat too much – hence the increasingly serious problem of childhood obesity. However, some children, especially girls, worry about being fat and attempt to lose weight by dieting.

Children who try to control their weight by extreme dieting are at somewhat greater risk of developing serious eating disorders such as anorexia and bulimia. Girls are at much greater risk of developing eating disorders than boys. The chances that an average adolescent will develop full-blown anorexia are less than 1 in 1000. However, many more will suffer from some degree of distress about dieting and dissatisfaction with their appearance.

Children are more likely to develop an eating problem if they are criticised or teased about their weight by their parents, siblings or peers, or if their parents use extreme methods such as crash dieting to control their own weight. Children are also at greater risk if their parents attempt to exert rigid control over their eating behaviour early in life. Many children whose parents encourage them to lose weight are actually of average or even below-average weight.

In this era of snacking, junk food and soaring childhood obesity, it might seem strange that almost 1 in 5 parents is concerned about their child not eating enough. What this perhaps underlines is our society's preoccupation with food, dieting and body image. We live in a world that stigmatises fatness and equates being attractive with being thin. The message that 'thin is good' is constantly beamed at us by the media and advertising industry, and some parents reinforce this by making critical remarks about their children's weight.

Children have taken the message on board. Research has shown that boys and girls as young as seven believe that being thin is important, while being fat means having fewer friends, doing less well at school and being unhappy. So it should come as no surprise that many children are dissatisfied with their bodies and would prefer to be thinner. Some of them act on these concerns by dieting to lose weight. As many as a third of boys, and half of all girls, resort to dieting at some stage. Ironically, the UK is at the same time witnessing an epidemic of childhood obesity, which many experts now believe presents the biggest threat to the health of future generations.

Perhaps another reason why so many parents are concerned about under-eating is the increasing difficulty they face in monitoring their children's food intake. There is a strong trend in the UK for children to eat more and more of their food outside the home and in the form of snacks. This change in eating habits obviously makes it harder for parents to keep track. Their children may be eating more (or less) than they imagine. Studies have found that many parents are also unaware of their children's attempts to lose weight.

So, how much food do children actually need? Setting aside the requirements for essential nutrients, vitamins and minerals, which should be provided by any reasonably varied diet (see Worry 35, page 187), how many calories of energy a day must a child consume to stay alive?

The answer depends, among other things, on the child's age, sex and activity level. The average energy requirement for children aged 4–6 years is about 1600 Calories a day.[3] This rises to 1900 Calories a day for 7 to 10-year-olds and just over 2000 Calories a day for 11 to 14-year-olds. Boys generally need more than girls; for example, boys aged 11–14 need an average of 2220 Calories a day, against an average of 1845 for girls. The fact that so many British children are overweight or obese suggests that many are consuming more calories than they actually need.

A short-term loss of appetite can be triggered by emotional upsets or anxieties arising from everyday situations, such as falling out with school friends, relationship problems with members of the opposite sex, or conflicts within the family. However, for some children a reluctance to eat is longer lasting.

Many children go through periods when they are driven to eat less because of their anxieties about food and weight. The desire to be thin is stronger among girls than boys. This sex difference emerges at around eight to ten years of age, and girls become even more dissatisfied with their bodies as they get older. By the age of ten, girls are also more likely than boys to have tried losing weight by dieting or exercise. Children who are concerned about their weight are often unhappy about other things as well. Research has found that children who diet because they are dissatisfied with their bodies also tend to have low self-esteem and low levels of satisfaction with other aspects of their life, including school.

Perhaps the biggest cause for concern is that children who diet because they want to look thinner are more likely to develop eating disorders. Dieting is associated with a significantly greater risk of developing a serious eating disorder such as anorexia nervosa or bulimia, especially if the weight loss is sudden. Even moderate crash-dieting has been shown to increase an adolescent girl's risk of developing an eating disorder by a factor of five, while

---

[3] Calorie (with a big C) = 1000 calories (with a small c) = 4200 joules = 4.2 kJ.

severe crash-dieting increases the risk 18-fold.

Anorexia nervosa literally means 'loss of appetite for nervous reasons', although the name is somewhat misleading. A person with anorexia does not simply lose their appetite, but rather, intentionally reduces the amount of food and drink they consume in a determined effort to control the shape and appearance of their body. Some do this to an extent that can threaten their health, and a few anorexics end up dying, either from medical complications or suicide.

The signs of anorexia in children and teenagers include weight loss (or failure to gain weight), an intense fear of gaining weight, ritualistic eating behaviour such as cutting food into tiny pieces, a distorted perception of weight and physical appearance, mood swings, secretiveness and a refusal to accept that there is a problem.

A related eating disorder is bulimia, which literally means 'the hunger of an ox'. The name reflects the disorder's most obvious feature, which is a cycle of binge eating and purging. Bulimics periodically pig out on large amounts of food and then purge themselves by vomiting, taking laxatives, or both. Some also try to work off the calories with strenuous physical exercise. The tell-tale signs include secretive visits to the toilet after meals in order to vomit, an obsession with food, and low self-esteem. Bulimia is harder to detect than anorexia because the sufferer may not actually lose much weight.

The core problem in both anorexia and bulimia is an excessive and distorted concern with weight and body shape. Sufferers judge their own worth almost exclusively in terms of their body weight and their ability to control it. The self-starvation is merely a means to an end. Bulimics also try to control their weight, but periodically succumb to binge eating; for that reason, they sometimes describe themselves as failed anorexics.

Fortunately, serious eating disorders such as anorexia and bulimia are rare in children. The risk that an average young person in the 10-19 age group will develop anorexia is about 3 in 10,000.

Anorexia is even rarer among younger children: only 1 per cent of anorexics are under ten years old. Female anorexics outnumber males by at least 10 to 1. Bulimia is somewhat more common than anorexia, affecting about 4 out of every 10,000 young people in the age range 10–19 years.

So, the vast majority of children who fret about being fat and go on diets do not become anorexic or bulimic. However, less serious problems such as chaotic eating patterns and an unhealthy preoccupation with food are much more common. There are no definitive statistics on the prevalence of these sorts of eating problems among British children, but most experts agree that they have become more common in recent decades. According to some definitions, up to 8 per cent of young boys and 14 per cent of young girls have some form of eating disorder or problem.

What causes eating disorders, and what can parents do to prevent them? Eating disorders such as anorexia do not have a single cause. They result from complex interactions between various factors, including family background, experience, genes, psychological state and cultural influences. Inherited factors are known to have some influence on anorexia, but they are only one part of the story.

Parents can play a pivotal role, either for better or worse, by helping to shape a child's early diet and experiences with food. Their own behaviour and attitudes towards food, body shape and dieting also provide powerful role models – children tend to prefer the same sorts of foods as their parents. Parents can also influence their children more directly and more negatively by criticising their weight or encouraging them to diet.

Research has found that children are more likely to become dissatisfied with their body if they think their parents are concerned about their weight, or if they have been teased about it by their parents, siblings or peers. (Girls who frequently discuss their body with friends are also more likely to be dissatisfied with it.) Children are more likely to diet if their parents use dieting themselves, or if their parents encourage them to lose weight. The risk is particularly great when parents use extreme methods such as crash dieting or fasting to control their own weight. Many children who are encouraged by their parents to lose weight are actually of average or even below-average weight.

The research evidence shows that mothers generally have a bigger influence than fathers on children's attitudes and behaviour towards food, weight and dieting, and that the influence that mothers have on their daughters is especially strong. Girls are significantly more likely to develop an eating disorder if their mother has an eating disorder herself, or if their mother frequently complains about her own weight.

So, parents can unintentionally heighten their child's risk of developing an eating disorder if they create a home environment where great value is attached to being thin, where dieting or excessive exercising are used as ways of attaining an idealised body shape, or where comments are often made about the child's weight or appearance.

Parents often under-estimate the impact of what they say to their children about a sensitive topic such as weight. A remark intended as a joke, or supportive encouragement to lose weight, can sometimes be perceived by the child as outright criticism.

Parents may sow the seeds of a problem early in their child's life by attempting to exert rigid control over the child's eating – for example, by insisting that the child eats everything on their plate. Research suggests that this can undermine the child's ability to regulate his or her own feeding, leading to later problems with dieting, chaotic eating and fluctuating weight. Parental attempts to control children's eating also tend to backfire in the short term: when parents try to make young children eat food they dislike, they usually end up disliking that food even more. Nagging can put children off healthy food for years.

What happens if your child is one of the tiny minority who does develop a major problem? Anorexia and bulimia are potentially serious illnesses that require expert medical care. They are also complex disorders for which there is no single cause and no simple remedy. The treatment involves a combination of approaches that tackle both the physical and psychological aspects of the problem. Some sort of counselling or psychological therapy forms the core of any treatment. When the sufferer is a child or adolescent, family-based therapy is often employed.

What can you do?

◆ **Encourage a healthy and balanced attitude towards food.**

It is generally a bad idea to use food as a frequent way of rewarding, punishing or bribing children. Avoid rigidly categorising foods as either 'good' or 'bad': some foods are nutritionally better than others, but even 'bad' food will do no harm if eaten occasionally and in moderation as part of a varied diet. Do not try rigidly to control a younger child's eating; for example, by always insisting that they eat everything on their plate. Be relaxed about food – it should be a source of pleasure, not an emotional battleground.

◆ **Don't encourage your child to diet unless he or she has a genuine weight problem, and only then under supervision.**

Any attempt at dieting should start by cutting out snacking and reducing the intake of fatty and sugary foods. Crash dieting is never a good idea. Children who diet are at greater risk of developing eating disorders, and those who crash-diet are at much greater risk. The best strategy for controlling weight is to eat a healthy, balanced diet and take regular physical exercise. ▶

◆ *Do not tease or criticise children about their weight or shape.*

Encourage them to feel good (or at least, accepting) about their appearance, even if it falls short of their ideal. If they are genuinely and significantly overweight for their age then you should broach the subject of healthier eating and exercise, but try to do this with diplomacy and tact.

◆ *Set a good example yourself.*

Your behaviour and attitudes towards food, eating and body shape can have a big influence on your children, especially in those crucial early years. So do not go on crash diets and do not constantly complain in front of your children about how fat you are. Eat healthily.

◆ *Encourage your child to take part in sport.*

Regular exercise will help them feel more confident about themselves, as well as keeping them slimmer and trimmer. As many adults discover, dieting alone is rarely successful in maintaining weight loss; if you want to look slimmer then you will need to change your lifestyle, and that includes being more active.

◆ *Help your child to be realistic about body shape.*

Be openly sceptical when the media and advertising portray ludicrously thin people as the ideal to which we should all aspire. Let your children know the truth – which is that the vast majority of real people look nothing like the skeletal supermodels and diet-obsessed celebrities we are all supposed to emulate.

◆ *Watch out for sudden weight loss.*

Serious eating disorders are rare in children. Nonetheless, you should seek medical advice from your GP if your child suddenly starts to lose weight for no apparent reason. A sudden unexplained loss of weight might result from some undiagnosed illness. In older children, keep an eye open for signs of an eating disorder, such as intense fear of gaining weight, secrecy about eating, denial of ever being hungry, cutting food into tiny pieces or eating very slowly, mood swings, compulsive exercising and social withdrawal.

Further advice

British Nutrition Foundation
Tel: 020 7404 6504
www.nutrition.org.uk
Facts on the nutritional needs of children and adolescents, and advice on what children should know about nutrition.

Eating Disorders Association
Adult Helpline: 0845 634 1414
Youthline: 0845 634 7650
Text-phone Service: 01603 753322
Helpline e-mail: helpmail@edauk.com
www.edauk.com/default.htm
Information and advice on all aspects of eating disorders.

NHS Direct
Tel: 0845 4647
www.nhsdirect.co.uk
Information on symptoms and treatments for eating disorders.

Related worries

3. Eats too much sugar and sweet foods
7. Eats too much junk food or convenience food
12. Will only eat a narrow range of food/has food fads
35. Doesn't get enough vitamins from his/her normal diet

WORRY **26**

Isn't reading or writing as well as he/she should

19% of parents worried

···

Chances: MEDIUM **Consequences: MEDIUM** **Control: MEDIUM**

Two-fifths of the adult UK population have such poor reading and writing that it causes them practical problems in their everyday lives. In 1998 the government launched the National Literacy Strategy to improve this situation. Since then there has been a significant improvement in standards, with 3 out of 4 children now achieving the desired level of literacy at age 11.

A child's ability to read and write is primarily influenced by the quality of the teaching they receive. However, parents can play a key supporting role. Research has shown that the more children read at home with their parents, the stronger readers they are likely to be.

Some children have severe difficulties learning to read and write, despite appropriate teaching, and may therefore be described as dyslexic. An estimated 4 per cent of children are seriously affected by dyslexia and may need additional teaching and support. With the right help, most of them can go on to do well in school and at work.

Being able to read and write reasonably well are fundamental requirements. Most jobs require basic literacy skills, such as being able to understand and act on written instructions or fill in forms. Statistics show that people with very poor literacy skills are more likely to be unemployed and more likely to turn to crime. According to one estimate, the cost to the country of poor literacy, in terms of lost business, remedial education, crime and benefit payments is more than £10 billion a year.

In 1998 the government launched the National Literacy Strategy to raise standards. In essence the strategy advises that every primary school child in England and Wales should spend an hour each day dedicated to literacy. The 'literacy hour' should comprise roughly 30 minutes of whole class teaching, 20 minutes of group and independent work and 10 minutes for whole class review, reflection and consolidation.

The National Literacy Strategy originally set out termly teaching objectives for the 6–11 age range in primary schools (Key Stages 1 and 2), but literacy is now also an integral part of the Key Stage 3 strategy for 11- to 14-year-olds in the first three years of secondary school. The strategy's objectives focus on three broad dimensions of literacy: word-level work (phonics, spelling, vocabulary and handwriting); sentence-level work (grammar and punctuation); and text-level work (comprehension and composition).

The results have been encouraging. The limited research evidence available suggests that standards of literacy among British primary school children changed little during the second half of the 20th century, with roughly half of all children achieving the expected standard by the age of 11. However, following the introduction of the National Literacy Strategy there has been a distinct improvement. Currently, around 3 out of 4 children achieve the desired standard in English at age 11.

Focused teaching is the key to improving children's reading and writing skills. But parents can also play a valuable role. The home environment has a substantial influence on a child's interest and motivation to learn: parents who spend time reading with their children at home are more likely to have children who are better readers. Creating the right environment does not necessarily mean having a lot of books in the house. The quality of the time parents spend with their children is more important than the sheer number of books they read together.

What do you do if, despite good teaching and support at home, your child is still failing to read and write as well as you think they should? The first thing is to talk to their class teacher. Some parents don't really know how well children of a particular age should be performing and may have unrealistic expectations of what their child should be able to do. The child's teacher can give an objective account of how the child is doing in comparison with other children in the class and relative to national standards.

Recognising a problem

Slow progress in learning to read and write during the early years of primary school does not necessarily mean that a child has a permanent problem. Some children develop more slowly than others. A child who is slightly below average in reading age when they are five or six will not necessarily still be below average when they are 13 or 14. Some individuals are just not ready to start learning to read and write when they are five years old, but they do catch up later.

Schools in many other countries start teaching children to read and write later than in the UK. Swedish children, for example, do not start formal full-time education until they are seven, but they nonetheless achieve higher levels of literacy than British children by the time they are 11. Remember, too, that a child with a summer birthday might be nearly a year younger than other children in their class. A year can make a real difference, especially in the early stages of primary school.

Children can have problems learning to read and write for a variety of different reasons. Some find it difficult because they lack confidence or because they have not been taught properly. In other cases, undiagnosed defects in hearing or vision turn out to be the root cause. For some children, however, the problem is less tractable. They continue to struggle with their reading and writing despite good teaching, and their perform-ance fails to improve at the expected rate. These children are usually said to have dyslexia.

Dyslexia is an umbrella term applied in cases where children have severe and persistent problems learning to read, write and spell fluently, despite receiving appropriate teaching. It can be hard to decide objectively whether a child should be labelled as dyslexic. (Indeed, in a few instances the label has been misused as a medical-sounding just-ification for children who fail to perform as well as their parents expect.) The British Dyslexia Association estimates that around 4 per cent of children – roughly one child per class on average – are severely affected by dyslexia, and that around 10 per cent of the population show some signs of the condition. Literacy problems are three times more common among boys than girls, and a person is more likely to be dyslexic if a parent or other family member also has the condition.

Contrary to one popular belief, dyslexia shows no clear correlation with intelligence, which means that dyslexics are no more (or less) likely than other people to score highly in IQ tests. In fact, children of all abilities, and from all types of back-grounds, can have severe difficulties acquiring fluent reading and writing skills.

Psychologists have identified a number of basic mental skills that are essential for reading and writing, and where a weakness can give rise to literacy problems. For example:

- *Phonological skills:* the skills that enable us to hear and distinguish between the component sounds that make up a word – for instance, knowing that the sounds C, A and T blended together make the sound 'cat'. If phonological skills do not develop well, the child becomes more reliant on learning to read whole words by recognising them visually, which may limit their capacity to learn.

- *Sensory integration:* the ability to process and integrate information coming via two or more senses. Reading requires us to integrate visual information (seeing the printed word) and aural information ('hearing' the corresponding sounds). Children who have problems with sensory integration take significantly longer to understand written words when they see them, or spoken words when they hear them.

- *Automatisation:* the process whereby basic processing skills become increasingly automatic through practice. Children with an automatisation deficit are in effect having to re-learn literacy skills each time they use them, rather than clicking into autopilot. This slows their performance.

Although dyslexia is defined by difficulties in learning to read and write, dyslexic children often have problems in other areas as well. Some dyslexic children may display a range of other difficulties, such as:

- difficulty following complex instructions
- difficulty with sequences (e.g., reciting the days of the week or the months of the year)
- poor short-term memory for sounds
- difficulty learning nursery rhymes and rhyming words (e.g., 'cat, mat, sat')
- difficulty organising themselves and their belongings
- later than expected speech development
- persistent difficulties in getting dressed efficiently and putting their shoes on the correct feet
- difficulty clapping to a simple rhythm
- difficulty remembering multiplication tables in maths

These days it is unusual for dyslexic children to be withdrawn from the mainstream education system, even if their literacy problems are quite severe.

Most dyslexic children receive support and additional teaching within their mainstream school. In the majority of cases this will enable the child to overcome his or her difficulties, take exams and gain good qualifications.

In addition to help from school, parents of dyslexic children are also being offered a raft of commercial products and programmes that claim to alleviate the problem. These often appeal to parents because they appear to offer a quick fix. However, many of these products and programmes have not been adequately evaluated and there is little solid evidence (other than anecdotal) that they are genuinely effective. Some of them may help some children, but parents are advised to proceed with caution and investigate the claims thoroughly before parting with their money.

The solution that is still by far the most likely to bring success is a well-structured teaching programme appropriate to the child's individual needs. The child will also need to be encouraged to practise, which is where parents can really help.

The harsh reality is that children with poor literacy skills will need to work harder than most of their peers at learning to read and write. Sadly, there are no quick or easy fixes.

What can you do?

◆ *Read to your child.*

You can help your child by regularly reading them stories from as young as six months of age. The evidence indicates that children whose parents read to them do better in primary school and are more likely to develop a love of reading in the longer term. As your child gets older, try shifting to paired reading, in which you and your child take turns to read aloud to each other. Research shows that paired reading is one of the most successful ways of helping children to improve their reading.

◆ *Don't turn literacy into a battleground.*

You should try to avoid making reading, writing, spelling or homework a source of conflict. If your child steadfastly refuses to read to you, don't immediately make a big issue of it. Do something else for a while instead, such as reading to your child or talking about the book. Leave the reading practice to one side for a few days and then try again. Major confrontations that damage your relationship with your child will probably do more harm in the long run than not practising their reading for a while.

◆ *Communicate with your child's teacher.*

The best way to resolve any nagging concerns you might have about your child's literacy is to talk to their teacher. There should be plenty of opportunities to do this, ranging from a quick chat to formal parents' evenings at the school. If your child does have some difficulty with reading or writing, their teacher will be able to discuss with you what can be done about it.

◆ *Give your child access to books.*

You can expose your child to books at home or by using the local library. Children who are introduced to the pleasures of books and reading at an early age tend to perform better in reading at primary school. Quality matters more than quantity, so don't worry if your house is not full of books. ▸

◆ *Little and often.*

It's generally better to practise with your child little and often. Several five-minute bouts of reading or spelling will usually be more productive than fewer, longer sessions.

◆ *Play games that involve co-ordination and rhythm.*

Games or activities that introduce children to patterns, sequencing and physical co-ordination can help them to develop some of the basic mental skills that underlie reading and writing. For children under five you could try teaching them songs and rhymes. For older children, you could encourage them to take part in activities such as dance, football or music. It might help, and it almost certainly won't do any harm.

◆ *Discuss your child's books with them.*

You can help to stimulate and reinforce your child's interest in reading by talking to them about it. Ask them what their favourite book is, why they like it, and how it makes them feel.

◆ *Set a good example.*

You can help to demonstrate the value and pleasure of reading and writing by doing it yourself – even if it's just reading the Sunday papers. If you are not a strong reader yourself, consider enrolling in an adult literacy course to brush up your skills. Even better, some excellent family literacy programmes are available through many local councils.

◆ *Encourage your child to read for pleasure.*

Reading should be a pleasure as well as a necessity. If your child comes to regard reading as just an irksome homework task then he or she may well be turned off it. Encourage your child to read as much and as often as they like, even if what they are reading is not terribly worthy or 'educational'. Let them choose mainly according to their own interests.

◆ *Try the Pause-Prompt-Praise approach.*

If your child gets stuck over a word while reading, try using the tried and tested approach:

* Pause to see if they can work it out themselves, then

* Prompt, then

* Praise when they get it right.

◆ *Get involved with your child's school.*

Research has found that one potential snag with parents helping their children with reading and writing at home is that they may use a different approach to teaching than that used at school, and thereby inadvertently confuse their child. It is therefore a good idea to find out how your child's school goes about teaching literacy skills. Many schools provide leaflets and other advice for parents on how to support their children's reading at home. The National Literacy Strategy also encourages parents to act as volunteers in the classroom. Helping out is a good way of seeing how reading and writing are being taught.

Further advice

The Parent Centre (Department for Education and Skills)

Tel: 0870 000 22 88

www.parentcentre.gov.uk

A comprehensive guide to the education system for parents, with links to other organisations and online discussion forums.

The National Curriculum Online

www.nc.uk.net

Details of all subjects covered in schools and the standards expected of children at different stages.

Reading Is Fundamental, National Literacy Trust

Tel: 020 7828 2435

E-mail: rif@literacytrust.org.uk

www.rif.org.uk

Promotes reading for children of all ages. Tips and advice for parents to help children realise their potential.

British Dyslexia Association

Helpline: 0118 966 8271

www.bda-dyslexia.org.uk

Information about dyslexia and contacts for local support.

Related worries

14. Will not be successful in adult life if he/she does not do well at school

27. Is bored or under-stimulated at school

36. Won't do his/her homework

39. Isn't as good at maths as he/she should be

40. Is only assessed on narrow academic achievements, not broader abilities

Is bored or under-stimulated at school

19% of parents worried

Chances: HIGH   Consequences: MEDIUM   Control: MEDIUM

Any normal child or teenager will occasionally complain that school is boring. And they are often right: school can be boring. What parents have to decide is whether there is a genuine and significant problem, and what that problem is. Children may claim that school is boring for a variety of reasons, including having a different idea of what 'boring' means. But some of those reasons, such as tiredness or social problems, may have little to do with their school.

One of the many reasons why some children become bored is that lessons are not sufficiently stimulating for their high level of ability. Schools are generally better nowadays at recognising gifted children and catering for their needs, but the system is not foolproof. Some children hide their talents because they don't want to stand out of the crowd. Alternatively, a 'bored' child may be concealing the fact that he or she finds school work too difficult. Boredom is not necessarily a sign of high ability.

Good communication is crucial. Talking to your child should help you to identify the real nature of the problem (if any) and talking to the school should help you to find a solution.

Many children go through phases when they complain of being bored at school. These phases usually pass. The truth is that school sometimes *is* boring, even for bright and well motivated students. Remember how it was when you were at school: not every minute of every day was totally riveting. Some teachers and some lessons are less exciting than others. And, like it or not, there is a mass of work that has to be got through.

Children (and adults) often have unrealistic expectations. Life *can* be boring at times. Every adult's job contains periods of extreme boredom. Sometimes a supposedly bored child is not really bored at all, but their parents think they must be bored because the parents themselves would be bored under the same circumstances.

However, if your child does genuinely seem to be bored and unhappy, day in and day out, there could be a real problem. A child who routinely feels bored in lessons may switch off and daydream, which the teacher might interpret as laziness. Or they may become disruptive and unruly. Either way, their learning will suffer and they will not get the most from their education. Boredom in small doses is an unavoidable hazard of being at school, but boredom in large doses can spell trouble.

A child's complaint that 'school is boring' cannot always be taken at face value. What a child means by 'bored' may not be the same as what an adult means. Various unrelated problems can be concealed under the catch-all label of boredom. For instance, a 'bored' child may in fact be experiencing social problems at school, but finds it easier to say they are bored than to admit feeling unpopular or being bullied. Or a child may have unrecognised problems with their hearing or vision, making it hard for them to follow lessons. Their difficulty may be passed off as boredom.

A child who just seems bored and lacklustre might in fact be depressed. Around 1 in 100 school-aged children are thought to suffer from depression, though their condition is often hard to recognise. Children with mild ADHD (Attention Deficit/Hyperactivity Disorder) can also appear to be suffering from boredom because of their short attention span and restlessness.

Tiredness is another problem that sometimes gets mislabelled as boredom. Many school-aged children and teenagers feel tired during the day because they are not getting enough sleep (see Worry 15, page 81). But their fatigue and inability to concentrate can feel to them like boredom, so that is how they describe it. If you are tired enough, almost any task can seem tedious.

One obvious way that parents can check whether their child's boredom is a general problem, or specific to the classroom, is to find out whether other children in the class are also complaining of boredom.

Understanding the system

Aspects of the education system can conspire to make children feel bored. Some parts of the National Curriculum for schools in England and Wales are (in our opinion) quite dull, even for the teachers, and the relentless regime of testing and assessment makes the dullness worse. Schools, teachers and pupils are all under pressure to perform well. Teaching inevitably focuses on raising performance in these tests, often at the expense of other aspects of education that are not so easy to measure.

Large class sizes can add to the problem. The quality of teaching can suffer in large, overcrowded classrooms if teachers use a narrower range of teaching methods that are less tailored to the needs of individual children. A teacher dealing single-handedly with a class of 30+ children cannot provide each individual with optimum stimulation all of the time. Discipline can be more difficult to maintain in large classes if the quality of teaching is not high, and disruptive behaviour by some pupils can make it harder for others to learn. Other things being equal, smaller classes tend to produce somewhat better results in terms of literacy, numeracy and academic achievement – although the biggest factor by far is still the quality of teaching. The children who benefit most from smaller classes are those in the early years of education and the less able children.

Despite improvements in recent years, class sizes and pupil-teacher ratios in the UK still compare unfavourably with those in many other wealthy nations, especially for primary schools. In 2003, the average class size in maintained primary schools in England was 26.3 pupils, while 16 per cent of primary school pupils were in classes of 31 or more. Classes are usually smaller in secondary schools, where the average size is about 22. The average class size in independent schools is roughly half that of maintained schools.

Class size is not everything, however. It has some influence, but the evidence clearly shows that the quality of individual teachers is far more important. Your child would almost certainly be better off in a large class taught by a good teacher than in a small class taught by a weak teacher.

Parents who are worried about their children being bored often believe it is because their children are bright and under-stimulated. But boredom is actually very widespread, especially among lower-ability children who make up the bulk of truants. In some cases, however, a child really is bored because the lessons are pitched too low to engage their interest.

By the time they start school, children already have a basic need to be mentally stretched and stimulated, and they soon become bored if this need is not satisfied. A gifted child who is not recognised as such is likely to become switched off and disaffected in school. They may also become disruptive, playing the fool or defying authority. For some, the whole experience of school becomes so irksome that they start inventing illnesses or playing truant in order to avoid it altogether. Identifying such children at an early stage is crucial; otherwise their intellectual, emotional and social development can suffer.

Maintained schools in the UK are generally better now than they once were at spotting gifted children and responding to their particular needs. All schools are expected to have specific policies for dealing with gifted and talented children. ('Gifted' pupils are defined by the government as those who have exceptional abilities in one or more subjects in the statutory school curriculum other than music, art and design or PE, while 'talented' pupils are those with exceptional abilities in art & design, music, PE or performing arts such as dance or drama.) Schools in England are inspected by Ofsted (Office for Standards in Education) on the basis of their provision for high-achieving children.

Over the past few years the government and local authorities have been running a number of special programmes for gifted and talented pupils. These are aimed at the most able 5–10 per cent of children in each year group in each school. For example, local education authorities run summer schools for gifted and talented children aged 10–14, while the National Academy for Gifted and Talented Youth has been set up at Warwick University.

How do you know if your child is gifted? This may not be obvious. One pitfall is that gifted children do not always score highly on conventional intelligence tests, particularly if their special abilities lie in other spheres. A child may have excellent powers of creativity and imagination, or highly sophisticated social skills, yet still get mediocre scores on intelligence tests.

Gifted children do not always perform brilliantly at school. Indeed, some may appear to be lazy and inattentive. Social pressures lead some gifted pupils to conceal their ability. They hide behind a mask of mediocrity because they do not want to be labelled as swots or nerds by their peers. In some schools it's not cool to be too clever, and blending into the crowd may be the best way to avoid being ridiculed or bullied.

No single characteristic definitively marks out a child as gifted. However, most exceptionally bright children display some or all of the following signs:

• starting to talk early and using a wide vocabulary

- learning faster than other children of the same age and asking lots of questions
- a very good memory
- strong curiosity and interest in the world
- good general knowledge
- keen powers of observation and reasoning
- a vivid and unusual imagination
- a strong (and perhaps slightly odd) sense of humour

- an enjoyment of problem-solving
- strong powers of concentration
- preferring the company of older children and adults

A gifted child's parents are usually the first people to notice that he or she is gifted. But parents sometimes remain oblivious, leaving the discovery to be made by a playgroup or nursery teacher, family friend, health visitor or doctor.

What can you do?

♦ *Communicate with your child.*

If your child complains of being bored, explore what they mean by this before jumping to conclusions. It may not be what you think. Try not to ask them leading questions that will simply reinforce their complaint. Instead, ask open-ended and specific questions about the best part of their day, their favourite and least favourite lessons, how their friends are getting on, what they think of their teacher, and so on. Check out whether their complaint of boredom might be masking some other problem such as feeling unpopular, being unable to see or hear properly, or feeling tired.

♦ *Communicate with the school.*

If your child seems to be genuinely bored at school, talk to their teacher. But do this in a non-confrontational way. Your aim should be to help your child by finding a practical solution to their problem, not just to punish the school. If you believe your child could achieve more highly than the level currently being aimed at, talk to school about the possibility of their being given more demanding work or moving to another class or set. The school should

have a written policy for dealing with high-ability children, including strategies for identifying them and responding to their needs. You might want to read this policy.

♦ *Communicate with other parents.*

Talk to other parents to see if other children in the class are also complaining of boredom. If they are, this might indicate problems with a particular teacher or subject.

♦ *Try to make learning more fun.*

If your child is truly uninspired by school, see if you can rekindle their interest at home by making learning a bit more fun. You can make a big difference by spending just 15-20 minutes a day having a stimulating conversation or reading aloud from an interesting book. It is crucial for children to have a positive experience of learning, and if this is not happening enough at school you might have to do more at home.

♦ *If all else fails, get an expert opinion.*

There is little point in rushing your child off to be assessed by a private educational psychologist before you have had ▶

thorough discussions with the school, who will want to do their best to resolve the problem. Schools and local education authorities are under no obligation to act upon the findings of private assessments, and they are unlikely to do so unless they agree with the recommendations. However, a private assessment might be worth considering if you have seriously tried but failed to reach some sort of agreement with the school about the best way to deal with your child. A competent psychological assessment should provide you with additional information about your child, which may help you to decide the best way forward.

Further advice

The Parent Centre (Department for Education and Skills)
Tel: 0870 000 2288
www.parentcentre.gov.uk
A comprehensive guide to the education system, with links to other organisations and online discussion forums.

The National Curriculum Online
www.nc.uk.net
Details of all subjects covered in English schools and the standards expected of children at different stages. Includes links to related sites for Wales, Scotland and Northern Ireland.

The National Association for Gifted Children (NAGC)
Helpline: 0870 770 3217
www.nagcbritain.org.uk
Aims to help gifted children, their parents, teachers, LEAs and others concerned with their development.

Related worries

13. Has difficulty concentrating/paying attention
26. Isn't reading or writing as well as he/she should
36. Won't do his/her homework
39. Isn't as good at maths as he/she should be
40. Is only assessed on narrow academic achievements, not broader abilities

WORRY **28**

Is being bullied

19% of parents worried

· ·

Chances: HIGH **Consequences: HIGH** **Control: MEDIUM**

Most children will experience some form of verbal or minor physical bullying at some point before they leave school. For a small minority, it can be severe and long term.

The impact of bullying can be profound, both for the victim and the bully. Children who are severely bullied are more likely to become depressed, are generally less confident as adults and tend to do worse in education and relationships. In later life they are more likely to attempt suicide than people who were never bullied.

Schools have a legal obligation to provide a safe and nurturing environment for children. They take the problem seriously, and many new measures have been introduced in recent years to control it.

Bullying is not easy to define. Sometimes it is blatantly obvious; sometimes it can be more subtle, but just as hurtful. Bullying can be divided into three main types:

- *Physical:* Pushing, kicking, hitting, pinching and other forms of violence or threats.
- *Verbal:* Name-calling, sarcasm, spreading rumours, persistent teasing.
- *Emotional:* Excluding ('sending to Coventry'), tormenting, ridiculing, humiliating.

The most frequent place for bullying to occur, not surprisingly, is in or around school, since this is where children mix with their peers. Bullying also occurs outside school, when it can be harder to stop because of the lack of direct channels for control.

One of the trickiest aspects of bullying is that children are often reluctant to tell their parents, teachers or anyone else. Research shows that less than a third of secondary school pupils are willing to tell a teacher when they are being bullied. Many feel ashamed, believing that somehow they should be able to deal with it on their own. Parents can ask their child directly, but sometimes it may require them to play detective and piece together the evidence.

Common signs of bullying include:

- coming home with cuts and bruises or torn clothes
- repeatedly asking for possessions to be replaced
- 'losing' dinner money or coming home hungry because their money has been stolen
- being unusually moody, bad-tempered or withdrawn
- reluctance to leave the house
- doing less well at schoolwork than before
- insomnia for the first time
- being frightened of walking to and from school, or changing their usual route
- not wanting to go on the school bus or asking you to drive them to school
- being consistently very unwilling to go to school ('school phobic').
- feeling ill in the mornings
- starting to truant
- asking for money or starting to steal (to pay the bully)

Most bullying is carried out by small groups rather one-on-one. Bullies like an audience. Although bullying is most common between the ages of about seven and 13, it seems to peak at the start of secondary school at around 11–12. Bullies are usually the same age or older than the victim and usually of the same sex. Generally speaking, the children most likely to be picked on are those who stand out for some reason, perhaps because they are too clever or too slow, too fat or too skinny, or from a minority ethnic group.

Minor bullying is very common. In a survey of 11- and 13-year-olds, children were asked whether they had been bullied at school within the past year. Over half the 11-year-olds and a third of the 13-year-olds said they had been. Verbal aggression was the most frequent type of bullying, but more than 1 in 10 children had suffered physical aggression for no reason and 1 in 20 (mostly girls) said they had experienced unwanted sexual touching.

Long-term studies have shown that most children experience some form of bullying at some time or another during their time at school. Verbal bullying is experienced by 9 out of 10 girls and 8 out of 10 boys, while 3 out of 4 boys and 2 out of 3 girls will have been physically bullied. Recent reports show a worrying trend among girls for their bullying to become markedly more physical. In the past few years violent physical bullying between girls has risen by almost half.

Electronic communication has emerged as a new mechanism for bullying, in the form of unpleasant text messages and e-mails. In the last few years one anti-bullying charity has taken legal action to close down a number of personally directed 'hate' websites.

The impact of bullying can extend far beyond

the actual event. Bullying, like any other intimidation, does not have to be continually inflicted on the victim to affect them – the fear of it can be just as damaging. When nine- to 16-year-olds were asked if they ever felt afraid of going to school because of bullying, the responses showed that girls were more afraid of bullying than boys, with a third of them fearing bullying at some time. Of all the boys questioned, those in the 11- to 12-year-old age range were the most fearful.

The consequences of bullying can be long term and affect victims throughout their adult life. A major retrospective study found that former victims had significantly lower self-esteem and less ability to make friends. On average, such individuals did less well in education, were less communicative and more fearful of new situations. Most of the respondents who were bullied had left school at or before the age of 16, many citing the bullying as the main reason for leaving. Nearly half said that bullying had affected their plans for further education. Many believed that the bullying would have continued if they had stayed at school. Nearly half of those who had been bullied had contemplated suicide, compared with 7 per cent of those who had not been bullied at school. The majority reported feeling angry and bitter about the bullying they had suffered as children. Most had received no help at the time, and telling someone was seen to have made matters worse or to have had no effect.

Bullying can also damage the bully in the long term, because bullies learn that they can get away with violence, aggression and threats, and that this sort of behaviour gets them what they want. A long-term study in Norway found that boys who were bullies were twice as likely as their peers to have criminal convictions and four times more likely to be multiple offenders later in life. Typical convictions were for aggression and violence and were often alcohol-related. Similarly, a survey conducted in the UK found that 9 out of 10 young offenders had engaged in bullying behaviour while at school. Parents and schools are right to take a firm line on bullying, for both the victims' and the bullies' sake.

Schools have a legal duty to provide a safe and nurturing environment for children and can be sued if they fail to do so. The great majority of schools take allegations of bullying very seriously. In the year 2000, the government set out new guidelines for schools, stating that there should be a written school policy on bullying and that schools should go through a stepwise process to create it, involving awareness-raising, consultation, implementation, monitoring and evaluation. Everyone involved with the school, including parents, should contribute.

Responding to bullying

A school might typically use a succession of progressively stronger responses to bullying. These might include:

- a warning
- calling the bully's parents into school
- detention
- fixed term exclusion
- permanent exclusion

Approximately 1 in 400 children end up being permanently excluded from school, and about a quarter of these cases are for persistent bullying. The overall number of exclusions fell by a quarter between 1996/7 and 2001/2.

Many schools have introduced broader anti-bullying programmes and training. Three common types of scheme are:

- *The no-blame approach.* The victim is interviewed and asked to draw a picture or write a poem about the effect their bullying has had on others. A meeting is then held between a teacher and a group of students, including the bullies, those who may have seen the incidents, and others who are not directly involved. The teacher explains to the group how the victim is feeling and the group then offers suggestions to find a solution. The idea behind this is that as the bullies are not being directly blamed for what they have done, they stop feeling threatened and can be part of finding a solution. Those who were bystanders are supposed to be able to see that by doing nothing, they were condoning the bullying. Research suggests that this method has a high success rate.

- *Circle time.* This approach is used in primary schools to help develop general social and emotional skills. The idea is that pupils sit in a circle and play games or do something enjoyable for a short time. They then discuss matters as a group, including bullying. This is an opportunity for everyone in the class to take part in a structured setting. Everyone is expected to listen to the person who is speaking without making remarks or laughing.
- *Peer group programmes.* Older pupils undergo training over a number of months on the effects of bullying and how to care for younger pupils who are affected by it. These volunteers are then identified by badges or ribbons. Other pupils therefore know they have someone of their own age who will listen and take their concerns seriously. Recognising that some children may feel left out, schools also set aside a quiet room where pupils can go to do their homework, play board games or just chat with others. Boxes are placed around school so that children who are upset and don't want to approach a volunteer directly can use the service by sending a note.

These sorts of schemes seem to be working well, especially in primary schools. Sixty per cent of primary pupils now believe their schools are good at dealing with bullies.

What can you do?

◆ **Talk to your child.**

If you are worried that your child is being bullied, ask him or her directly. Children who are being bullied are often frightened to talk about what is happening, so be prepared for your child to deny that there is anything wrong at first. Encourage your child by saying you are concerned and that you want to help and support them, whatever the problem. Take whatever your child says seriously and try to find out what exactly has been going on. Do not promise to keep the bullying secret, but do reassure your child that you will help them sort out the problem.

◆ **Talk to the school.**

If you think your child is being bullied, get in touch with the school. It is usually best to start with the child's form teacher. Ask them to investigate the situation and request a follow-up meeting to discuss what, if any, action they think should be taken. The school should have a written policy on dealing with bullying, together with experience of dealing with past cases. If after a few weeks there is no improvement, then you can request to discuss the situation with the head teacher and, ultimately, the school governors if necessary.

◆ **Try to build up your child's self-confidence.**

Victims of bullying can end up believing that somehow they deserve to be taunted. They can feel vulnerable and powerless, with their self-esteem considerably reduced. If you find yourself in this position as a parent, you might need to rebuild their self-confidence with plenty of praise and affection. Ways of doing this include regularly telling your child that you ▶

love them very much and that you are 100 per cent on their side, reassuring them that the bullying is not their fault, and encouraging activities at which they excel and which involve different groups of friends.

◆ *Practise responses with your child.*

Practise with your child saying 'no' firmly and walking away from a bully. Together you could think up some simple responses to the bully's most frequent taunts. These don't have to be brilliantly witty or funny, but victims report that it helps to have some sort of reply prepared in advance. Explain that reacting to bullies by crying or becoming upset will only encourage them. If bullies can't goad their victim into a response, they may get bored.

◆ *Try to minimise opportunities for bullying.*

Discourage your child from taking valuable possessions to school. Advise them not to be the last person in the changing room and not to linger alone in empty corridors. Encourage them to stick with a group, especially on their way to and from school. There is safety in numbers.

◆ *Talk to other parents.*

Try asking other parents if their children are experiencing similar problems. Your child might not be the only target and you could find that other parents are keen to develop a joint plan of action with you and the school.

◆ *Keep a record.*

If you discover that your child is being seriously bullied, keep a diary of incidents and make a note of any injuries, with photographs and details if a visit to the doctor or a hospital is required. A written record makes it easier to check facts later, and will be helpful if you need to take any formal action. Make a note of the people you speak to about the bullying and keep copies of any letters you write.

◆ *Go to your GP.*

If the bullying is very bad and your child is extremely distressed, your doctor may decide that spending some time away from school would help him or her. Once you have a sick note from the doctor advising a spell at home, you can legitimately keep your child away from school for the duration of the sick note.

◆ *Go to the police.*

If your child has been assaulted, or has had property stolen at school, then consider making a complaint to the police (as well as talking to the school, of course). Police forces have school liaison officers who are experienced at dealing with school-related issues. They can be very effective at warning bullies off in front of their parents. Physical attacks by older pupils could result in a reprimand, a final warning or prosecution, particularly if injury is involved.

◆ *If the bullying persists ...*

Most schools will try hard to deal effectively with bullying. Agreeing a way forward with the child's school should certainly be the first stage in any response. However, in a minority of cases where the bullying persists and the school seems powerless to stop it, parents might have to consider more extreme options. These could include:

* Switching the child to another school. This might seem like an easy answer at the time, but parents need to think carefully about ▸

the many implications. Will the child be any happier in the new school? Will the child miss his or her friends? How easily will the child fit into an established year group? Might their exam results be affected – for example, if the school uses a different exam board with different syllabuses? Do the bullies have friends at the new school? Will the travel arrangements be more difficult? And so on. Trying to sort out the problem in the child's current school will often turn out to be the less troublesome option.

* Withdrawing the child from the school system completely. Once a child reaches the age of five, parents have a legal duty to ensure that he or she receives a suitable full-time education, either by regular attendance at school or 'otherwise than in school'. This means that parents can educate their children at home if they choose to do so.

However, parents may risk prosecution if their child fails to go to school and is not receiving an appropriate full-time education at home. When children stay at home without good reason this is regarded as truancy or an unauthorised absence, and there has been a well-publicised case where a mother was jailed. Again, this is not an easy option.

* Taking legal action against the school. Schools are charged with a duty of care towards their pupils. If a child's education is being severely disrupted by bullying, parents have a right to claim that the school is failing in its duty of care. Several legal cases have successfully been mounted against schools who failed to deal with bullying and were seen in be in breach of this duty of care. Of course, suing the school will by itself do little to solve the child's problem.

Further advice

Kidscape
Tel: 020 7730 3300
www.kidscape.org.uk
Advice for parents and children about dealing with bullying.

Anti-Bullying Campaign
Tel: 020 7378 1446
www.bullying.co.uk
Advice and information for parents and children on all aspects of bullying, including the legal situation, school policies and tips for youngsters.

Bullying website (Department for Education & Skills)
www.dfes.gov.uk/bullying
Government website dedicated to providing information and support to those concerned about bullying in schools.

Parentline Plus
24-hour helpline: 0808 800 2222
www.parentlineplus.org.uk
Advice and support for parents.

Children's Legal Centre
Tel: 01206 873820
www.childrenslegalcentre.com
Publications and free advice on legal issues concerning children, including specific information on bullying.

Related worries

6. Might be the victim of crime
8. Has friends who are or could be a bad influence
10. Might be the victim of physical violence
37. Is not safe on public transport

WORRY *29*

Is disorganised/loses things

18% of parents worried

....

Chances: HIGH   **Consequences: LOW**   **Control: MEDIUM**

Being untidy, disorganised and losing things comes naturally to children. The organisational life skills that most adults possess, to varying degrees, must be learned and require some motivation.

Children lose things for reasons other than just poor organisational skills. When they start secondary school their lives suddenly become more complex and losses can mount. Many young people have money or mobile phones stolen from them in street crime. Others fail fully to appreciate the value of possessions because they have never needed to. Sometimes, disorganisation and losses may be concealing more serious personal problems such as low self-esteem or being the victim of bullying or crime.

Parents have a big to role to play, both by being good role models and by teaching children some basic tactics for self-management. It helps to start early. But remember that order and tidiness are not the most important things in life.

We all need a basic modicum of organisational ability in order to cope with our busy lives, keep track of all the many things we have to do, manage our time, decide on priorities and think straight. Being neat, efficient and highly organised comes easily to a few lucky adults, though most of us find it a bit of a struggle.

Children, of course, are not born into the world knowing how to organise their lives as an adult would (let alone an obsessively tidy adult who reads self-help books on time management). They need to learn how to do this, just like you had to. In the meantime, they will lose things, forget things and make a mess of the house. Wishing that children were tidier, better organised and less prone to losing their possessions is probably a universal experience of parenthood.

By the time they start school, most children in the UK have amassed a large number of clothes, toys and other items, but their ability to organise these and keep them tidy is not well developed. And the situation usually gets worse before it gets better. Children's lives become more complicated when they start primary school, and *much* more complicated when they start secondary school.

The transition to secondary school suddenly confronts the 11- or 12-year-old with the need to cope for the first time with lots of different teachers rather than just one, together with many different classrooms, subjects, books, timetables, homework schedules and games kits. Schools are aware of this and most have strategies to help. Even so, parents often find that the first year of secondary school is when children are at their worst on the organisational front. Items of clothing and games kit go missing and homework deadlines fail to be met. Fortunately, even the most shambolic pupils usually adjust after a while. But those who fail to develop basic organisational skills will find school more of a struggle.

Losing things and being generally disorganised are not always the result of simple carelessness; they can sometimes be symptomatic of deeper emotional problems such as low self-esteem. Children who care little about themselves are unlikely to care greatly about their possessions or physical surroundings either.

A less obvious reason why some children lose possessions and money is because they are robbed. The risk that a child might be the victim of robbery has risen sharply over the past decade and is now depressingly high (see Worry 6, page 32). Moreover, research suggests that when children are robbed, there is a good chance that they will not tell their parents.

Recent government crime figures reveal that more than a fifth of all personal robberies involve victims under the age of 16. The most common items to be reported stolen are cash and mobile phones. (That said, some mobile phones are falsely reported as stolen in order to obtain a free replacement.) The number of child victims and offenders has increased considerably since the early 1990s. For example, a major survey of British children in 2002 found that 1 child in 5 said they had been the victim of crime. Almost half of these young victims did not tell their parents, let alone the police, that they had been robbed.

Some children just cannot help being disorganised and losing things – notably the small minority who are diagnosed with Attention Deficit/Hyperactivity Disorder (ADHD). Indeed, two of the diagnostic criteria for ADHD are that the child often has difficulty organising tasks and activities and often loses things necessary for tasks or activities. However, there is much more to ADHD than losing things and being disorganised. And for a child with severe ADHD, losing things is probably the least of their problems.

When children lose items of clothing, toys, books or other possessions, parents may be inclined to assume that this is because they do not appreciate how much things cost. There is often an element of truth in this, although it is rarely the whole story. And, in so far as it is true that children do not appreciate the value of things, some parents have only themselves to blame. If parents readily give their child everything he or she asks for, including replacements for lost items, then that child is hardly likely to develop a sense of value or responsibility. The child will just assume that as soon as a possession is broken or misplaced, a new one will automatically appear.

The best antidote to this form of carelessness is to gently educate children from an early age to appreciate the cost of material possessions and the value of money. When they accompany you to the supermarket, for example, point out how much things cost and relate this to their pocket money. If they have to save up for a coveted item and pay for it with their own money, they will probably take more care of it than if you just give it to them.

Organisational ability is to some extent a life skill, and parents are often the best people to teach it, if only by setting a reasonably good example. By teaching your children how to be better organised, you will be doing them – and yourself – several favours:

• You will be equipping them with life skills they will need when they get older. Someone who learns as a child to put their dirty clothes in the clothes bin rather than scatter them on the floor is slightly less likely to end up in a complete shambles as an adult.

• You will be helping them to become independent and self-confident individuals. Children with good organisational skills are better placed to be happy and do well at school.

• By providing more structure and order in their life you will be making them feel more secure.

• You will benefit yourself from having a less chaotic house and fewer hassles.

Of course, teaching your children how to be better organised will be of no use if they still lack the motivation to do anything about it.

Finally, it is important to hang on to the simple fact that there is much more to life than being neat and tidy. If your only problem as a parent is that your child is disorganised and loses things then you are an extremely fortunate person.

What can you do?

◆ **Resist the temptation to do everything for your child.**

If you insist on organising and arranging their entire lives, and always tidying up behind them, they will not learn to do things for themselves. You can help them to become more capable and independent by making them increasingly responsible for organising themselves. By all means give them guidance on how to perform tasks, but leave them to do the actual work.

◆ **As far as you can, try to set a good example.**
Show them how you sort your own life out. People have many different ways of organising their lives, and yours may be just as effective as anyone else's. Even if you are one of nature's scatterbrains, you can at least encourage them to learn from your errors. Show them how you would like to run your life.

◆ **Teach your child some basic tactics.**

Encourage your child to sort out what they will need for school the next day before they go to bed, so that you can all avoid the early-morning scramble. Disorganisation is usually worse when people are in a hurry. Most schools issue students with homework diaries or planners. Encourage your child to use theirs effectively, and if they don't have one then buy them one. Suggest that they ▶

keep a to-do list of important tasks and store school papers in a folder. Consider fixing a specific time each week (e.g., Saturday mornings) when they will sort through their school bag, books and homework planner, discard rubbish and review what needs to be done.

◆ *Start when your child is young.*

Pre-school children are obviously not equipped to absorb adult time-management techniques. But they can start to take on board some basic principles by doing things like helping you sort the laundry and put it away in the right places. Young children generally prefer their world to be well-ordered and predictable, so they will respond better to your teaching. You will face a tougher challenge if you leave it until they have become stroppy adolescents with entrenched habits of slovenliness. However, think about whether you are expecting them to do things that are simply beyond their capabilities for their age.

◆ *Keep things in perspective.*

Avoid going over the top and trying to turn them into pernickety control freaks. Most people manage to live happy and effective lives without having to consult timetables, lists, planners, personal organisers and stopwatches, and without having to impose obsessive order and tidiness on everything around them. When you show them how to be better organised, approach this task in the same way you would teach them anything else. Try to be calm, gentle and patient. Use humour to lighten the atmosphere. The subject in question may be the untidiness of your house, but that is no reason to be bad-tempered and authoritarian. Take a balanced approach. Remember that being well organised is merely a means to an end, not an important life goal in its own right.

Further advice

UK Parenting
www.ukparents.co.uk
Advice and tips for parents.

Related worries

6. Might be the victim of crime
13. Has difficulty concentrating/paying attention
24. Won't listen to me/is disobedient
33. Won't help with household chores
34. Is always asking for things or money

WORRY **30**

Might be harmed by mobile phone masts or overhead power cables

18% of parents worried

···

Chances: LOW   **Consequences: LOW**   **Control: HIGH**

A lot of scientific research has been done to investigate the possible health effects of the radiofrequency radiation given off by mobile phone masts and the electromagnetic fields surrounding overhead power cables. Most of it supports the conclusion that there is no clear health risk associated with the very low levels of exposure that the majority of adults and children encounter in everyday life. For example, there is no firm evidence that you are more likely to develop cancer if you live near a high-voltage power line. Similarly, no firm evidence has yet emerged that using mobile phones is harmful.

However, there are some grounds for taking a moderately cautious approach towards children's usage of mobile phones. The radiofrequency radiation emitted by mobile phones has been shown to produce a minor heating effect on brain tissue. Some researchers believe that children might be more susceptible to any as-yet unrecognised health risks because their nervous systems are still developing and because children have thinner skulls than adults.

Current government guidelines err on the side of caution. They recommend that children under the age of 16 should only use mobile phones when it is absolutely necessary, and should use them for as short a time as possible.

There has been an explosion in mobile communications technology since the 1980s. There are now at least 47 million mobile phones in use in the UK and half of all children between the ages of seven and 16 own one.

The UK has more than 35,000 base stations that receive and send the radio signals used by mobile phones. The whole country is covered by mobile phone cells, each served by its own base station. These cells are usually no further than 10 kilometres (6 miles) apart, but they can be as close as a few hundred metres apart in areas where usage is high. Base station antennae usually stand 10–30 metres (32–98 feet) above ground level and can be erected on stand-alone masts or attached to existing structures or buildings. They require no special planning permissions and can be erected anywhere and without consultation with local residents. Some are hidden in petrol station signs, on the tops of building or even in church steeples.

Should we be worried by this? The radiofrequency radiation emitted from mobile phone base stations has been shown to have a minor heating effect on body tissue. The more intense the radio signal, and the closer you are to its source, the greater the heating effect. Research shows that the areas of the body most vulnerable to this heating effect are the eyes and the testes, and there is evidence that very high levels of radiofrequency radiation exposure can promote cataract formation and reduced sperm counts. Some scientists have found evidence of behaviour changes in humans as a result of thermal changes in the brain.

For these and other reasons, radio emissions have for many years been tightly regulated. In 1993 the government put in place national guidelines on the maximum levels of radiofrequency radiation that mobile phones, base stations and other sources could emit. These guidelines were based conservatively at levels where no long-term thermal damage could be shown and they were endorsed by a large international commission in 1998.

Since 2001 the Radiocommunications Agency has been monitoring the emissions from mobile phone base stations, with a particular focus on those sited on or near schools. Obviously, if there were to be a health issue, children's safety would be the top priority. The highest levels of radiation are usually some way away from the mast itself, rather than at its base, because the main beam is tilted slightly downwards. Therefore, even if a base station or mast is situated in a school, the highest level of radiation at ground level might still fall outside the school grounds. So far, no mobile phone masts have been found to be in breach of the safety guidelines and no scientific research has been published showing any clear health problems associated with their emissions.

There is no legislation to prevent mobile phone masts from being located in schools, and many are still being erected. A school can receive several thousand pounds a year in rental income from mobile phone companies for agreeing to place a mast or base station on school property, making it an attractive proposition. Currently, the only restriction on schools doing this comes from the Radiocommunications Agency, which stipulates that the beam of greatest intensity from the base station should not fall on any part of the school grounds or buildings without agreement from the school and parents.

Media reports that mobile phone masts and base stations are 'frying our brains' have little basis in fact. And if there were any cause for concern, it should probably be the mobile phones themselves rather than the base stations. Even here, though, the highest intensity phones create a temperature rise of no more than 0.1 degree C in human tissue, which has so far not been shown to have any adverse effects on health.

While most scientists agree that the health risk from mobile phones and their base stations is probably negligible, some feel there are still grounds for remaining cautious. Again, the risk, if there is one, appears to be greater from the phones themselves than from the base stations. Laboratory experiments have shown that when isolated human cells are subjected to radio waves similar in intensity to those emitted by mobile phones, tiny changes in their biological functioning can be detected. However, opinions are currently very mixed as to whether these changes have any adverse health implications.

Many large-scale and well-funded research studies have so far failed to find long-term health implications from mobile phone use or exposure to the radio waves emitted by mobile phone base stations. Long term studies in the UK and US have found no significant health differences between people who have used mobile phones frequently over extended periods and those who have never used them. Despite this, some scientists are still concerned by the cellular changes they have observed in laboratory experiments. They suggest that until we understand exactly how and why these changes are occurring, we cannot be absolutely sure that mobile phone technology is completely safe.

The government advisory committee of experts that recently investigated the safety of mobile phones took a similarly cautious approach. The committee's report concluded that there was little or no evidence for any health risks from mobile phone base stations, but that the case was inconclusive with regard to the signals emitted by the phones themselves. While they could find no evidence that mobile phones caused any damage to people's health, the committee decided to send a precautionary message to parents about children's usage, recommending a restriction of use by children until further research was conducted.

The story concerning overhead power cables in not dissimilar. For many years, some people living close to power lines have worried that they might be harming their health. In particular, concerns have been expressed that the electromagnetic fields generated by the cables might cause cancer.

In laboratory experiments, the sorts of electromagnetic fields produced by power lines can be shown to influence the functioning of isolated human cells. But, just as with research on mobile phones, the health implications of this are controversial. Some researchers have found that animals living below power lines have impaired immune systems, more stillbirths and higher blood pressure. Studies on humans, however, have failed to find any adverse health effects, including any increased cancer rates, even amongst people living directly below high-voltage cables. For instance, one study which looked at the health records of cable repairmen, who are exposed for extended periods every working day, failed to find any evidence of damage to their health. Similar conclusions have emerged from studies looking specifically at the health risks to children.

So, where does this leave us? Exposure to radiofrequency radiation, of the sort produced by mobile phones and base stations, can produce measurable changes in living cells. So, too, can the sorts of electromagnetic fields generated by overhead power cables. However, there is as yet no firm evidence that the levels encountered by people in daily life pose any significant health hazard.

Mobile phones have been in widespread use since the 1980s, and if they did harm people's health then some evidence of this would probably have become apparent by now. The same is true of power cables, which have been part of the scenery for many decades. If there are any as yet undetected health effects, these are likely to be subtle and long term.

What can you do?

◆ **Try to limit your child's mobile phone usage.**

The safest approach would be to encourage your child to follow the government's precautionary guidelines. These advise that children under 16 should only use mobile phones when it is absolutely necessary, and should use them for as short a time as possible. We recognise, however, that this may be easier said than done, given the central role that mobile phones now play in many young people's daily lives.

◆ **Encourage your child to text rather than talk.**

You can reduce your child's exposure to the radio emissions from mobile phones by encouraging them to text rather then talk, and to use a hands-free set when they do talk. Mobile phones emit far more radiation when the user is talking into them. Hands-free sets have been shown to reduce radiation exposure by up to 80 per cent, although it is important to choose the right one.

◆ **Check the emission levels of your child's phone.**

When you do buy your child a mobile phone, check the radiation levels for that model. Different phones emit different amounts of radiation and shops must provide information on the relative ratings for each. That said, all mobile phones sold in the UK fall within the international guidelines.

◆ **Find out the school's policy on mobile phones.**

Partly due to health concerns, and partly because of the disruption they can cause, many schools have banned mobile phone usage on school grounds.

Further advice

Department of Health
Tel: 020 7210 4850
www.doh.gov.uk/mobilephones/index.htm
Authoritative information about safety and government policy on masts and overhead cables.

Radiocommunications Agency
Tel: 020 7211 0211
www.radio.gov.uk
Provides audit results for the safety of mobile phone base stations.

National Radiological Protection Board
Tel: 01235 822742
www.nrpb.org.uk/
Information and advice about the hazards of radiation.

Report of the Stewart Group
www.iegmp.org.uk/
The report of the Independent Expert Group on Mobile Phones, which investigated the safety of mobile phones.

Related worries

9. Might get a serious illness

FACE THE FACTS 8
Mobile phones

- Half of all children aged 7–16 have a mobile phone, and more than three-quarters of 14- to 16-year-olds have one.

- According to market research, children aged 5–9 are the fastest expanding group of mobile phone users in the UK. In 2003, 1 in 9 children aged 5-9 had a mobile phone. This is predicted to rise to 1 in 5 by 2006.

- Girls are more likely than boys to own a mobile phone.

- Children in the 7–16 age range send an average of two or three text messages a day and make an average of two voice calls a day.

- The first mobile phones went on sale in 1985.

WORRY **31**

Might have an accident in the home

18% of parents worried

....

Chances: HIGH   **Consequences: HIGH**   **Control: HIGH**

Parents should be worried about accidents in the home. The number of domestic accidents involving children each year is huge, with consequences ranging from trivial to fatal. Parents can do a lot to reduce many of the risks.

Pre-school children are at greatest risk, both because they spend more time in the home and because they lack physical coordination and awareness. Boys have more accidents than girls. Falls are the most common form of non-fatal accident in the home, while house fires account for the most deaths. Alcohol or drug use by parents or carers greatly increases the risk.

Children should be allowed to play and explore, so the occasional cut or bruise is an inevitable part of growing up. However, by taking basic precautions, parents can usually insulate children from the most serious and avoidable risks such as fire, scalding, poisoning and drowning. It is highly desirable for parents and older children to learn basic first aid.

Accidents in the home injure huge numbers of children. Every year in the UK, about a million children are taken to hospital following a domestic accident. That's 20,000 children a week. And this is only the tip of the iceberg: many more accidents never appear in the official statistics because they are treated at home or by a family doctor.

Domestic accidents also kill a lot of children. In fact, accidental injury is the single biggest cause of death among children and young people, and a substantial proportion of these fatal accidents occur at home or in the garden. During an average week, two or three children die in a domestic accident. Fortunately, the number of serious accidents involving children has been falling in recent years.

Who is affected? The risks vary greatly according to the child's age. Toddlers and pre-school children spend most of their time in the home, so that is where most of their accidents occur. Children under the age of five account for a large proportion of domestic accidents. School-aged children and teenagers do have accidents, of course, but many of these occur outside the home.

Sex matters too. Boys are at much greater risk than girls, and overall, are about twice as likely to have an accident. This is partly because boys expose themselves to more risks by engaging in more vigorous physical play. Children from poorer homes are also at greater risk of being injured or killed in domestic accidents, compared to children from more affluent backgrounds.

What types of accident do children have in the home?

- *Falls* are the single most common cause of non-fatal injuries to children in the home, accounting for nearly half of all incidents. More than 400,000 children a year are taken to hospital after falling at home. Children under the age of five are most at risk.
- *House fires* cause the largest number of deaths. Each year, 40–50 children die in house fires and a further 2000 are injured. Many house fires are caused by children playing with lighters or matches.
- *Scalds and burns* result in 40,000 children a year being taken to casualty. More than half of them require further hospital care and many are left with permanent scarring. The most common type of accident is scalding by hot drinks, usually when a child overturns a mug or cup. Several hundred children a year are severely injured by falling or climbing into a bath of very hot water, and several hundred more are severely injured by pulling the hot contents of a kettle or saucepan onto themselves. Pre-school children account for the majority of these cases.
- *Suspected poisoning* sends more than 30,000 children a year to hospital, when their parents or carers think they might have swallowed harmful substances such as medicines, household cleaners or gardening chemicals. Again, the large majority are less than five years old. Fortunately, only a small proportion of these cases turn out to be serious. Alcohol presents a real hazard to older children: each year there around 1400 cases of alcohol poisoning involving children aged 10–14 years.
- *Choking* accidents in the home account for a further 4000 children being taken to hospital each year. More than half are under the age of five. Asphyxia (i.e., choking, suffocation or strangulation) is the third most common cause of accidental death among children, after road traffic accidents and house fires. Each year in England, about 15–20 children die from choking, most of whom are under five. Most of these accidents involve choking on food.
- *Drowning* kills around 50 children a year in England and Wales. Three-quarters of them are boys. On top of this death toll, hundreds of children require hospital treatment after nearly drowning, and some suffer long-term health problems. On average, eight children a year under the age of six drown in garden ponds, although most of these deaths occur in ponds

belonging to a relative, friend or neighbour rather than the victim's own garden. A few children drown in domestic swimming pools each year, and one or two drown in buckets, water butts or other containers.

Why do domestic accidents happen? In some ways, it is surprising that there aren't even more of them. For a start, our houses are full of potential hazards that adults take for granted, such as stairs, glass panels, boiling liquids, toxic and corrosive chemicals, mains electricity, fireplaces, windows, cookers, alcohol, matches, scissors, knives, and ponds.

Into this environment we place young children, who are naturally playful, inquisitive and keen to explore. They lack the understanding and judgment needed to appreciate hazards such as trailing kettle flexes or unguarded fires, and they may not have the physical co-ordination needed to avoid some of them. Moreover, their small physical size means they are sometimes unable to see hazards such as boiling kettles, or to be seen by other people.

Older children have better physical co-ordination and a better understanding of the dangers in their environment, but they are also more likely to take risks. Boys, in particular, are prone to acts of bravado, which partly explains why they have far more accidents than girls.

Domestic accidents often happen at times of stress, when people are distracted or hurrying, or when something has happened to disrupt their normal routine. Many an accident has occurred when a family is rushing to leave the house for some reason. Children are also more likely to have an accident when their surroundings are unfamiliar – for example, when visiting someone else's house or shortly after moving into a new home. Alcohol and, increasingly, illicit drugs also play an important role. Many serious household accidents are caused, either directly or indirectly, by a parent or carer being drunk or under the influence of drugs.

Ultimately, children must learn how to deal with the potential dangers in their everyday environment. A normal childhood involves playing and exploring, both indoors and outside. Along the way, children will inevitably collect the occasional cut or bruise. Parents cannot feasibly insulate their children from every conceivable hazard – no house can reasonably be made 100 per cent 'childproof'. And even if they *could* remove every possible source of risk, their children might actually end up at greater risk when they were older because they would lack the skills and experience needed to live safe, independent lives in the real world.

What parents *can* do is to insulate children from serious and avoidable hazards that could injure or kill. Doing this requires some thought, however, because they will need to try looking at the world, and their home, from the child's perspective – literally. Parents need to think about their child's current interests, behaviour patterns and physical abilities, while remembering that these can change rapidly over time. What sorts of objects might attract the child's attention, and which ones could they reach? What if they opened that cupboard or went through that door? What if they turned on that tap or tripped over that step?

Child safety equipment, such as stair gates and electrical socket covers, can provide some additional protection, especially for very young children. But it can never be a substitute for the careful thought and attention of adults.

What can you do?

Excellent safety advice is available from sources such as the Royal Society for the Prevention of Accidents (RoSPA) and the Child Accident Prevention Trust (CAPT); see Further advice, below. But here are some of the basic precautions that any sensible parent should take as a matter of course.

◆ *Try looking at your home from the child's point of view.*

Walk around the house, room by room, looking for child hazards. Think about their physical abilities and interests and get down to their eye level to see what they can see and reach. This should make you more aware of the risks they might face.

◆ *Don't get drunk or take mood-altering drugs when you are looking after children.*

If you have been drinking or taking drugs, you are much more likely to cause an accident in the home.

◆ *Learn basic first aid.*

Parents of school-aged children should be aware of basic first aid, in case of an accident. It could save someone's life. If you regularly leave your child to be looked after by someone, ask if the carer knows first aid. When your children are old enough, they should learn first aid too. (After all, you might be the one who has the accident.) Find out what training in first aid is provided by their school. As soon as your children are old enough, teach them how to dial 999 in an emergency.

◆ *Fit your house with smoke alarms and test them regularly.*

They could save your life as well as your children's. Work out escape routes from the house in the event of fire and make sure that everyone in the family is aware of it. Close all internal doors when you go to bed each night. This will help to prevent fire and smoke spreading quickly through the house.

◆ *Keep dangerous substances out of sight and out of reach.*

All medicines, household cleaners, gardening chemicals and other dangerous substances should be kept out of sight and out of reach of young children, preferably in a locked cupboard. (Children may try to climb up to reach 'forbidden' places such as high shelves.) Remember, even 'healthy' things like vitamins can be poisonous if swallowed in large quantities. It is not a good idea to put medicines in the fridge, since this is tantamount to inviting someone to eat or drink them. Do not overlook possible sources of danger outside the house, such as garages and garden sheds. Medicines, household cleaners and other hazardous substances should also be kept in their original containers, because these usually have child-resistant closures and are clearly marked. If you suspect that your child might have swallowed something poisonous, seek immediate medical advice from your GP, a hospital A&E or NHS Direct (tel: 0845 4647). Keep the bottle or packet and anything that remains of the pills or substance, and take these with you. Do not try to make your child vomit, as this might do more harm than good.

▶

◆ *In the kitchen ...*

Never leave a chip pan or deep-fat fryer unattended. Turn pan handles so that they do not stick out over the edge of the cooker. Make sure your electric kettle has a short, curly lead and keep this well out of reach of children. Avoid overhanging tablecloths as well.

◆ *In the bathroom ...*

When you run a bath, put cold water in first and then add hot water. Adjust the thermostat on your hot water system so that the hot taps (especially on the bath) do not deliver water at more than about 46 °C. Always supervise young children when they are in or near water. Never leave a child under the age of six alone in the bath.

◆ *Elsewhere in the house ...*

Never pick up a child when you are holding a hot drink, or drink one when a child is sitting on your lap. Fit safety glass in any glass-panelled doors or low-level windows that a child might collide with.

◆ *In the garden ...*

If you have young children, or if other people's young children visit your house, fit a strong cover over your garden pond. Many children have drowned in garden ponds belonging to neighbours, relatives or friends. Remember that a young child can drown in water that is only 5 centimetres (2 inches) deep.

Further advice

Child Accident Prevention Trust (CAPT)
Tel: 020 7608 3828
E-mail: safe@capt.org.uk
www.capt.org.uk
Factsheets, frequently asked questions and personalised advice on all aspects of safety in the home.

Royal Society for the Prevention of Accidents (RoSPA)
Tel: 0121 248 2000
E-mail: help@rospa.co.uk (to register personal questions)
www.rospa.com
A range of advice about safety in the home.

British Standards Institution (BSI)
Tel: 020 8996 9000
www.bsi.org.uk
Information on the standards governing domestic safety equipment such as safety gates, household glass, fireguards and smoke alarms.

St John Ambulance
Tel: 08700 104950
www.sja.org.uk
Provides training in first aid for parents and children.

Related worries
1. Might be knocked over by a vehicle
9. Might get a serious illness
19. Is reckless and not sufficiently aware of dangers

WORRY **32**

Does not get enough physical exercise

17% of parents worried

....

Chances: HIGH   **Consequences: HIGH**   **Control: MEDIUM**

Most children don't get enough exercise. A third of school-age boys and half of all girls get less than the recommended minimum of at least one hour of moderate physical activity a day.

Children walk less, engage in more sedentary pastimes, and do less sport at school now than in previous generations. A third of children are driven to school and TV has become their number one leisure activity. In addition, the amount of time and facilities allocated to sport in schools has fallen significantly over the last 25 years.

The implications for children's health can be serious. Lack of exercise contributes to many illnesses, and childhood obesity is reaching epidemic levels.

Parents can have a strong positive influence by presenting a good role model and actively encouraging children to be more active. Children who establish the habit of being physically active when young are more likely to remain active in adulthood.

Regular physical activity should be a central part of growing up. Throughout the early years of life, physical activity plays a key role in physical, social and mental development. All forms of activity are potentially valuable, whether in the form of informal play, games, physical education, sport, walking, cycling or exercise in a gym.

Yet a worrying number of children are living sedentary lifestyles. A major survey found that between 1994 and 2002 there was a consistent rise in the proportion of young people who do not regularly take part in any sport in school.

Health experts and government guidelines recommend that school-aged children should participate in at least one hour of moderate activity a day. This means any activity that raises heart rate and warms the body, and can include brisk walking, cycling, and most games and sports. According to research, however, about a third of seven- to 14-year-old boys and half of all seven- to 14-year-old girls are routinely getting less than this amount of exercise. This picture is seen in all social groups and in all parts of the country.

Perhaps even more remarkable is some research suggesting that the average teenager takes less exercise than the average pensioner. Young people in the 8-19 age range were found to spend on average just under an hour a day being physically active, compared to nearly two hours for the average pensioner.

The consequences of inactivity for children's health can be profound. A strong body of evidence shows that regular physical activity is one of the cornerstones of mental and physical health. Unless children establish regular patterns of activity in their early years it becomes increasingly hard to do so later in life. They might also have sown the seeds for serious health problems in the future.

Regular exercise, sport and other forms of physical activity have been shown to:

- reduce the risk of dying prematurely
- reduce the risk of developing heart disease and stroke
- reduce the risk of developing colon cancer by up to half
- reduce the risk of developing type II diabetes by half
- help prevent or reduce hypertension, which affects approximately 13 per cent of the adult population of England
- help prevent or reduce osteoporosis, reducing the risk of hip fracture in women by up to half
- promote psychological well-being, reduce stress, anxiety and feelings of depression and loneliness
- help control weight and lower the risk of becoming obese by half compared to people with sedentary lifestyles.

The British Heart Foundation has published research suggesting that more than a third of deaths from coronary heart disease can be attributed to physical inactivity – more than to smoking. Yet this message does not seem to be getting across – at least, in terms of changing people's behaviour. Publicity about the health risks of smoking has helped bring about a decline in smoking to less than a third of the population, but two-thirds of adults are still not active enough. If our children turn into even less active adults then the long-term prognosis for the nation's health looks grim.

For children, the most immediate health risk from inactivity is obesity. Childhood obesity levels have doubled in the UK in the last ten years, leading some experts to describe it as an epidemic. The UK is now seeing large numbers of children and young people developing diseases such as diabetes as a consequence of obesity. One in 5 children are now overweight by the time they are four years old, and at least 1 in 10 are classified as obese. It is estimated that by the year 2010 a quarter of the UK population will be obese.

Physical activity, particularly sport, has many other benefits for children beyond improving physical health. The evidence shows that children who take plenty of exercise tend to be more confident, more sociable, less prone to depression and have higher self-esteem. Sport gives them a common topic of communication and makes them feel part of a group. Research also shows that physically active children are less likely to turn to smoking or drugs, and, in the case of girls, less likely to become pregnant before they leave school. Schools with well-developed activity programmes suffer less truancy, and some recent research hints that regular exercise might even help to boost scores in maths and reading.

Beyond its benefits to the individual, sport can also help break down social and community barriers. Sports programmes and clubs have been used to help reduce juvenile crime, regenerate community areas and alleviate racial tensions.

For a whole host of reasons, then, it is worrying that so many children in the UK are not getting enough physical exercise. Why is this? Our lifestyles and those of our children have changed considerably over the past 50 years. Today, most children do little manual work around the home and many are driven places more often than they walk. TV and computer games have become their most popular leisure 'activities', and they spend an average of three hours a day sitting in front of a screen.

Research has revealed a clear link between the number of hours of TV watched and a reduction in activity levels, together with its associated health risks. It has been estimated that a child's risk of becoming obese increases by about 12 per cent for each hour of TV they routinely watch each day. The problem is exacerbated by the growth in advertising. British children are exposed to several food commercials every hour when watching TV, and many of these adverts are for fast food, soft drinks, sweets or sugar-laden breakfast cereals. It is not surprising, then, that researchers have found clear links between children's calorie intake and watching TV.

On the positive side, children do at least seem to be receiving the message that exercise is important. Nine out of 10 children agree that it's important to keep fit and the great majority say they enjoy sport. In 2002, 7 out of 10 young people considered themselves to be a 'sporty type of person' – the highest percentage recorded over the previous decade.

Responding to the risk

The problem of inactivity seems to be more one of opportunity and time than motivation. In previous generations, much of a child's exercise would have been taken during school time. This is, unfortunately, no longer the case. Many children have been receiving less rather than more exercise in school. Between 1994 and 2002, the proportion of young people who did not take part in any school sport on a regular basis (defined as at least ten times a year) rose from 15 per cent to 18 per cent. As well as a reduction in the time allocated to sport, many sports facilities have been cut. In 1994 every secondary school had access to playing fields. Five years later only three-quarters had regular access. In 2002, 4 out of 10 secondary school teachers said their school sports facilities were fairly or wholly inadequate.

However, the tide appears to be turning. For England, the government has recently recommended two hours a week of physical activity in school. This activity does not all have to take place in PE lessons: it includes activity outside core curriculum time. Even so, the challenge to meet the target is huge. Currently, only about half of all secondary school children and less than a third of primary school pupils achieve the two-hour guideline.

In addition, the government introduced legislation in 2000 that requires all planning applications involving playing fields or open spaces to be referred to Sport England, the sports governing body. Sport England has the power to block an application which they believe would seriously damage sports activity in the area. This legislation is about to be extended to sites as small as 0.2 hectare (about half the size of a football pitch).

What can you do?

◆ **Practise what you preach.**

Try to be a good role model by taking regular exercise yourself. Generally speaking, the more active the parents the more active the child is likely to be. Children with active parents often adopt similar habits.

◆ **Help your child to take part in sport.**

This is easier said than done. Sporting children need kit, lifts to and from clubs, and even altered meal and bed times. However, there is good evidence that the more practical support and encouragement that parents, siblings and friends provide, the more likely a child is to participate in sport.

◆ **Believe that your child can be good at sport.**

Parents who expect that their children can be successful in sports or physical activity, and who value participation in sport, are more likely to be successful in encouraging them to take part. Children are quick to pick up on parental doubts about their basic ability.

◆ **Encourage your child to get outdoors.**

Obviously, children are more likely to be active when outdoors than when inside.

◆ **Try to limit TV-watching.**

Watching a lot of TV cuts into valuable time when your child could be being active. It also encourages bad eating habits and weight gain.

◆ **Encourage your child to walk or cycle to school, if feasible.**

If it is practical to do so, leave the car at home and get your child to walk or cycle instead. The risks to children of being harmed while walking to and from school are generally less than the health risks associated with chronic inactivity. Walking also makes them more road-aware and therefore better equipped to be safe pedestrians.

◆ **Consider becoming a sports volunteer.**

Local clubs are always looking for coaches, managers and helpers. Nearly 1.5 million people act as sport volunteers in the UK each year. You would be able to enjoy an activity together with your child, while also signalling to them that exercise is something you value and are willing to invest your time in.

Further advice

PE and School Sport (Department for Education and Skills)
Tel: 0870 000 2288 (DfES main switchboard)
www.dfes.gov.uk/pess/
Information about the government's physical education programmes.

British Heart Foundation
Heart Information Line: 08450 70 80 70
www.bhf.org.uk
Information and materials to encourage children to have a healthy and active lifestyle.

Sport England
Tel: 020 7273 1500
E-mail info@sportengland.org
www.sportengland.org
Organisation responsible for delivering government objectives in sport.
(Sports Council for Northern Ireland:
www.sportni.org/
Sport Scotland: www.sportscotland.org.uk/
Sports Council for Wales: www.sports-council-wales.co.uk)

Youth Sport Trust
Tel: 01509 226600
www.youthsporttrust.org
Develops physical education and sports programmes for young people aged 18 months to 18 years in schools and their communities.

Related worries

3. Eats too much sugar and sweet foods
7. Eats too much junk food or convenience food
4. Spends too much time watching TV or playing computer games
9. Might get a serious illness

Won't help with household chores

17% of parents worried

....

Chances: HIGH   **Consequences: LOW**   **Control: MEDIUM**

Household chores are one of the most frequent causes of disputes within families, with parents often on the losing side. Contributing to housework is good for children. Among other things, it helps them to develop practical skills and a sense of responsibility. And busy parents need all the help they can get in this era of long working hours and smaller families.

If you want your children to help around the house, you should get them into the habit from an early age. More than a third of parents pay their children to do housework.

They haven't tidied their bedroom in weeks. Rarely, if ever, do they put their dirty clothes in the dirty clothes basket, and they are always leaving damp towels lying around. There is no chance of them offering to do the dishes or sort the laundry ... This litany may sound familiar to the many parents who have little success in getting their children to help with household chores, despite nagging, bribery and threats. According to one survey, 4 out of 10 children do less housework than their parents have instructed them to do. That sounds to us like an under-estimate.

Solid information about how much housework children in the UK actually do is hard to find. However, according to published data, American children appear to be paragons of virtue from an early age. Researchers in the US have reported that by the age of four, a third of American children are being given tasks to do in the house, and around 90 per cent of them are regularly performing chores by the time they are ten. One study found that children under the age of 13 were spending a remarkable 5½ hours a week on housework, although this impressive figure included time spent accompanying parents while shopping. Whether a similar picture applies to the UK is unclear.

The amount of housework done by children is known to vary according to their age, their sex and the family structure. Parents of older teenagers will be unsurprised to read that 16-year-olds do far less housework on average than younger children: the statistics suggest that children contribute most between the ages of about 11 and 15. Children whose mothers work part-time do the least housework: less even than children whose mothers don't work. Unsurprisingly, children in single-parent households do the most. Family size also makes a difference, with children in large families tending to do more than those in small families.

The research also shows that girls generally do more housework than boys, possibly because they are expected to do more. Boys and girls also tend to be given different tasks that fit with their gender stereotypes, such as mowing the lawn for boys and cooking for girls.

Getting your children into the habit of doing household chores is good for several reasons:

- It helps children to develop independence, self-confidence and a sense of responsibility.
- It teaches children to co-operate and help other people, rather than expecting everything to be done for them.
- It teaches children practical life skills that they will need later in life, such as cleaning, shopping, cooking and managing their own time.
- It creates extra opportunities for you to spend time together, which can help communication.
- You probably need all the help you can get, especially if you are a busy working parent.

American research has even uncovered some statistical associations between children's participation in housework and their later success as young adults, measured in terms of outcomes such as completing their education, getting a good job and not taking drugs. But findings such as these should not be taken too literally, because many different factors affect how much housework an individual child will do, let alone how successful they will become when they grow up.

Despite all the obvious attractions of having extra help around the house, there are also worthier reasons why parents may be reluctant to heap domestic work on their offspring. Some parents feel it would interfere with their children's homework or extracurricular activities, or eat into their free time when they should be playing or relaxing.

Other parents conclude that it's simply easier to do the work themselves, because experience has taught them that persuading their child to do the work, supervising it, and then clearing up the mess afterwards, is just not worth the effort. Although we have some sympathy with that viewpoint, because getting children to help around the house can be tricky, it strikes us as defeatist. Starting them when they are young and then being patient will usually pay dividends in the long run.

Sharing the burden

So how much housework is there to be done, and who does it? Women still do the lion's share, despite the increasing numbers who work full-time. Government figures show that women in the UK spend an average of nearly three hours a day on household chores other than shopping and child-care, whereas men contribute only 1 hour 40 minutes. (On the other hand, men spend nearly two hours a day more than women working or studying.) The least popular household chore is reported to be ironing clothes.

Various trends in society are acting to reduce the burden of housework, while other trends are pushing in the opposite direction. In recent decades British families have generally become wealthier, acquired more labour-saving devices and taken to eating more of their meals outside the home. But people are also getting busier, and the typical household now contains fewer people to share the burden.

The average British home is far better equipped with labour-saving devices than was the case for previous generations. More than 9 out of 10 British households now have a washing machine, more than half have a tumble drier, and more than a quarter have a dishwasher. We are consuming an ever-growing proportion of our meals outside the home or in the form of pre-prepared convenience foods. And more families are wealthy enough to pay for various types of household help such as cleaners, nannies, au pairs, laundry services and meal deliveries. In 2002, for example, 2.6 million British households used the services of a home cleaner.

On the other hand, parents' lives are getting busier as more of them work, and households are getting smaller. The size of the average British household has fallen from almost three people in the early 1970s to just over two people now, and a quarter of all families are headed by a lone parent. Smaller families mean that the same household chores have to be divided among a smaller number of people. (Cleaning, shopping and cooking for five people does not take five times longer than cleaning, shopping and cooking for one person.)

Around two-thirds of all mothers now have some form of paid employment, and a fifth of women with school-aged children work full-time. British fathers work the longest hours in Europe – the average is 48 hours a week – and more than a third of fathers work more than 50 hours. Moreover, many parents work non-standard hours or shifts. On top of this, a growing slice of each working parent's day is eaten up by travelling to and from work. The great British commute has grown longer and nastier in terms of the distance travelled, time taken and frustration incurred. The average journey is now more than eight miles and lasts 25 minutes, but these figures conceal a wide range of variation: people working in central London take an average of an hour to get to work each day, which adds up to ten hours' commuting a week. Some commuters spend far longer.

Our children are busier too. They are under increasing pressure at school from the intensive regime of testing, assessment and public exams. As society becomes more affluent, children are presented with more opportunities for leisure and entertainment, thanks to computers, video games, multi-channel TV, CDs and DVDs. Add to this their complex social lives, hobbies, extra-curricular activities and part-time jobs, and you will see why school-aged children can feel busy, just like their parents. All things considered, it's hardly surprising that housework is so often a source of conflict between busy parents and their busy children.

Should children be paid for helping with housework? Opinions differ. Purists argue that payment is wrong in principle, because everyone in the family should contribute something towards it and children should not be brought up as though they were living in a luxury hotel. However, many parents take a more pragmatic approach: they expect their children to do some basic tasks for free, but are willing to pay for other jobs such as washing the car. According to one British survey, more than a third of parents pay their children to help clean the house, and 1 in 5 parents believe their children would not do any housework unless they were paid.

What can you do?

◆ *Start your child young.*

Experience suggests that children are more likely to be willing helpers around the house if they get into the habit young. If they reach adolescence having always had everything done for them, you could face an uphill struggle persuading them to mend their ways.

◆ *Involve your child in the decision-making.*

Give your child some degree of choice about which chores to do and when. If you are really lucky, they might quite like doing one of your less favourite tasks. Once the tasks have been chosen and agreed, it's best to make these a part of the weekly routine, rather than continually re-opening the debate as to who does what. Invite your children to help you draw up a rota of chores for the whole family, including you. They might be impressed when they realise just how much their parents have to do. Try to include at least one task of communal value, such as watering plants, feeding pets or sorting laundry. They should not expect to do only chores that are exclusively of benefit to them.

◆ *Be reasonable.*

Be clear and consistent about what you expect your child to do. Make sure you are not giving them too much, or expecting them to do things that are beyond their abilities. Just because they have seen you perform a task many times does not mean they will know how to do it without further instruction. Don't demand perfection. If you criticise your child for not performing a task to your own exacting standards, you will only demotivate them. Be satisfied with good-enough.

◆ *Say thank you.*

When your child has completed a chore, acknowledge the fact and thank them. If they have done a job well, then say so. None of us likes to be taken for granted.

◆ *Think about your child's safety.*

A household chore that might seem mundane to you, such as cooking a meal or mowing the lawn, could be dangerous for a child. Large numbers of children are injured or killed each year in household accidents (see Worry 31, page 166).

◆ *If your child still won't lift a finger ...*

Do not issue empty threats. Once they have successfully called your bluff, your authority will have been further undermined. Gently remind them that until relatively recently in history children were regarded as economic resources, and that sorting the laundry for half an hour is a lot better than working a 12-hour shift down a coal mine.

Further advice

Parentline Plus
Free helpline: 0808 800 2222
www.parentlineplus.org.uk
Advice on all aspects of parenting.

Practical Parenting
www.practicalparent.org.uk
Tips and support on child behaviour and family relationships, with specific articles on household chores.

Related worries

24. Won't listen to me/is disobedient
29. Is disorganised/loses things
31. Might have an accident in the home
34. Is always asking for things or money
36. Won't do his/her homework

WORRY 34

Is always asking for things or money

17% of parents worried

Chances: MEDIUM   **Consequences: MEDIUM**   **Control: MEDIUM**

Many parents believe that children (and adults) have become more materialistic in recent decades. Children recognise brand names from as young as one year of age. They have considerable spending power, both directly and indirectly (through 'pester power').

Marketing and advertising reinforce this consumerism, along with parents' own attitudes to possessions and wealth. Other things being equal, materialistic parents tend to produce materialistic children.

Being overly focused on acquiring possessions has little to recommend it. While there is the initial pleasure when an item is bought or received, this tends to be short lived. In the longer term, children who are highly materialistic tend to do less well academically. They are also somewhat more likely when adult to be less happy and to turn to crime, alcohol or drugs. This is probably because highly materialistic children learn to define themselves in relation to, and derive their pleasure from, possessions and status symbols. In comparison, less materialistic people tend to have a stronger sense of their own worth and feel less need for external validation.

Most people in the UK have never had more disposable income, or been so readily able to borrow money to satisfy their desires. Rather than developing into a post-materialist culture, as some pundits predicted back in the 1960s, we are instead becoming an increasingly acquisitive one. And this consumerism is certainly not limited to adults. Young children are also acquiring more: they have indirect purchasing power through influencing their parents, as well as being able to buy things themselves using pocket money, allowances and earnings.

One survey found that in 2002 children in the 7–16 age range received an average of almost £6 a week in pocket money, while another estimated that pocket money gave five- to 16-year-olds a combined spending power of £60 million a year. In addition to their direct spending power, it is estimated that children indirectly control 15 times that amount by influencing parents, friends and family into buying things for them – so-called pester power.

Growing numbers of children are taking on paid work to top up their incomes. Nearly 1 in 4 11- to16-year-olds now have some form of part-time job, such as doing a paper round, earning them an average of just over £27 a week. There is even a possibility that credit and debit cards will be made available to children to buy goods and services over the Internet.

Vast commercial enterprises have developed to cater for children and their money. Over the past two decades there has been at least a five-fold increase in the amount of advertising and the number of brands deliberately targeted at the children's market. Children have considerable spending power, and they are potential customers for life. Children in the 9–12 age group are especially susceptible. Midway between childhood and adolescence, they have been labelled 'tweenies'. The accumulation of possessions has become a preoccupation for many of them.

Research generally supports the suspicion that people in Western nations have become even more materialistic in recent decades. Long-term studies of materialism among American college and high school students have found significant changes over the last 30 years. In the late 1960s, two-thirds of college students said that developing a meaningful philosophy of life was very important to them, while less than one third said the same thing about making a lot of money. By the late 1990s, those figures had reversed, with the majority giving priority to money. British research has found that schoolchildren typically judge people who appear affluent to be also more intelligent, hardworking and successful.

Historical evidence shows that children from previous generations were more likely to save some of the money they acquired. But the saving habit has declined, with most children now tending to spend everything they have. Only a quarter of seven- to 10-year-olds now save a large proportion of their money, with girls saving less than boys. In the 11–16 age group, only 1 in 10 save most of their money; nearly half claim to be no good at managing their money and say they spend without thinking. The most common purchases are everyday items such as sweets and magazines, but there is increasing spending on costly items such as mobile phones and games consoles.

Children's desire for possessions is natural. Below the age of about six, children are still primarily self-focused and have not yet acquired the social skills or maturity to be able fully to understand the needs of other people. Their primary objective at this age is to fulfil their own needs and wants. Combine that with a growing awareness of what others have, and the developing desire to fit in with the group, and you have an almost perfect recipe for materialism.

So, the basic seeds of a materialistic desire for possessions are already there in children, whether their parents like it or not. Advertising can reinforce this desire hugely. The UK now has more advertising aimed directly at children than any other country in Europe, and is third in the world behind only the USA and Australia. American children see an average of 50 TV commercials a day and are exposed to over five hours of media in the form of TV, music, magazines, video games and the Internet.

In the UK there are no specific restrictions on the amount or type of TV advertising shown to children, beyond those that apply generally to all advertising, such as questions of taste, decency and accuracy. Many other countries are stricter. Sweden and Norway do not permit any TV advertising to be directed specifically towards children under the age of 12, and no adverts at all are allowed during children's programmes. Australia does not allow adverts during programmes for pre-school children.

Research suggests that children under the age of five tend to see adverts as sources of information and entertainment. They recall the music, colours and characters, but often fail to register the advertiser's intention to make them buy something. However, between the ages of about five and nine, their awareness develops strongly. By the time they are about 11, most children have become experts in the subtle ways of marketeers and advertisers.

The consequences of materialism

Advertising certainly works. Generally speaking, the more heavily a product is advertised to children, the more they will go and buy it. Even when children don't buy an advertised product, they still develop an awareness and recognition of the product brand. And research shows that this brand awareness can strongly influence their desire to buy, both then and later in life. By the age of three, before they can even read, 1 out of 5 American children are already making specific requests for brand-name products. One study found that among young children ranging in age from 3½ to 6½ years, those who watched more commercial TV also requested a greater number of items from Father Christmas and requested more branded items. While few pre-schoolers can identify the flag of their country, most can identify the Coca Cola logo and the McDonald's 'yellow M'.

Despite this media bombardment, parents can do a lot to influence children – either reinforcing or counteracting this materialism. They are, after all, their children's primary role models. The more parents express their own desire for possessions and brands, the more their children will probably do the same. It is unfair if parents complain about their children's insistence on brand-name trainers when they wouldn't dream of wearing own-label themselves.

Parents are right to be concerned about children becoming too fixated on possessions and brands. For a start, people who rely too much upon material possessions to gain pleasure and acceptance are less likely to be happy. Rather than feeling good because of who they are or what they're doing, they learn to get immediate pleasure from the brands and objects they buy. The research evidence shows that short-term pleasure does not necessarily lead to long-term happiness.

Researchers have found that highly materialistic people are more likely to suffer from depression and anger and tend to be less satisfied with their life than less materialistic people. Highly materialistic people typically judge success or failure on the basis of personal possessions and social comparisons. When they are unable to support their self-esteem by buying the latest high-status possessions, they can quickly start to feel dissatisfied and unhappy.

A second reason for concern is that we might be raising a generation who believe they should be able to have everything now. Instant gratification is the order of the day. However, research suggests that individuals are more likely to be happy as adults if they have developed the self-awareness and capacity to wait for things, work for what they want, and make choices.

Psychologists refer to this desirable capacity as delayed gratification. In one classic experiment, scientists offered children a choice between one marshmallow now, or two marshmallows later if they were willing to sit quietly and wait until the researcher returned. The same individuals were then assessed in a follow-up study ten years later. This revealed significant differences between those who had waited when they were children and those who had sought instant gratification. On average, the children who had grasped the concept of waiting to earn something better had achieved more in school, were more verbally and socially advanced, better able to handle stress and frustration, and had better concentration. As college students they were less likely to smoke, drink heavily or take drugs. In real life, people usually do better by taking a longer-term view rather than always going for the instant pleasure.

On a more practical level, greater materialism is thought by some experts to be one of the driving forces behind the rise in juvenile crime. Frustrated by their inability to buy the branded items they desire, some youths may be turning to street crime to acquire them. A recent government report cited the desire for branded items as one of the main factors behind rising crime rates. The individuals who are most likely to go down this route are those living in households where both parents are unemployed, or those living in low-income households located near affluent areas.

Teaching children the life skills needed to manage their desires, manage their spending and make choices is obviously very important. And most parents do take it seriously. One study found that six out of ten parents said they were teaching their children either a fair amount or a great deal about managing money, which was more than respondents said their own parents had taught them.

What can you do?

◆ **Don't give in too easily to your child's requests.**

Children who get everything they ask for are not learning how to wait, how to work for things they desire, or how to handle disappointment. Do yourself and your child a favour by saying no to unending requests, even if that provokes tantrums. Enlist the aid of friends and grandparents who might otherwise delight in spoiling your child.

◆ **Explain why you are saying no.**

Children can get resentful if they are just told they cannot have something without being told why. Giving the reasons for saying no helps to teach them about the realities of life. They might not like the fact that you cannot afford an item at the moment, but they should at least be able to understand it.

◆ **Spend more time rather than more money on your child.**

It's not easy, in the hectic lives that most parents lead, to give young children enough time and attention, but spending more time with them is nonetheless one of the best ways to ward off the 'gimmes'. The temptation is to give things to children as a substitute for giving them time.

◆ **Help your child resist peer pressure.**

It can be hard thinking that your child might feel left out because of something you haven't bought for them, which is why parents often cave in when peer pressure is mentioned. You can counteract this by pointing out that everyone has to make choices.

◆ **Give your child pocket money or an allowance.**

Receiving pocket money is good for children. It gives them a sense of independence and a measure of choice in making decisions about how money is spent. Receiving pocket money also helps children to understand the value of money, and forces them to think about whether they want to spend it all straight away or save for something special. Deciding how much money to give can become more complicated as children get older and friends receive differing amounts. If possible, talk to other parents to find out the going rate before deciding what you think is reasonable. Many parents increase the amount once a year, on each birthday. Sticking to a single 'annual award' can help to stop continual negotiations and pleas for more.

◆ **Make your child contribute.**

Aside from birthdays and Christmas, aim to make your child contribute from their pocket money or savings if they want something special. If they have to fork out a month's pocket money for something, they will have a greater understanding of its value. If they do not have enough money, consider asking them to do some paid jobs around the house to earn it.

◆ **Be consistent.**

Children have a strong sense of fairness, so try not to be seen to give in and buy extras for one child who has already spent all their money, if their sibling has had to save to buy theirs.

◆ **Try to be a good role model.**

Your example is very influential. Try not to talk too much about wanting lots of new things yourself, and try to avoid making envious comparisons between, say, your house or car and other people's. If you want to discourage your children from developing an insatiable appetite for material possessions, let them see you behaving with restraint. Take them along to the shoe repair shop and explain why it's worth re-heeling your favourite shoes instead of buying new ones. Enjoy window-shopping together without having to buy something.

◆ **Turn off the TV occasionally.**

From cereal boxes and Saturday morning cartoons to clothing emblazoned with store names and Disney characters, advertising is everywhere in our culture. TV is the most pervasive medium and it wields the greatest influence on young children.

◆ **Teach your child about value.**

Talk to your child about how much things cost when you're out shopping. Explain the differences between needs and wants. They might want that new computer game, but you really *need* the family's food for the week.

Further advice

BBC family finance information
www.bbc.co.uk/parenting
Information on all aspects of family finances, including pocket money and teaching children to value money.

Financial Services Authority (FSA): Learning and Education department
Tel: 020 7066 1000
www.fsa.gov.uk
Information for parents to help their children with finances.

Advertising Standards Agency
Tel: 020 7580 5555
www.asa.org.uk
Industry regulator which investigates the effects of advertising on children.

Related worries

4. Spends too much time watching TV or playing computer games
29. Is disorganised/loses things
33. Won't help with household chores

WORRY **35**

Doesn't get enough vitamins from his/her normal diet

16% of parents worried

Chances: LOW   **Consequences: MEDIUM**   **Control: HIGH**

The vast majority of school-aged children (and adults) should be able to get sufficient vitamins and minerals from their normal diet without having to take supplements. The key is to have a balanced and varied diet that includes a range of foods and at least five portions a day of fruit and vegetables.

However, not all young people do eat a balanced and varied diet. Some individuals, notably some adolescent and teenage girls, could benefit from having more iron, calcium or zinc in their diet.

Parents who are concerned about the poor quality of their child's normal diet should aim to improve it before falling back on vitamin pills as a substitute.

Taking excessive amounts of vitamin and mineral supplements can be harmful.

What are vitamins and how much do people need? Vitamins are complex organic chemicals that our bodies must have to function properly. They include, for example, vitamin A (retinol), vitamin B1 (thiamin), niacin, vitamin C (ascorbic acid), vitamin K and folic acid. Most vitamins cannot be made by the body and must therefore be provided by what we eat and drink.[4] Minerals are inorganic substances that our bodies also require for various reasons; they include calcium, iron, magnesium, potassium, sodium, phosphorus, zinc and iodine.

We need vitamins and minerals only in tiny quantities, measured in milligrams (thousandths of a gram) or micrograms (millionths of a gram) a day. Someone who consistently gets insufficient amounts of a particular vitamin or mineral for long enough will eventually develop a deficiency disease; for example, a severe lack of vitamin C causes scurvy and a severe lack of vitamin D causes rickets. Deficiency diseases such as these are now rare in the UK, although they were once more common.

The Department of Health publishes what are known as Reference Nutrient Intakes (RNIs) for all vitamins and minerals, based on the best available scientific evidence. RNIs are the levels of intake that will satisfy the requirements of almost everyone in the population. To give just two examples, the RNIs for children aged 7–10 years include 500 milligrams a day of vitamin A and 0.7 milligrams a day of thiamin.

Our bodies need different amounts of each vitamin and mineral. These amounts also vary between individuals, depending on the person's age, sex, health and level of activity. For instance, the RNI of vitamin C is 30 milligrams a day for children aged 7–10 years, but rises to 40 milligrams a day for adults. (To give you some idea of what that means, an average-sized orange contains somewhere between 50 and 70 milligrams of vitamin C.) Other factors can also alter a person's requirements for certain vitamins or minerals. For example, smokers and people who are under stress need more vitamin C, while individuals recovering from illness may have increased requirements for several vitamins and minerals.

People in the UK are buying ever-increasing amounts of vitamin and mineral supplements. The consumers are mostly adults, but around one fifth of young people aged 4–18 now take vitamin and mineral supplements too. The total amount spent on supplements in 2002 was almost £400 million, or about £7 for every man, woman and child in the nation. Moreover, prices have dropped sharply in recent years, so the same sum of money now buys much larger amounts of vitamins and minerals.

Ironically, research with British adults has found that the people who take vitamin and mineral supplements also tend to have diets that are richer in vitamins and minerals than people who don't take supplements – presumably because these people are generally more health-conscious and more concerned with nutrition. So those taking the tablets may actually have less need for them.

Certain vitamins are widely believed to have beneficial effects if taken in larger-than-normal quantities. For example, some people take very large amounts of vitamin C in the belief that it will prevent or cure the common cold, but the scientific case for this remains as yet uncertain. Other evidence has suggested that antioxidants such as vitamin E and beta-carotenes may contribute to the body's defences against heart disease and some forms of cancer, leading growing numbers of people to consume large amounts as dietary supplements. However, research has not yet confirmed that high doses of these substances do actually confer significant protection against illness. Either way, the best means of getting more vitamin C and antioxidants is to eat plenty of fruit and vegetables.

More generally, vitamins and minerals tend to

---

4 The two exceptions are vitamin D, which can be made by the action of sunlight on the skin, and niacin, which our bodies can synthesise from the amino acid Tryptophan.

be regarded as good things, with the implication that the more we have, the healthier we will be. But this is not true. Consuming *too much* of a particular vitamin or mineral can be harmful. For instance, vitamin D, vitamin B$_6$ and niacin can all be toxic if consumed in excessive amounts.

The Food Standards Agency (FSA) has issued warnings that many vitamin and mineral supplements can be harmful if taken in excess. For example, too much vitamin C, calcium or iron can cause diarrhoea and abdominal pain. The FSA also advises that taking large amounts of beta-carotene, nicotinic acid, zinc, manganese or phosphorus supplements for long periods can do irreversible harm. The message is clear: swallowing excessive amounts of vitamin and mineral supplements, far from making you healthier, could actually harm you.

Another point to bear in mind is that it can be misleading to think about individual vitamins or minerals in isolation. This is because certain vitamins and minerals affect the way your body absorbs other vitamins and minerals. For instance, vitamin C helps your body to absorb iron from plant sources, while vitamin D is essential for the absorption of calcium. Conversely, too much iron can interfere with the absorption of zinc. So, consuming too much or too little of one vitamin or mineral may have knock-on effects on others.

Do children get enough vitamins and minerals?

As pointed out in Worry 7 on page 37, the typical diet of many British children is far from ideal in terms of healthiness. A major national study of nutrition found that the foods most commonly eaten by children are white bread, savoury snacks, potato chips, biscuits, potatoes and chocolate – none of which is especially known for being packed with vitamins and minerals. Young people in Scotland, and to a lesser extent northern England, tend to have lower intakes of most vitamins and minerals, as do children from poor backgrounds (for example, those living in homes receiving benefits).

On the other hand, some everyday foods that do not appear to be particularly 'healthy' are in fact fortified with additional vitamins. The law in the UK requires that margarine must be fortified with vitamins A and D and that bread must be fortified with iron. Many breakfast cereals are fortified with various vitamins and minerals, most commonly thiamin, niacin, vitamin B12, folic acid and iron.

The upshot is that even a fairly unpromising-looking diet can still deliver the necessary vitamins and minerals, provided it is reasonably varied. Indeed, the national survey of nutrition found that, for children and young people, average intakes of all vitamins except one were well above the minimum (RNI) levels. The one exception was vitamin A, where intakes fell short among older teenagers. Children's average intakes of most minerals were also found to be above the RNI levels, with the exception of zinc. More than a third of 11- to 14-year-old girls were found to have zinc intakes below the recommended lower limit.

Average intakes of two important minerals – iron and calcium – have been gradually decreasing in the UK over recent years, partly because of the trends for eating less meat and dairy products. Most people still get enough iron and calcium despite this. However, some adolescent and teenage girls may be deficient in one or both. A national survey found that 45 per cent of girls aged 11–14 had iron intakes below the lower recommended level. Girls and women who regularly lose a lot of blood during menstruation are at greater risk of iron deficiency.

So, should our children (or anyone else, for that matter) be taking supplements? Most experts agree that the vast majority of children and adults should be able to get all the vitamins and minerals they need by eating a balanced and varied diet. Food is definitely the best way of obtaining vitamins and minerals, because it provides the complex combinations of other nutrients and fibre that tablets and supplements cannot provide.

However, there are certain groups of people who might benefit from supplements. Department of Health guidelines recommend that most young children would benefit from receiving supplements of vitamins A, C and D between the ages of six months and two years (or until five years of age if the child is at particular risk of deficiency because of a restricted diet). Families receiving income support are entitled to receive these vitamins in droplet form, free of charge, for children under the age of five. Other groups who might benefit from supplements include people with a chronic illness or those recovering from an illness.

The case for taking vitamin and mineral supplements also becomes stronger if someone is trying to lose weight by radical dieting. Our society's obsession with thinness is driving increasing numbers of children and teenagers, especially girls, to try reducing their weight, and some of them use harmful methods such as smoking or extreme dieting (see Worry 25, page 135). The evidence suggests that about 1 in 6 teenage girls are dieting. A diet that simply involves eating a bit less of everything, cutting out snacks and very fatty or sugary foods, and taking more physical exercise should present no problems in terms of vitamins and minerals. However, a radical diet that involves eating only a very restricted range of foods can make supplements more desirable.

What about vegetarians and vegans? Vegetarianism has become much more common in the UK over the past 50 years, and has now been adopted by up to 7 per cent of the population. Of course, the term 'vegetarian' can mean different things, ranging from people who normally eat no red meat to strict vegans, who avoid everything of animal origin including fish, eggs and dairy products. About 1 in 10 girls aged 15–18 say they are vegetarian or vegan.

Vegetarianism has been around for centuries, and is believed by many to be healthier than having an omnivorous diet containing meat. There is indeed some evidence that vegetarians tend to be healthier and to live slightly longer on average than non-vegetarians, but this may be largely because vegetarians also tend to have generally healthier lifestyles in other respects. Healthy-living non-vegetarians have similar mortality rates to vegetarians.

As a general rule, vegetarian diets can be very healthy and need present no significant problems in terms of vitamins and minerals – provided, like any other forms of diet, they are reasonably balanced and varied. It is particularly important for a vegetarian diet to contain alternative sources of vitamins A, D and B_{12}, calcium, iron and zinc, which would otherwise have come mainly from meat and fish. Good sources include milk, cheese, eggs, butter, fortified breakfast cereals, green leafy vegetables, bread, nuts, dried fruit, pulses and yellow/orange vegetables.

A strict vegan diet presents a bigger challenge, particularly as far as vitamin B_{12} is concerned. The vitamin B_{12} in our diets normally comes exclusively from animal sources, which means that a strict vegan would get virtually no vitamin B_{12}. Vegans therefore need to take vitamin B_{12} supplements, either in tablet form or in a fortified food such as yeast extract or fortified breakfast cereals. Vegans are also at risk of having a low iodine intake, which is easily rectified by consuming small amounts of seaweed or iodised salt.

Finally, remember that even a perfect diet containing optimum amounts of every vitamin and mineral will not by itself guarantee a long and healthy life. No vitamin or mineral supplements can erase the damaging effects of smoking, obesity, lack of physical exercise, drug abuse or depression. Maintaining good physical and mental health requires a rounded approach, of which diet is only one component.

What can you do?

- **Try to ensure that your child has a balanced and varied diet.**

    By far the best way to give children all the vitamins and minerals they need is to make sure they have a balanced and varied diet. That means one containing at least five portions a day of fruit and vegetables, together with a good mix of bread, pasta, fish, meat, cereals, eggs and dairy products. If your child is vegetarian, check that they have good alternative sources of iron, such as green vegetables, pulses or fortified breakfast cereals, plus plenty of vitamin C (which helps the body to absorb iron from plant sources). As a general rule, try to avoid falling back on vitamin and mineral supplements as a substitute for a healthy diet, other than as a stop-gap measure. Think twice, think three times and then take expert medical advice before putting a child onto a highly restrictive macrobiotic or vegan diet. Children have different nutritional requirements from adults, so even if the diet keeps you in good health it might not be good for them.

- **Make sure your child eats breakfast.**

    For parents of adolescents or teenagers, breakfast is often the best opportunity to influence their diet seven days a week. Encourage them to eat breakfast cereals that are fortified with vitamins and minerals (as most of them are) and to drink fruit juice, but try to steer them away from cereals containing large amounts of added sugar. Skipping breakfast can be bad for children.

- **Set a good example.**

    Try to set a good example yourself, especially when they are young. Your child is less likely to develop healthy eating habits if he or she routinely sees you skipping breakfast, avoiding fruit and vegetables and surviving mainly on junk food.

- **Don't believe everything you read.**

    Parents are exposed to many sources of information, advice and propaganda about vitamins, minerals and nutrition. Some are scientifically dubious and some are trying to sell you things. If in doubt, take your guidance from an independent, non-commercial and trustworthy source that draws upon the best available scientific evidence, such as the Food Standards Agency.

- **Some children may benefit from more iron, calcium or zinc.**

    Adolescent and teenage girls may be at greater risk of having insufficient iron in their diet, especially if they have heavy periods. Good sources of iron include fortified breakfast cereals, red meat (especially liver), dark green leafy vegetables (such as spinach), beans, dried fruit, whole grains (such as brown rice) and nuts. The other minerals to think about are calcium, which growing children require in larger quantities, and zinc. Good sources of calcium include dairy products (such as milk, cheese and yogurt), dark green leafy vegetables (such as broccoli and cabbage), bread, canned fish, nuts and soybean products. Zinc is found in milk, cheese, meat, eggs, fish, wholegrain cereals and pulses. In other words, a balanced diet should be able to provide plenty of all three.

Further advice

Food Standards Agency
Tel: 020 7276 8000
www.foodstandards.gov.uk.
Information on all aspects of diet, including vitamins and minerals.

British Nutrition Foundation
Tel: 020 7404 6504
www.nutrition.org.uk
Information on the nutritional needs of school children and adolescents.

The Food Commission
Tel: 020 7837 2250
www.foodcomm.org.uk
Independent advice and information on healthy eating.

Related worries

3. Eats too much sugar and sweet foods
7. Eats too much junk food or convenience food
12. Will only eat a narrow range of foods/has food fads
25. Doesn't eat enough

WORRY **36**

Won't do his/her homework

15% of parents worried

....

Chances: HIGH   **Consequences: LOW**   **Control: MEDIUM**

Many children resent or refuse to do homework at some point. This typically happens because they are bored, tired or fail to see its relevance. Parents can have a big influence on their child's willingness to do homework. Providing the right routine, environment and support can make children more likely to do, and perhaps even enjoy, their homework.

There is little solid evidence that doing a lot of homework helps children of primary school age do better academically. It can, however, play a valuable role in overcoming a specific problem with, say, reading. Homework also helps to create stronger links between parents and school, which in turn helps children to realise that learning is something their parents value.

At secondary school level, homework plays a more central role in education. The evidence shows that secondary school pupils who regularly do their homework perform substantially better academically than those who do not.

Homework can be a frequent cause of conflict in families. Surveys show that the vast majority of parents believe their children should be doing homework and that it will help them academically. However, many parents are unable to persuade their children of this, resulting in regular arguments. Parents tend to have more trouble persuading boys to do homework than girls.

The homework demands placed on most children are considerable. While stressing that it is the quality of the work that is important, not simply the time spent on it, the government has published homework guidelines for schools and parents. According to these guidelines, children are expected to spend roughly the following amounts of time on homework tasks:

5- and 6-year-olds:	1 hour a week
7- and 8-year-olds:	1–1 1/2 hours a week
9- and 10-year-olds:	30 minutes a day
11- and 12-year-olds:	45–90 minutes a day
13-year-olds:	1–2 hours a day
14- and 15-year-olds:	1–2 hours a day

International opinion is mixed on what constitutes the right amount of homework, with some countries expecting substantially more than the UK and some less. Countries also differ in their attitudes to homework for younger children. The UK starts homework at a younger age than many other countries, and also requires primary school-aged children to do more of it each day. In comparison, British secondary school pupils appear to get off relatively lightly. The recommended amounts are lower than in many other countries, and in practice teenagers often do still less. For example, it is reported that 14-year-olds in Hungary, Poland, the Netherlands, Israel, Italy and Japan actually do between eight and nine hours of homework a week, compared with an average of six hours a week in the UK.

What is the theory behind homework? The reasons for giving children homework include:

- reviewing and practising the material covered in class
- getting ready for the next day's lessons
- learning to use resources such as libraries, reference materials and the Internet to find information about a subject
- exploring subjects more fully than classroom time permits
- extending learning by applying existing skills to new situations
- integrating children's learning by applying various skills to a single task, such as writing a report on a book or completing a science project
- developing independence, self-discipline and motivation

Some critics argue that not all of the homework being given to children is well thought-out. One survey found that some primary school teachers are assigning homework more as a response to parental expectations than because they genuinely believe it will aid children's development. The survey also found that with a packed curriculum, homework is often being set simply to complete a task that children have insufficient time to do in class, rather than as a specific learning tool in its own right. Findings like these make it easier to understand why children sometimes find homework irksome and boring.

Research suggests that for homework to interest children, it should relate to their school classes but somehow take things further, and that the work should be challenging but achievable and varied. Children also need to see the relevance of the task to their lives. Furthermore, children need feedback. If they are putting in the effort to complete a task, they can become demotivated if they get no comments back on how well they did. Research suggests that the method of feedback doesn't much matter: a written note from the teacher or a group discussion in class can both work well. With hectic school timetables, many teachers find it hard to give homework planning and marking as much time as they would like.

The evidence suggests that the educational value of homework varies considerably according to the age of the children. Studies show that students over the age of 14 who regularly do homework tend to perform better in tests and exams than those who do not do homework. Considering the importance of factual information and coursework in the secondary curriculum, this is hardly surprising.

For children in the 11–14 age group, the evidence still shows that those who do homework perform better on average in school. But for children in primary school, there is no consistent evidence that homework boosts their academic performance. Indeed, some researchers suggest that the wrong kind of homework can have a negative effect in this younger group, because some children become bored and disengaged if made to do repetitive and boring tasks. In addition, some critics argue that too much homework can prevent children from engaging in more active pursuits after school and that it can encourage some individuals to copy or cheat.

Despite the lack of clear evidence that homework has major academic benefits for primary school children, the Department for Education and Skills (DfES) remains keen to promote homework for children as young as five. They do this for one good reason: homework aims to provide one of the few practical points of contact between a child's home life and school. By helping their children with homework, the theory goes, parents become more actively involved in their education. Homework helps to inform parents about what their children are studying at school and allows them to monitor their progress.

These benefits may be more important than any short-term improvement in the child's academic performance. A significant predictor of academic success in the long term is how much interest and involvement a parent shows in their child's education. The children of parents who talk to them about what they are learning at school tend to do better in exams, other things being equal. If parents become actively involved in supporting and helping with homework, the results tend to be even more positive. By showing they are interested, parents signal that school is something they value. Over time children notice this and become more motivated.

The government believes so strongly in promoting closer links between home and school that they have asked every school to produce a written home–school agreement. This agreement must be jointly created by the school and parents, and must set out the responsibilities of both. Home-school agreements usually describe the general learning approach and ethos of the school. They set guidelines on attendance, discipline and behaviour, and describe what information the school and parents should provide for each other.

Home–school agreements should clearly state what is expected from both sides in terms of homework. Teachers are expected to plan and mark all homework, while parents are expected to support and encourage their children's learning at home and help them to deliver work on time. Most parents are given a copy of the home-school agreement when their child joins a new school.

Most secondary schools broadly follow these guidelines on homework, but the position in primary schools is less clear-cut. Only about 60 per cent are regularly setting homework or achieving the level of home-school involvement recommended by the government.

What can you do?

◆ *Try to provide a suitable place for your child to work.*

A child's homework area doesn't have to be fancy: a desk in their own bedroom is nice, but for many children the kitchen table or a corner of the living room can be just as good. The important thing is for them to have a regular, quiet and well-lit place where they can go to complete their work. For households unable to provide a quiet space at home, an increasing number of schools now offer study clubs or homework groups. These can take place at the school or in a local library or sports centre. Find out what is available in your area.

◆ *Try to avoid distractions such as TV or loud music.*

Research consistently shows that having a TV or music on in the background really does reduce children's ability to concentrate. The only exception to this is quiet background classical music, which has been shown to improve memory – but whether most children would be willing to listen to quiet classical music is, of course, highly doubtful.

◆ *Develop a regular homework routine.*

Establishing a routine for doing homework helps to avoid excuses such as 'I'll do it after this programme' or 'I forgot'. It's important for children to learn to take responsibility rather than having to rely on their parents to remind or cajole them. For many children, the best time for homework is an hour or so after they return from school. They can enjoy some wind-down time and grab a snack, but they are not so tired that homework becomes an unbearable chore.

◆ *Show an interest and give praise.*

Try to make time each day to chat about school and the subjects covered. It is important to praise children for their efforts and achievements. Positive comments are generally more effective at changing children's behaviour than critical ones. A child may become disaffected if continually reminded of their shortcomings. Remember that the objective of homework is to learn, not to achieve perfection.

◆ *If you don't have a computer, consider getting one.*

Personal computers are not essential for successful home study, but they obviously have benefits in terms of being able to prepare written reports and access information from the Internet or CD-ROMs. For many children they also make homework more fun.

◆ *Communicate with the school.*

The school's broad approach to homework should be set out in the home–school agreement, but it may be worth talking to teachers about specific help or support you could give your child. Many schools find it helpful to maintain a regular dialogue with parents through homework diaries, in which both teachers and parents record their comments.

◆ *Try to be available.*

Many primary school children like to have someone with them to answer questions as they work on assignments. If your child is ▶

cared for by someone else, talk to that carer about how to deal with homework. For an older child, you might want to offer to read through a completed piece of work. But remember, your primary role should be one of support and help: resist the urge to step in and do the work for them. That helps no one in the long run and makes it harder for the teacher to spot if your child is finding the work difficult.

◆ *Keep it in perspective.*
Homework is valuable, but there is more to developing healthy minds in healthy bodies than working at a desk. It is just as important for children to enjoy sports and hobbies after school.

Further advice

The Parent Centre (Department for Education and Skills)
Tel: 0870 000 22 88
www.parentcentre.gov.uk
A comprehensive guide to the education system for parents, with specific guidance on homework.

Department for Education and Skills (DfES)
E-mail: homework.policy@dfes.gsi.gov.uk
www.standards.dfes.gov.uk/homework
Models of best practice for schools regarding homework and a reference point for parents on standards.

BBC Schools
www.bbc.co.uk/schools
A wide range of materials to help make learning more interesting at school and at home.

Channel 4, Homework High
www.channel4.com/learning
Online homework library for children aged 6–16.

Related worries

13. Has difficulty concentrating/paying attention
14. Will not be successful in later life if she/he does not do well at school
26. Isn't reading or writing as well as he/she should
27. Is bored or under-stimulated at school
39. Isn't as good at maths as he/she should be

WORRY 37

Is not safe on public transport

15% of parents worried

Chances: HIGH **Consequences: HIGH** **Control: MEDIUM**

The risk that a child travelling on public transport might be attacked by an adult stranger is small. However, children and young people travelling on public transport are often on the receiving end of lower-level unpleasantness, intimidation and crime, much of which comes from other young people.

Young people are also the source of much trouble and low-level crime on public transport. Some are viewed with suspicion or hostility by adult passengers and transport staff. A small but significant amount of intentional risk-taking behaviour is associated with the journey home from school.

Another potential concern is that children might be injured or killed in a crash while travelling on public transport. In fact, the risk is small, and certainly much smaller than with alternative means of transport. A journey by bus or rail is much less likely to result in accidental death or injury than a journey by car, bicycle or on foot.

Most of us travel a lot nowadays, and our children are no exception. If you add up all the miles covered in cars, trains, buses, on foot and by other modes of transport, the average person travels almost 7000 miles a year within Great Britain, compared with less than 5000 miles a year in the mid-1970s. A significant fraction of that travel is on public transport.

Children and young people are major users of public transport, especially buses and coaches. Several million of them use public transport every weekday to get to and from school. Almost a third of secondary school children make the school journey by bus and more than half of all 13- to 14-year-olds travel by bus at least once a week. In addition, from around the age of 12 onwards, children increasingly use buses, taxis and, to a lesser extent, trains for leisure and social purposes such as shopping, visiting friends or going to the cinema. By this age they are more likely to travel alone or with friends, and to make journeys at weekends or in the evenings. Some adolescents and teenagers also use bus stations, train stations or bus shelters as places to hang out and meet other young people.

Crime is a rational concern for anyone travelling on public transport, regardless of age. According to recent survey data, about 4 per cent of passengers say they have been the victim of theft within the past year, 5 per cent say they have been threatened with violence, and 11 per cent have been stared at in a hostile or threatening way. Most of these incidents are not reported at the time and do not find their way into the official crime statistics. Even so, more than 50,000 crimes a year are reported on the railways and more than 14,000 a year on London Underground. Unsurprisingly, crime rates are highest on routes that travel through high-crime areas, notably some parts of large cities.

Fear of crime is perhaps an even bigger problem, for children and adults alike. For every passenger who is actually mugged or threatened there are many more who feel anxious or frightened when travelling on public transport, especially at night. Research has found that one of the main factors contributing to this fear is the presence of drunks and beggars, who are widely perceived as unpredictable and potentially violent. Litter, graffiti and signs of vandalism add to passengers' anxieties because they imply a lack of control or supervision.

Children and young people who travel on public transport share many of the same concerns as adults. Research has found that although most feel safe if travelling unaccompanied during the day, their sense of insecurity grows after dark. One of their least favourite activities is waiting for a bus or train at night. Boys tend to be most worried when groups of young males are in the vicinity, whereas girls are most worried by the presence of lone men. Partly for that reason, many girls and young women dislike travelling alone in a taxi.

Surveys show that many young people have a negative perception of public transport. They do not feel it offers a friendly and secure environment in which their custom is valued, and feel that adult passengers and staff often appear to regard them as unwelcome troublemakers. Recent research found that almost a third of 13- to 14-year-olds said that a member of staff or adult passenger had been rude to them within the previous year. Reports of being treated badly by hostile or impatient bus drivers are common. But despite their negative feelings towards bus drivers and other transport staff, children and young people say they still feel safer when there are members of staff around, especially at night.

The unfavourable impression of public transport held by many children and young people has unfortunate long-term implications: research indicates that people who do not become regular users of public transport when they are young are less likely to use it in later adult life.

Of course, anxieties about crime occasionally turn into realities. The evidence shows that young people travelling on public transport are often on the receiving end of unpleasantness, intimidation and low-level crime, both from adults and other young people. Common experiences include being bullied by groups of older youths, having mobile phones or other personal possessions stolen, and being approached by men. For instance, one survey found that 15 per cent of 10- to 12-year-olds said they had been bullied by other young people while using or waiting for public transport within the previous year, 16 per cent had had something stolen from them, and 13 per cent had been frightened or upset by an adult. Most of these incidents are never even reported to the children's parents, let alone the police.

A small proportion of incidents are more serious, involving physical violence. Police crime statistics show that in more than a quarter of all recorded assaults on bus passengers, the victim is under the age of 16. (In contrast, elderly people account for only 6 per cent of assault victims.)

But young people are not just victims of unpleasantness and crime: they can also be the perpetrators. British Transport Police estimate that 90 per cent of vandalism on the railways is committed by young people, mostly older teenagers. Bus companies also experience widespread problems with rowdy behaviour and damage by young people. In surveys, adult passengers and transport staff frequently report that they have been troubled or intimidated by rowdy groups of young people behaving in an anti-social manner. On the other hand, many young people claim to be unaware of the effect their behaviour can have on other passengers.

Parents who conclude that public transport is far too nasty for their children to use must also think about the alternatives. Public transport might have its risks, but are other modes of travel any safer? If you had a choice between letting your children travel by rail, bus, coach, car, bicycle or on foot, which would be safest?

If you are worried about your child being killed or seriously injured in an accident while travelling, then the statistics point firmly towards a simple conclusion: travelling by rail, bus or coach is much safer than travelling by car, bicycle or on foot.

The chances of being killed or seriously injured while travelling in a car is nearly four times greater than that for travelling on a bus or coach. Walking is only marginally safer than travelling in a car. And if you really want to consider the extremes, the risk of being killed or injured if you travel on a motorbike or moped is more than 200 times greater than on a train journey.

Public transport is safer even than air travel, in terms of the risk per journey. You are roughly twice as likely to reach your destination intact after travelling by bus, coach or rail than if you travel by air (though of course you are likely to have travelled a shorter distance). Although a child might be less likely to be bullied or mugged if driven everywhere by their parents, their chances of being killed or injured in an accident are much higher. Despite its problems, public transport is still a relatively safe way of travelling.

What can you do?

◆ *Apply the three Ws: Where, Who and When.*

Make sure you know *where* your child is going, *who* they are with and *when* they will be back. Also make sure they know where you are and how to contact you. If they have a mobile phone, make them promise they will use it to let you know of any problem or change of plan. If they don't have a mobile, equip them with a phonecard or change so they can use a payphone. Try never to find yourself in a situation where your child is late back and you suddenly realise you have no idea where they are and no way of contacting them.

◆ *Make sure your child knows what to do in an emergency.*

Give your child clear instructions about what to do if they have a problem while travelling. Make sure they know how to contact you or some other responsible adult, whether you are at home or at work. Unless they know the relevant phone numbers off by heart, write them down or check that they are stored on your child's mobile phone. It can be a good idea to equip older children with the phone number of a trustworthy local taxi firm plus emergency cash for a taxi fare in case they get stranded.

◆ *Teach your child the basic elements of personal security.*

For example:

* Be discreet with your mobile phone and don't to flash it about in a way might attract unwelcome attention. Mobile phones are great in emergencies, but they can also be a lure for muggers and bullies.

* Don't flaunt other valuables such as wallets or jewellery in public places.

* Keep your keys apart from your wallet or anything else that might reveal your address.

* Plan your route in advance.

* Beware of pickpockets, especially in crowded places. Any bag containing valuables should be worn on the front of the body, closed, and with the fastening facing in towards the body.

* Try to keep to well-lit areas, preferably where there are other people about.

* Sit near other people on a train or bus, rather than in an isolated position.

* Never accept lifts from strangers.

* If someone is threatening you, make lots of noise and run away.

* When in public places, don't reveal personal information such as where you live.

* Try to appear confident.

◆ *Tell your child to hand over their valuables if they ever get mugged.*

A golden rule is that a child's personal safety must always take priority over their possessions or money. If in any doubt about what to do in a confrontation, they should hand over their wallet or mobile phone rather than risk being hurt. Boys, in particular, should be told to resist any macho instinct to fight. It is far better to run away than to end up being injured.

◆ *Tell your child to be aware of what is going on around them.*

Young people are much more vulnerable if they cannot hear what is going on around them because they are listening to loud music through earphones. Explain why it is a bad idea to use a personal stereo in public places, especially when moving around on foot. The same applies to chatting on a mobile phone.

◆ *Consider giving your child a personal alarm.*

If your child's journey is such that they face a real risk of being bothered, consider providing them with a personal alarm ▸

◆ *Complain if there is a problem.*

If your child travels on a route where there are specific problems or hazards, such as broken lighting, drunks or inadequate staffing then consider doing something about it, such as informing a member of staff or complaining to the relevant bus or rail company. You should not assume that things cannot be improved.

Further advice

Government Crime Reduction website

Tel: 020 7273 4000 (Home Office public enquiries team)

www.crimereduction.gov.uk

Advice on personal safety from crime, including when using public transport and taxis.

British Transport police

Tel: 0800 40 50 40

www.btp.police.uk/travel_safe.htm

Guidance on how to stay safe on public transport.

BBC Crime Prevention website

www.bbc.co.uk/crime/prevention/

Personal safety advice, including public transport.

The Suzy Lamplugh Trust

Tel: 020 8392 1839

www.suzylamplugh.org

Materials to promote personal safety, including for children and on public transport.

Related worries

1. Might be knocked over by a vehicle
2. Might be abducted or murdered
6. Might be the victim of crime
10. Might be the victim of physical violence
18. Is at risk if he/she goes on a school trip
38. Might get into trouble with the authorities or commit a crime

WORRY **38**

Might get into trouble with the authorities or commit a crime

14% of parents worried

Chances: HIGH   **Consequences: MEDIUM**   **Control: HIGH**

Few children are persistent law-breakers. However, many will truant from school or even commit a minor crime once in their youth. Around 1 child in 800 will end up being excluded from school and about 1 in 50 will be formally reprimanded or convicted of a crime.

Schools are often the first places to spot the early signs of delinquent behaviour. Bullying, truanting and poor academic achievement in primary school all correlate with committing crime as teenagers.

In England, Wales and Northern Ireland, children are legally responsible for their own behaviour from the age of ten and can receive custodial sentences from the age of 12. Parents of children below the age of 16 cannot be held legally responsible for their child's behaviour, but they can receive fines or court orders to encourage them to take a more active role in the discipline of their child.

Most children who commit a crime and are caught receive a reprimand or final warning. However, in recent years a growing number of children have received some sort of court order that seeks to control their future behaviour. Very few children receive custodial sentences.

Rebelling against parents and society is to some extent a rite of passage for teenagers. As they try to carve out an individual identity, many will test the boundaries to see what they can get away with. In the majority of cases the consequences are relatively minor and short-lived; the young person ends up broadly adhering to the rules and norms laid down by their parents, school and society. But for those who do get into serious trouble with the authorities, it can be the start of a downward spiral of misbehaviour which they may find hard to break out of.

As a broad rule of thumb, if children are going to get into trouble with the authorities, things tend to start going wrong when they are about 11–13 years old, with misbehaviour peaking in the mid-teens. By around the age of 15, 1 in 3 boys claims to have committed a crime within the previous year. For girls the figure is 1 in 6. The most common offences for which young people are convicted include criminal damage, shoplifting, buying stolen goods and bodily harm. Over half of all convictions are for some form of stealing.

Only a small proportion of the crimes committed by children and young people result in formal action. Many are considered too minor to warrant the time and cost. Approximately 1 in 10 incidents lead to a formal reprimand or a prosecution. This figure has been relatively stable over the past 20 years, although there has been an increase in the number of girls being prosecuted. For many children, getting caught the first time will shock and scare them enough to ensure that they never re-offend. For some, however, the first incident marks the start of repeated offending.

One of the obvious early warning signs that a child might be heading for the courts is that they are repeatedly getting into trouble at school. A quarter of all secondary school children claim to have truanted for at least one day, but those who do so regularly are nearly twice as likely to be convicted later of a crime. Children who get into trouble for bullying in school are also statistically more likely to turn to crime, especially assault.

A child's behaviour can be so disruptive that he or she ends up being excluded from school, either temporarily or permanently. In the 2001/2 academic year, there were 10,000 permanent exclusions from schools in the UK. More than 3 out of 4 excluded pupils are boys. Once a child has been permanently excluded, the risk that they will fall into a pattern of crime rises sharply.

A 2002 survey of children aged 11–16 found that almost 7 out of 10 excluded pupils claimed to have committed a crime, compared with 1 in 3 mainstream pupils. More than half of these young people claimed they were carrying a weapon when they committed the crime. Worse still, they claimed to have committed an average of 44 crimes within the previous year. This small but highly active subset of criminal youths have been referred to as 'personal crime waves'.

Boredom was the most common reason given for committing a crime. More than a fifth of the young people said they had misbehaved because of alcohol or drugs, while others cited the bad influence of friends as a factor. Nearly three-quarters of all youth crimes are committed by two or more youths together, and trying to impress friends is the third most common reason given for committing a crime. Obviously, these are the reasons given by the young offenders when asked: the true underlying causes of their behaviour could be different.

What happens if your child *does* get into trouble? Below the age of ten, children in England and Wales cannot be held criminally responsible for their actions. If a child under ten commits an act which, if they had been ten or over would have been an offence, the courts have the right to impose a child safety order. This means that the child can be placed under the supervision of a social worker or a Youth Offending Team (YOT) worker to ensure that he or she receives appropriate care, protection, control and support, and is prevented from repeating the behaviour which led to the order being made.

For children and young people over the age of

ten, three different levels of response are possible. By far the most common is a reprimand or final warning. The final warning scheme replaced the system of cautioning young offenders that was used in England and Wales until June 2000. Depending on the seriousness of the offence, a reprimand is usually given for a first offence and a final warning for a second offence. The hope is that by acting swiftly, a reprimand or final warning will dissuade the young person from offending again. At least half of youth offenders are dealt with in this way.

The final warning system goes further than the old-style caution that it replaced. Following a final warning, the police are required to refer the young offender to the local YOT. If a young person who has received a final warning commits a further offence, he or she must be charged.

For more serious crimes, or for serial offenders, the young person will normally be charged and taken to court. This could be a juvenile court or, if the allegations are serious, a crown court. If the young person is found guilty, several different levels of punishment can be applied, ranging from a discharge to a fine, community sentence or custody. Discharges are given when it is considered 'inexpedient' to punish the young person. Fines tend to be given when a rap on the knuckles is seen as necessary.

Community sentences are the most common outcome; the number of young people being punished in this way has risen steadily over the past decade. Community sentences can include:

- *Supervision Order.* A supervision order can be made in relation to an offender aged 10–17 years. It may require the young person to live in a particular place, or to attend a specified place at a specified time to receive training, counselling or to take part in other activities.

- *Curfew Order.* A curfew order requires the young person to remain at a particular place for a period of between two and 12 hours a day. The offender may be required to wear a device or tag that alerts the authorities to where they are at any given time.

- *Action Plan Order.* This is designed to provide a short but intensive and personalised programme that targets both the offending behaviour and the causes of that behaviour. The action plan may require the offender to participate in prescribed activities such as anger management classes, educational projects, or programmes to combat drug or alcohol misuse. It may also require the offender to present him- or herself at specific places at specific times, to help establish a routine in their life.

- *Reparation Order.* Under a reparation order a young offender can be required to make reparation to the victim, if they agree, or to the community at large. The aim is both to recompense the victim and to help the young offender understand and face up to the consequences of their actions.

Custodial sentences are used with young offenders only if the offence is so serious that no other punishment would be suitable. Custody is also appropriate if the offence was violent or sexual, or if the young person refused to consent to, or had breached, a community order. Only young people over the age of 12 can be kept in custody, and this usually means a detention centre.

Parents can be reprimanded if their child is a persistent troublemaker. While they are not legally responsible for the criminal acts of their children, parents can be compelled to attend court and can be served with a parenting order, which can require them to attend a maximum of 12 parenting guidance or counselling sessions over a three-month period. The parents may also have requirements imposed upon them concerning the care and control of their child. Failure to comply with a parenting order can result in a fine.

In Scotland, young offenders under the age of 16 are normally dealt with by the Children's Hearing system, which involves a local Children's Panel of three specially trained volunteers from a variety of backgrounds. Children under 16 are only considered for prosecution in court in the case of serious offences such as murder or life-threatening assault.

Why do some children turn to crime? Research has consistently identified three key factors as increasing an individual's chances of ending up in trouble with the law.

First, the circumstances in which a child grows up obviously have a profound effect. On average, children born to young mothers or into unusually large families are more likely to turn to crime; so too are children who grow up in poor housing or with a low household income. Disadvantaged communities and those with a high turnover of residents are associated with more crime. Children who frequently move school or home are also more likely to turn to crime.

A second big influence is school. As mentioned earlier, children who truant or are excluded from school are more likely to get into trouble with the law. Some of these children seem to fail to form any strong relationship or attachment to their peers or the school and they often perform badly aca-demically. They tend to be less able and many have learning difficulties.

Finally, parents play a huge role. Research suggests that certain types of parental behaviour can significantly increase the risk of their child turning to crime. The key things to avoid include:

- *Neglect:* where parents spend too little time with their children and are unaware of mischief-making. Neglectful parents provide too little direct supervision.
- *Conflict:* where parental discipline is physical, cruel or just very inconsistent, leading to an inability to control their child.
- *Deviant behaviour and attitudes:* where law-breaking by parents, or parental attitudes that reveal contempt for the law, encourage their children to do the same.
- *Disruption:* where family life is disrupted by chronic conflict between the parents, or actual separation.

What can you do?

◆ **Be consistent about rules and discipline.**

When you make a rule, stick to it. Children need structure in their lives, with clear expectations for their behaviour. Setting rules and then not enforcing them is confusing and invites children to see what they can get away with. Try to establish a consistent approach to discipline early, as it becomes increasingly hard to do this when children get older.

◆ **Apply the three Ws: Where, Who and When**

Always try to ensure that you know *where* your child is, *who* they are with, and *when* they will be back. Try to get to know their friends, at least by name and sight. It should be possible to apply the three Ws without infringing too much on their freedom or independence.

◆ **Keep in touch with the school.**

The school will probably be the first to spot signs of learning difficulties, bullying, aggression, or other problems which could later develop into truancy or crime.

◆ **Try to make sure your child has enough to do.**

Remember that young offenders often cite boredom as the main reason why they turn to crime. Boredom can be a ▸

particular problem during school holidays. Check out what is available locally in terms of activities.

◆ *Lead by example.*

Obviously, never break the law or indicate to your children that it is acceptable to do so, even with seemingly minor things like speed limits. Talk about the reasons why society needs rules and how laws help all of us, even if we don't always like them.

◆ *Get your child involved in your local community.*

Children are less likely to commit crimes against people they know, or when they think it will harm places or people they care about. You could volunteer to help in your neighbourhood's anti-crime efforts or in programmes to make schools safer for children. Encourage your child to get involved in community groups.

◆ *Watch out for early signs of alcohol or drug abuse.*

Children who abuse alcohol or drugs are much more likely to get into trouble with the authorities.

Further advice

Nacro
Tel: 020 7582 6500
e-mail: communications@nacro.org.uk
www.nacro.org.uk
Crime-reduction charity with specific projects to help young people move away from crime.

NCH (formerly NCH Action for Children)
Tel: 020 7704 7000
www.nch.org.uk
Charity that helps vulnerable children, including young people who have committed crime or are at risk of committing crime.

Children's Legal Centre
Tel: 01206 873820
www.childrenslegalcentre.com
Publications and free advice on legal issues affecting children.

Related worries

8. Has friends who could be or are a bad influence
19. Is reckless and not sufficiently aware of dangers
24. Won't listen to me/is disobedient

The Law

- Parents are legally responsible for their children until the child reaches the age of 16.

- Children from the age of ten onwards can be held legally responsible if they commit a criminal offence.

- Children under the age of 12 cannot be given a custodial sentence. (In Scotland, offenders do not become subject to the adult system of prosecution and punishment until the age of 16.)

- Children are not legally liable for their debts until they are 18.

- It is *not* against the law for parents to leave their children alone in the house. However, a parent could be charged with 'wilful neglect' if the child might have been harmed or injured as a result.

- There is *no* legal minimum age for babysitters.

- Any person who is paid to look after more than one child under the age of eight for more than two hours a day, on a regular basis, must by law be registered with the local authority as a childminder. All childminders are subject to police checks and their homes are assessed for health and safety.

- The law covering childminders does not apply to nannies. A nanny does not have to be registered or checked.

- Parents have a legal duty, once their child reaches the age of five, to ensure that he or she receives a suitable full-time education. However, parents have a right under the Education Act 1996 to educate their child 'otherwise than in school'. Parents can choose to educate their children at home and do not need teaching qualifications to do this. However, they must still ensure that their child receives an efficient full-time education suitable to his or her age, ability and aptitude.

- It is against the law for a child under the age of 14 to work.

- It is against the law for children under the age of 16 to buy cigarettes or for shops to sell them cigarettes. However, it is *not* against the law for children under 16 to smoke.

- It is against the law for children under the age of 18 to buy or drink alcohol in a bar. However, it is *not* against the law for children to drink alcohol at home once they reach the age of five.

- It is against the law to tattoo any person under the age of 18, except for medical reasons.

The legal position above refers to England and Wales. The law is different in Scotland and Northern Ireland.

WORRY **39**

Isn't as good at maths as he/she should be

14% of parents worried

....

Chances: HIGH   **Consequences: MEDIUM**   **Control: MEDIUM**

Maths is a subject that many adults and children find difficult and anxiety-provoking. For someone to say they 'can't do maths' is socially more acceptable than admitting they have trouble reading or writing.

Individuals with 'maths phobia' tend to be genuinely less competent at maths, but their anxiety makes their problem worse by further impairing their performance. About 1 in 20 children have particular difficulties learning how to do arithmetic. However, very few children or adults are truly incapable of learning basic numeracy skills, given suitable teaching.

In England in 2002, 1 in 10 seven-year-olds, just over a quarter of 11-year-olds and a third of 14-year-olds did not reach the national expected standard in maths, as measured by the National Curriculum assessments (SATs).

Numeracy is just as important as literacy. People who lack a basic understanding of numbers are more likely to end up unemployed or in poorly paid jobs. Mathematical concepts such as probability and averages are essential tools for making sense of the complexities of modern life.

Parents can help children by taking maths seriously, talking about numbers, playing mathematical games, and engaging them in activities that involve counting, measuring or dealing with shapes. Ultimately, though, the key to success in maths is good teaching – which makes the current shortage of well-qualified maths teachers all the more worrying.

We were not surprised to find that more parents in our national survey were concerned about their children's ability to read and write than about their ability to do maths. It's far more socially acceptable for a person to claim that they 'can't do maths' than to admit that they have difficulty reading and writing. Some otherwise intelligent and well-educated adults virtually boast of their innumeracy, but would be horrified if someone accused them of being illiterate. This double standard towards maths is regrettable, because maths really matters.

A basic grasp of numbers, shapes and mathematical reasoning is essential for anyone living in a complex modern society. At the most mundane level, we all need simple arithmetic in our everyday lives – for example, when deciding whether we have received the right change, how far the shopping money will stretch, whether we have the right fare for a bus ride, how long a journey will take, how big a mortgage we can afford, and so on. Moreover, anyone who wants to be an active, informed and rational citizen needs at least a basic grasp of mathematical concepts such as probabilities, averages and percentages before they can make well-informed decisions about many of the choices and problems they will face in life.

Numeracy has a major bearing on earning power and employability. Employment opportunities for those who lack basic skills in numeracy and literacy are dwindling, as more and more jobs involve brain work rather than muscle power. Someone with numeracy problems is likely to be at a significant disadvantage in adult life, despite the availability of calculators.

In fact, the evidence shows that a person's level of numeracy has an even bigger impact on their earning power than does their level of literacy. Individuals with poor numeracy are even more likely to find themselves unemployed or in poorly-paid jobs than those with low levels of literacy.

Despite its importance, more adults have problems with numeracy than with reading and writing. Experts estimate that about 2 out of 5 British adults have some sort of numeracy problem; about half of these (i.e., 1 in 5 adults) have *very* low levels of numeracy, which means they cannot perform even simple calculations. To give two specific examples, surveys found that 1 in 3 British adults could not calculate the floor area of a room measuring 21 feet x 14 feet, even with the help of a calculator; and 1 in 4 adults could not calculate the change they should get from £2 after buying one item for 68p and two items at 45p each.

One worrying aspect of poor numeracy is that it tends to pass down through the generations. Parents who have problems with numbers are statistically more likely to have children with similar problems (though this probably has much more to do with parental attitudes and education than genes).

Maths phobia

Many people blame their innumeracy on 'maths phobia' or 'maths anxiety' – a generalised fear or dislike of anything to do with numbers. This gives them a blanket reason for avoiding numbers and maths after they leave school. The evidence shows, not surprisingly, that individuals with high levels of anxiety about maths take fewer maths courses and perform less well at maths than people with less anxiety.

Does 'maths phobia' really exist, or is it just an excuse? There is clear evidence that individuals who have high levels of anxiety about maths also tend to be less competent at it. So, 'maths phobia' may be more a consequence of poor mathematical ability than a cause. However, that's probably not the whole story. Experiments have shown that mental arithmetic problems can induce a state of anxiety, even in intelligent and well-educated people. Anxiety reduces the capacity of the working memory, which could explain why high-anxiety individuals find it harder to do mental arithmetic.

Of course, understanding mathematical concepts and performing mental arithmetic are two different things, and there is no obvious reason why anxiety should impair people's general ability to learn basic number skills or mathematical concepts. The safest conclusion is that individuals with 'maths phobia' perform worse at maths partly because they are simply less competent at it, and partly because their anxiety further impairs their ability.

The evidence suggests that only a very small minority of children are fundamentally incapable of acquiring basic numeracy skills, if they are properly taught. Where problems do arise, these often happen because the child has failed to understand a basic concept upon which other concepts are built, and hence feels increasing anxiety and a growing sense of failure. Good teaching is the key.

What is being done?

That said, some children clearly do find maths – and specifically arithmetic – much harder than other subjects. Psychologists have identified a condition known as dyscalculia, in which the individual has particular problems learning how to deal with numbers. The Department for Education and Skills (DfES) defines dyscalculia as a condition that affects the ability to acquire arithmetical skills. Dyscalculic learners may have difficulty understanding simple number concepts, lack an intuitive grasp of numbers, and have problems learning number facts and procedures. Even if they produce a correct answer or use a correct method, they may do so mechanically and without confidence.

How common is dyscalculia? The evidence is not yet clear-cut, but experts estimate that about 1 in 20 children who are otherwise of at least average intelligence have a particular difficulty with numbers. However, a substantial proportion of these children also have problems with literacy. Indeed, dyscalculia often goes hand in hand with dyslexia. Around 2 out of 5 children who have reading difficulties also have difficulties learning maths. Far fewer children have learning difficulties that are restricted to numbers alone. American research suggests that only about 1 child in a hundred has 'pure' dyscalculia, without the presence of other learning or behavioural difficulties. And anyway, even the tiny minority of children who do have severe and specific difficulties with numbers can still be helped by the right kind of teaching.

The current approach to teaching maths in maintained primary schools in England is shaped by the national numeracy strategy, which the government introduced in 1999. In September 2003 the national numeracy and literacy strategies were incorporated into a broader national primary strategy. The numeracy strategy reflected extensive international research into what helps children become successful and confident at maths. All pupils have a daily maths lesson, which should be based around specific teaching aims.

The numeracy strategy sets out detailed descriptions of what children should be able to do at various ages. For example, it states that by about the age of seven most children should be able to count, read and write whole numbers up to 100, put numbers in order, double or halve numbers, tell whether numbers are odd or even, predict how a shape would appear in a mirror, and tell the time to the half- and quarter-hour. By around the age of 11, most children should be able to, for example, multiply and divide decimals by 10 or 100 in their head, reduce a fraction to its simplest form, work out simple percentages of whole numbers, use a protractor to measure angles to the nearest degree and solve problems involving time on a 12- or 24-hour clock. By 14, most children should be able to, among other things, multiply and divide any whole number by 10, 100 and other powers of 10, express one number as a fraction or percentage of another number, find and use prime factors of numbers, know and use the formulae to calculate the circumference and area of a circle, and use algebra to describe the nth term of a simple sequence.

Primary school children are also expected to know the multiplication tables off by heart. Seven-year-olds should know the 2- and 10-times tables, eight-year-olds should know the 5-times table, nine-year-olds should know the 3- and 4-times tables, and ten-year-olds should know all the tables up to 10-times.

In England, each child's achievement against the expected standards is assessed in the National Curriculum tests (SATs), which children take when they are seven, 11 and 14 years old. Maths is assessed at all three ages, with additional tests of mental arithmetic at 11 and 14. At each age, written tests are accompanied by teacher assessments.

How well do children actually perform in these assessments? In 2002, 1 in 10 seven-year-olds, more than a quarter of 11-year-olds and a third of 14-year-olds in England did not reach the national expected standard for maths. (At the next stage, just under 1 in 10 15-year-olds in England who attempted GCSE maths did not pass it.) If your child is one of those who fell short of the expected standard, then you may have some grounds for believing that they are not doing as well as they should at maths.

That said, individual children move forward at very different speeds. Some children's understanding of maths improves in a gradual, progressive manner, while other children may get stuck for a while before making a sudden leap forward. A child who seems to be falling behind at one stage might catch up, given a little more time and some extra help.

Another point to bear in mind is that the maths syllabus involves several very different strands, and that children rarely find all of these strands equally easy. Some children, for example, find it hard to grasp concepts of shape and space, but have no great difficulty with number skills. So, a child's problems with maths may often be limited to specific aspects of maths rather than a general inability.

Good teaching is crucial for learning maths – perhaps even more so than for learning to read and write. After all, most parents are better equipped and motivated to help their children with reading and writing than they are with maths. However, the national outlook for maths teaching is mixed.

On the positive side, the quality of maths teaching has improved over the past few years, at least according to Ofsted (the Office for Standards in Education). In English primary schools, 90 per cent of maths lessons are now rated as at least satisfactory and 60 per cent are rated as good. Ofsted, together with many teachers, believes that children's confidence and enjoyment of maths have improved since the start of the national numeracy strategy.

On the downside, there is a worrying shortage of suitably qualified maths teachers. A survey of English secondary schools, conducted in 2001/2, found that a fifth of all vacancies in maths teaching posts were unfilled. Perhaps even worse was the finding that almost a quarter of secondary school maths teachers had 'weak' or 'nil' qualifications in maths, and that the proportion of maths teachers with qualifications in their subject had fallen since the previous major study in 1996.

The obvious worry here is the creation of a vicious cycle in which a shortage of good maths teachers results in poorer teaching, fewer pupils going on to do maths at A-level and university, hence fewer qualified maths teachers for the next generation of children, and so on. Pupils and teachers increasingly complain that A-level maths, compared with other subjects, is a hard course with an over-full curriculum, and many children avoid it at A-level unless it is required for a university course they want to do later. Whatever the reason, fewer children are doing A-level maths than ten years ago.

Maths is not a particularly popular subject at university either. Currently, just over 4000 people a year graduate with a first degree in maths, down from more than 5000 a year in the late 1990s. Mathematicians now make up a mere 1.5 per cent of all university graduates. By comparison, British universities turn out more than twice as many law graduates and eight times as many graduates in business and administrative studies.

To add to the problem, the need for maths teachers has grown by at least 10 per cent since the mid-1990s, as the number of children in secondary school has increased. If this trend persists, Britain will continue to face a shortage of qualified maths teachers unless virtually every maths graduate emerging from university goes into teaching.

What can you do?

◆ *Take maths as seriously as reading and writing.*

Try to show your child that you value their achievement in maths at least as much as in other subjects, and that you don't regard numeracy as being somehow less important than literacy. It's unhelpful for children to hear their parents or other adults saying that they themselves are hopeless at maths, because this reinforces the idea that a lot of people simply 'can't do' maths. This is a myth.

◆ *Tell your child to ask for help when they need it.*

Encourage your child to put their hand up in class and say if they do not understand something. Other children will probably be in the same position. Learning maths is a cumulative process, with each step forward building upon existing understanding. Therefore, a child who has failed to grasp one concept – perhaps because it was poorly explained or because they were absent at the time – may find it even harder to understand other concepts that build upon it. A child who is reluctant to ask for help, or to admit that they have not understood something, will be at increasing risk of getting left behind.

◆ *Talk to the school.*

If you think your child might have a problem with maths, talk to their teacher. Discuss the nature of your child's difficulties, find out how their achievement relates to the expected levels for their age, and ask for advice on how you can help them at home. If your child's problems are significant, the school might offer additional help.

◆ *Get involved.*

Parents of primary school-aged children are encouraged to be as involved as possible in their child's learning of maths. Ask your child to explain what they have been learning in maths lessons at school. Talk to them about numbers and shapes in real life. Encourage them to do mental arithmetic; for example, when you are out shopping together. Play number games with cards, coins, board games, dice, phone numbers or food shopping. Ask them to help you with everyday tasks that involve counting, measuring, weighing or dealing with shapes; for instance, comparing the costs of items in shops or catalogues, weighing out ingredients for cooking, measuring a floor for a carpet or deciding how to arrange tiles. Your aim should be to make maths seem both relevant and fun (hard though that may be for some parents truly to believe). ▶

◆ **Help your child with their maths homework as much as you can.**

(But don't just do it all for them, of course.) When you do help them with homework, bear in mind that they may well have been taught to perform calculations differently from the way you were taught. If so, try not to confuse them by insisting that your method is right and the school's method is wrong; let them do it the way they have been taught. Help them to learn their multiplication tables by heart: the expectation is that children should know up to their 10-times table by the time they are ten years old.

◆ **Point your child at the TV.**

Encourage them to watch some of the good radio and TV programmes about maths that are broadcast by the BBC and Channel 4.

Further advice

The Parent Centre (Department for Education and Skills)
Tel: 0870 000 22 88
www.parentcentre.gov.uk
A comprehensive guide to the education system, along with links to other organisations and on-line discussion forums.

Education Standards Site
www.standards.dfes.gov.uk/numeracy
Aims to provide models of best practice for schools to follow with regard to numeracy and gives parents a reference point for standards.

Education Standards Site: It all adds up website
www.mathsyear2000.org/standards/index.html
Tips for helping your child with numeracy.

The Basic Skills Agency
Tel: 020 7405 4017
www.basic-skills.co.uk
Programmes and advice aimed at improving the general standard of reading, writing and maths.

The Mathematical Brain
www.mathematicalbrain.com
Information on dyscalculia.

TV and radio programmes for children about maths:
www.bbc.co.uk/education
www.channel4.com/schools

Related worries

14. Will not be successful in adult life if he/she does not do well at school
26. Isn't reading or writing as well as he/she should
27. Is bored or under-stimulated at school
36. Won't do his/her homework
40. Is only assessed on narrow academic achievements, not broader abilities

Is only assessed on narrow academic achievements, not broader abilities

13% of parents worried

Chances: HIGH   Consequences: MEDIUM   Control: LOW

Schoolchildren in England are among the most intensively tested in the world. Most of the formal testing and assessment they undergo is focused on their academic abilities rather than on broader aspects of their development.

Academic skills and qualifications are obviously important for success in life, but they are not the only things that matter. Developing a child's social and emotional skills can contribute just as much, if not more, to their long-term happiness and success.

Despite the current focus on assessing academic skills, most teachers and schools remain very conscious of the need to develop the child as a whole and will be aware of individual children's broader social, emotional, physical and creative capabilities.

British children, and especially those being educated in England, are among the most intensively tested and assessed in the world. Before embarking on GCSEs, children in maintained schools are formally assessed in English and maths at the age of seven (the end of Key Stage 1) and in English, maths and science at 11 (the end of Key Stage 2) and 14 (the end of Key Stage 3).

These Standard Assessment Tests (SATs) generally happen during May each year and take three to eight hours, depending on the child's age. Independent schools are under no obligation to teach the National Curriculum or to enter their pupils for SATs, although most do in practice follow something similar to the National Curriculum.

SATs focus on children's core academic skills. The theory behind these assessments is that they allow the government to judge how well the education system is working across the country, and to get an indication of the achievement levels of specific groups of pupils as well as the population as a whole. The results provide schools with feedback that helps them to tailor and improve their teaching. They can also give children a sense of achievement from seeing themselves make progress.

SATs were not designed primarily to measure the performance of individual children. Nonetheless, many parents find their children's test scores give a useful indication both of how they are doing relative to other children and of how they are progressing over time.

Unfortunately, however, SATs seem to have had some unintended and undesirable outcomes too. Evidence suggests that some children, especially lower-achieving children, find the tests stressful and that this can damage their enjoyment of learning in the longer term. More noticeably, SATs have created a generation of parents who use league tables as a simple way of identifying the 'best' schools.

Perhaps more important, though, is their effect on teaching. The emphasis given to SAT league table results by the media, parents, local government and central government has encouraged most schools to become more focused on strategies for passing the tests. Partly for this reason, the authorities in Northern Ireland and Wales decided to stop publishing national league tables in 2001, judging them to be unhelpful.

Even setting aside the SAT regime, primary school education does focus on the teaching and assessment of core academic skills, notably literacy and numeracy. All maintained primary schools are required to teach a range of other subjects, including music, art, physical education, and personal, social and health education (PSHE). However, the amount of time teachers have available to devote to these other subjects has been restricted by the emphasis on literacy and numeracy. For example, although there is a guideline that all children should spend at least two hours a week on physical exercise, only 3 out of 10 primary school children are currently doing this.

What are the consequences of this focus on teaching and assessing academic skills in the early years? The core skills of literacy and numeracy are certainly essential for success, both in education and later in life. Children who do not learn to read, write, spell and handle numbers to at least a reasonable standard will find their future options in life severely limited. Formal qualifications such as GCSEs and A-levels are needed for many, if not most, attractive careers, and with more than a third of all 18-year-olds now going on to higher education, they certainly matter. That said, most experts (and probably most parents) would agree that there is more to education, and much more to life, than qualifications alone. Success and happiness also depend on other qualities, such as social and emotional skills, motivation, conscientiousness and good health.

Most psychologists now recognise that there is more even to intelligence than the reasoning abilities measured by traditional IQ tests. Intelligence comes in many different forms, not all of which are recognised or assessed by the kind of testing that goes on in schools. One well-known classification, for example, distinguishes between seven different types of human intelligence:

- linguistic intelligence
- logical mathematical intelligence (the ability to reason logically and to use mathematical symbols)
- spatial intelligence (the ability to form spatial images and to find one's way around in an environment)
- musical intelligence (the ability to perceive and create pitch and rhythmic patterns)
- body-kinaesthetic intelligence (the gift of graceful motor movement, as seen in surgeons or dancers)
- interpersonal intelligence (the ability to understand other people, how they feel, what motivates them, and how they interact)
- intrapersonal intelligence (the individual's ability to know him- or herself and to develop a strong sense of personal identity)

The current systems of teaching and assessment are focused more on the first two types of ability, perhaps at the expense of other areas such as social and emotional development.

However, the position is by no means one-sided. Children do receive continuing teacher assessments and termly reports covering all aspects of their development, including non-academic abilities and social skills. Despite the emphasis on academic skills, the vast majority of teachers and schools are very conscious of the need to develop the child as a whole. Moreover, they generally have a good feel for how each child is progressing in these non-academic spheres. In that sense, at least, it is not fair to say that children are *only* being assessed on their narrow academic achievements.

Furthermore, the approach in primary schools has recently shifted slightly away from the focus on core skills. From 2003, the national literacy and numeracy strategies have been incorporated into a new national primary strategy, which emphasises 'excellence and enjoyment'. The new strategy still concentrates on core academic skills, but it gives greater weight than before to creativity and the enjoyment of learning.

The secondary school system also offers children greater scope than before to pursue and excel in non-academic areas and non-traditional subjects. Students now have a much wider range of subjects and qualifications to choose from than was the case in the past. Moreover, the trend in recent years has been to introduce new and more flexible ways of assessing students' achievements, besides formal exams. Coursework and continuous assessment are now standard, even for more academic qualifications such as GCSEs. Children no longer need to be highly academically-minded, or good at passing lots of written exams, in order to do well and obtain valuable qualifications.

Generally speaking, those children who do well academically in primary school tend to do well academically in secondary school. But this correlation is far from perfect, and many other factors play important roles. One of the most important is self-confidence. Other things being equal, children who believe they are capable of doing well tend to do better than those who lack confidence in their own abilities. Another important personal attribute is conscientiousness. Numerous studies have shown that children who have the self-discipline and emotional intelligence to persist with tasks in the face of difficulties tend to do better on average, even allowing for differences in their academic ability.

Given the crucial importance of social and emotional skills, together with personal characteristics such as self-confidence and conscientiousness, many would argue that the education system should place even greater emphasis on their development and assessment.

What can you do?

◆ **Think about what is meant by a 'good' school.**

A 'good' school is one that will provide the best possible education, in the broadest sense, for your individual child. A school that performs very well in national league tables for SATs, GCSEs or A-levels may, or may not, be the right school for your particular child. Even academically-minded children benefit greatly from opportunities to engage in non-academic pursuits that help to develop their social, emotional and physical abilities.

◆ **Try to build your child's confidence.**

Self-confidence and self-esteem can have a big influence on a child's achievement in school, so praise your child when he or she does something well. But steer clear of hollow praise. Children are not stupid and they will soon realise if they are being praised indiscriminately, regardless of what they actually do. Praise must be meaningful to have any real value, and should preferably be linked to specific actions, rather than just delivered as a generalised statement. For example, saying 'I like the way you've used colour in your painting: you're very good at noticing the detail in things' is likely to have more impact than just saying 'This is a good picture'.

◆ **Help the 'whole child' to develop.**

Parents have a crucial role to play in helping their children to develop social, emotional and other non-academic skills – especially if their children are being educated in a highly academic school. Helping your child's social and emotional development is just as important as helping them with their reading and writing.

◆ **Pay attention to the school's broader assessment of your child, and not just their test results.**

Formal assessment results such as SAT scores by themselves will obviously not give you a full picture of your child's development and achievement. Look carefully at other sources of information, such as the annual reports that schools write for each child.

Further advice

The Parent Centre

Tel: 0870 000 22 88 (Department for Education and Skills)

www.parentcentregov.uk

A comprehensive guide to the education system for parents.

Education Standards Site

www.standards.dfes.gov.uk

Website explaining the testing and curriculum regime for all ages.

Schoolsnet

Tel: 01273 740200

www.schoolsnet.com

Web resource for parents and teachers covering all aspects of education. Includes articles and links on non-academic abilities.

Department for Education and Skills: performance tables

Tel: 0870 000 22 88 (DfES switchboard)

www.dfes.gov.uk/performancetables

Archive of current and previous school performance tables, as well as information on how to read them and how to choose a school.

Related worries

14. Will not be successful in later life if he/she does not do well at school
27. Is bored or under-stimulated at school

And Ten Questions from Us

The bulk of this book has focused on specific worries that parents have about their children. For this final section we have produced a set of ten questions that we believe parents might like to ask themselves. These questions are intended to highlight some of the fundamental themes that emerged from the 40 worries. They are in no particular order.

Do I spend enough time with my child?

We all know that our personal relationships develop over time, partly through sharing experiences and being together. The strength and depth of a relationship between two people depend both on the quality of their interactions and the quantity of time they spend together. The relationship between parent and child, though very special in many ways, is no exception to this general principle.

In the 1980s, a beguiling concept known as 'quality time' emerged. The basic idea was that the *quality* of interaction between parent and child could be traded off to some extent against the *quantity* of time they spent together. In practical terms, it meant that a parent should be able to substitute, say, half an hour of intense and highly structured 'quality time' for hours of just being there. The idea of 'quality time' holds obvious appeal for busy working parents trying to juggle the conflicting demands of parenthood and job. There is something comforting about the thought that parents can forge close and loving relationships with their child without having to spend too much time over it.

The notion of 'quality time' contains a strong grain of truth. The quality of the interactions between two people clearly does have an important bearing on their relationship; that is why, for example, you can remain close friends with someone despite spending little time with them. But, like most simple ideas, it can only be taken so far. There are limits to how far the parent–child relationship can be compressed into short bouts of 'quality time'. Quantity is still important.

The value of 'quantity time' (as opposed to 'quality time') is especially relevant when it comes to communication. Our national survey revealed that many parents are concerned that their children don't tell them what they are really thinking or feeling. Getting an uncommunicative adolescent or teenager to open up is not easy, and trying to force the issue in a short burst of intense 'quality time' may not be the best way to get results. Quite often, it takes patience and a certain minimum *quantity* of time. One simple reason why parents sometimes feel their children don't talk to them is that they are not around long enough for their children to talk to.

Spending time together need not mean spending every minute of that time earnestly trying to engage in 'quality time' activities or worthy discussions; just hanging out together, without trying too hard, can create the relaxed conditions in which communication can flourish. Moreover, many of us would probably do better by spending a bit less time talking and more time listening. Spending more unstructured time together in a relaxed atmosphere can help parents get into the habit of listening.

Just being around should improve your chances of reading your child's moods and picking up clues about what is going on in their lives. This becomes increasingly important as children get older and perhaps less inclined to volunteer information. Interrogating them doesn't always work. Simply being around will also help to strengthen their sense of security and stability, which cannot always be conveyed through words alone.

We are certainly *not* implying that working parents should give up work to stay at home and spend more time with their children, nor that 'quality time' is a bad idea. However, we *are* implying that some busy parents might do better by trading off a bit of quality for a bit of quantity and spending more of their free time with their children. So, if you are cooking, just let your child potter in the kitchen with you, but don't feel you must turn every such occasion into a cookery lesson, or you might be less likely to do it in the first place. If you are going shopping, invite your child to come with you, but don't feel you must turn each expedition into a structured lesson in life skills, or you might be more tempted to leave them at home. If your child needs to go somewhere, take the opportunity to spend some time with them by giving them a lift, but don't feel you must use the journey to question them about their progress in school. Just be there.

The more time you and your child can spend together, the more you will discover about your child and the less you should need to force the pace by questioning them. Which brings us on to communication.

Are we communicating as well as we can?

All parents go through difficult patches in their relationships with their children. As children grow up and assert their independence, disagreements and conflicts are bound to arise. Arguing with parents is a normal part of growing up, as children test the boundaries. Despite the squabbling, things usually work out all right in the long run – provided the lines of communication remain open.

Communication is crucial. If parents and children stop communicating with each other, real problems can start to arise. The children who no longer talk or listen to their parents are the ones who will be at greater risk of getting into trouble or failing to reach their potential. They are also the ones who are more likely to feel unloved and insecure, making them candidates for unhappiness and failure in their future lives. Conversely, many problems are soluble if you keep communicating with each other.

Communication is a two-way process. That may seem like an obvious point, but it is no less true for that, and many people behave as though it were not true. Too often in a relationship, the tendency is to talk rather than listen. Parents are sometimes prone to acting as though communication simply means conveying information and instructions to their child. And then they complain that their child won't tell them anything. But if parents aren't listening, they aren't really communicating.

Listening is an active process that requires the listener to be genuinely interested in what the other person is saying, thinking and doing; just because someone has stopped talking for a few seconds doesn't mean they are listening. If you want your child to tell you what they're really thinking and feeling, you may need gradually to tease the information out of them over a period of time. When you ask questions, try to make them open ones, such as 'What did you do in school today?' Closed questions, such as 'Are you OK?', just invite them to give a yes/no answer.

Remember, too, the power of silence. If you just keep quiet for a while, your child might eventually fill the silence by saying something. But if you immediately fill every silence for them, they may just prefer to keep quiet and let you get on with it.

Of course, listening to your child (or anyone else for that matter) doesn't mean you have to agree with them or do what they say. Children often complain that 'You're not listening to me', when what they really mean is 'You're not doing what I want you to do'. That's OK. You can listen, acknowledge their viewpoint, and then explain why you disagree. The important part is to listen in the first place. By listening, you not only find out what they are thinking, you also demonstrate that you respect them as an individual and are willing to hear them out.

A common pitfall is to take communication for granted when the going is good, and only start worrying about it when problems arise. Some problems might not have arisen in the first place if the communication had been better. The odd remark that might have given you a warning sign was never made and the problem continued to fester. So, keep talking – and listening – even when things are going well.

Am I allowing my child to be a child?

Children are not just miniature and slightly incompetent versions of adults. They are built differently and think differently from us. The process known as childhood has evolved during the course of human evolutionary history, and it has a purpose.

The core purpose of childhood is to enable the developing individual to acquire experiences and develop essential skills in a relatively safe environment, where he or she is looked after by parents and other adults. During those early years, the growing child acquires specific intellectual skills such as speaking, reading and writing one or more languages. But childhood is also a period when the individual develops socially, emotionally and physically.

Nature has equipped children (and young animals of other species) with a special mechanism that helps them to acquire experience and develop skills. That mechanism is known as play behaviour. When children and young animals play they are not just wasting their time, though it may often look like that. They are in fact learning important things about themselves, about other members of their species, and about the world in which they are growing up.

Through play, young children learn how to compete and cooperate with other individuals. They learn how to deal with their own emotions and other people's. They learn about, and extend, their physical capabilities, exploring ideas and exercising their creativity in ways that most adults have long since lost. Children are 'designed' to play, and they benefit enormously from doing so. The benefits of play are mostly delayed, and the dividends may not be realised until adulthood, but they are benefits nonetheless. Depriving children of play can have long-term costs.

We have banged on about the importance of childhood and play because they are under pressure for at least two reasons: excessive anxiety about safety, and excessive concern about measurable (usually academic) achievement. In their eagerness to protect their children from dangers, both real and imaginary, some parents try to insulate them from the real world. And in their eagerness to give children the best possible start in life, some parents and schools push them too early or too hard to perform academically, at the expense of other things.

Parents who become excessively anxious about their children's safety often respond by restricting their freedom and depriving them of opportunities for free play. The social scientist Frank Furedi has referred to this tendency as 'paranoid parenting'. One of its most obvious manifestations has been the trend in recent years for parents to drive their children everywhere rather than letting them walk with their friends. Driving them might reduce their risk of being mugged, run over or abducted, but it also deprives them of opportunities for play, social interaction, independence and physical exercise.

According to one piece of research, almost half of all school-aged British children are not allowed to play with water, more than a third are prevented from climbing trees and more than a quarter are forbidden to play on climbing equipment. Protecting children's safety is obviously essential, but parents and other responsible adults may sometimes need to step back and think more about the costs of such restrictions, in terms of lost opportunities for the child. There is a balance to strike between the desire for total safety and the need to let children have a normal childhood.

Excessive concern about measurable achievement ('pushiness') can also impinge on childhood and play. For a combination of reasons, some parents and schools seem to have become preoccupied with pushing children of younger and younger ages to perform in ways that can be measured, quantified and compared. Testing, assessment and league tables have fuelled this tendency. At their worst, they can distort the priorities of parents and schools by diverting their attention away from other important things such as children's social, emotional and physical development.

We're certainly not suggesting that it is wrong for children to receive a challenging and rigorous academic education, reinforced with regular testing and assessment. Pushing children is not inherently bad: the real issue is *how* they are pushed.

One form of pushing that we do find questionable, however, is the belief that formal education should start at the earliest possible age. According to this view, the true measure of success for a child (or their school) is how young they can be taught, say, to write English or perform maths to a defined standard. The assumption seems to be that the younger they start, the better. However, problems can arise if children are pushed to learn certain things too soon. A child who is not yet ready to read and write may not respond well to formal teaching. They may under-perform and experience failure. Indeed, some children can be turned off education for life.

Other countries do things differently, yet still manage to achieve levels of literacy and numeracy that compare favourably with the UK's. In countries such as Germany, Norway, Sweden, Finland, Denmark and Greece, children start formal schooling later than in the UK – in some cases, not until seven years of age. Nursery schools and kindergartens in these countries rely more on informal learning through play rather than formal tuition. Children are not systematically taught to read and write until they enter school at six or seven, but when they do start learning to read and write, they tend to make faster progress. Evidence like this casts doubt on the belief that the earlier a child is taught to read and write, the better. The best age might not always be the youngest age.

Am I providing a sufficiently stable and loving environment?

In an ideal fantasy world, every child would have two loving parents who are in a loving and stable relationship, a safe and comfortable home in a safe and friendly community, lots of good friends, and freedom from poverty, violence, crime or bereavement. Of course, the reality for many parents and children falls short of this cosy ideal, often for reasons beyond their control. Relationships break down, people get ill or die, they lose their jobs, or they run short of money. In real life, children experience turbulence and disruption. Does this matter?

To put a great deal of research in a very small nutshell, children can be remarkably resilient and weather many storms – if they feel truly loved and secure. For children to thrive and develop into happy, successful people, they need to feel safe, loved and accepted for who they are. However, they don't necessarily have to grow up in a comfortable and predictable environment where nothing bad ever happens. Conversely, a child who feels unloved and insecure will be more vulnerable to the vagaries of everyday life, no matter how affluent and stable their environment.

Of course, the vast majority of parents do love their children and don't need to be told that love is a good thing. However, some parents could perhaps do more to demonstrate their love through their everyday behaviour. One very simple rule of thumb, for example, is to criticise the behaviour, not the child. Children should be told when they do something wrong, and there is no reason why parents should not express genuine annoyance. However, the focus should be on the child's actions, not the child as a person. So, tell your daughter it was wrong for her to shirk her homework, rather than calling her lazy. Tell your son you are cross because he ran across the road, rather than calling him an idiot.

Persistently criticising children as individuals, rather than for their actions, can undermine their confidence and store up problems for the future. For similar reasons, parents should avoid mocking their children or making fun of them. The same applies to making mocking or critical remarks about them to other people such as their friends, siblings or other adults. Such remarks have a dreadful habit of getting back to the child, who will end up feeling doubly wounded, both because they have been criticised by someone they love and because it was done behind their back.

Do I really understand the world my child lives in?

Many parents feel they basically understand and can relate to their children's generation. The fashions and music are different, of course, but not so different that they are completely beyond comprehension, in the way that long hair and mini-skirts were to some middle-aged parents of an earlier generation. It's easy, however, to underestimate the differences that do exist.

In school, our children are under greater and more continuous pressure to perform in tests and public exams. For many, the process starts with National Curriculum tests (SATs) at the age of seven and continues, with little respite, until they leave school after A-levels at 18. And with more than a third of school-leavers now going on to higher education (compared with less than 1 in 10 a few decades ago) the pressure to get good results is no longer confined to the academically-minded minority.

At the same time, children are under enormous pressure from the advertisers, the media and their peers to conform to various stereotypes and to aspire to own various branded products. Young people drink larger amounts of alcohol now than a decade ago, and many of them will be experimenting with drugs. On average, they start having sex younger as well. They are physically bigger than us and more of them are overweight. And, of course, the ubiquitous mobile phone has transformed their ability to remain in continuous communication with their friends, and to be nagged by their parents.

However, despite the impression sometimes fostered by the media, the world has become a better place in at least some respects for our children. On average, they should live slightly longer and healthier lives than us, with less risk of being killed in a vehicle accident or dying prematurely from an illness. Many children will also have more interesting and more varied careers than their parents. Most will be considerably better off in material terms.

Life is not uniformly harder for our children than it was for us, but it is certainly different. The more you can understand the details of their world, the better placed you will be to communicate with them.

Am I practising what I preach?

The point here is a simple one. Children are heavily influenced – for better or for worse – by how their parents behave. They watch, they listen and they learn. The need for parents to set a good example has been a recurring theme throughout the book.

So, if parents want their children to eat a healthy and balanced diet, to take regular exercise, be safe pedestrians, not smoke, be streetwise, avoid violence, get sufficient sleep and be honest, they should try to avoid doing the opposite themselves. Actions speak louder than words.

Remember, too, that parents are not the only influence. If you regularly leave your child to be looked after by someone else, you might want to think about the examples they are setting as well. For instance, your efforts to encourage healthy eating habits might be undermined if your child's carer routinely grazes on junk food.

By setting a good example you will of course be helping yourself as well as your children. Many adults find that becoming a parent is a good discipline for them. Having children to think about can help us to recognise our own shortcomings and, perhaps, do something about them.

Am I laying the foundations for good health?

Compared with previous generations, people in the UK generally live longer, healthier lives nowadays. But there is certainly no reason to be complacent as far as our children's health is concerned. In certain respects, the outlook is worrying.

The UK, along with many other wealthy nations, is currently experiencing an epidemic of a life-threatening condition. It's called obesity. More than 1 in 5 school-aged children are overweight and at least 1 in 10 are obese. Obese children face a significantly greater risk of diabetes, heart disease and premature death. Obesity also has psychological consequences. In a society that places inordinate value on being thin, fat people are made to feel unattractive and inferior. Fat, unfit children are more likely to have fewer friends and to suffer from lower self-esteem, as well as living shorter lives.

The main reasons for all this obesity are not hard to identify. British children are consuming more calories and taking less physical exercise. They are spending more of their time sitting in front of the TV or in cars, and less time out playing with friends or walking to school. They are eating more high-calorie snacks, junk food and ready meals, drinking more sugary colas and doing less sport. No wonder they're putting on weight.

We all want our children to be successful in life. But success means more than just passing exams or getting a well-paid job. If we truly want our children to live long, happy and healthy lives, we should be doing our best to encourage them to eat a healthy, balanced diet, take regular exercise and avoid smoking. You might think you are being kind by giving them a junk food treat or letting them watch TV, but in the long run you could be doing them a disservice.

It may have become a Victorian cliché, but there is still much good sense in the ancient Roman ideal of 'a sound mind in a sound body'.

Am I helping my child to develop a lifelong love of learning?

We live in a knowledge economy. The days of leaving school or university, then settling down to do the same job until retirement, have largely gone. It has become the norm for people to have two or more careers during the course of a working lifetime, and to continue learning and developing new skills throughout adulthood.

The notion that learning stops the day you leave school is long since dead. As the pace of change in society quickens, children will face an even greater need to continue learning, changing and developing throughout their adult lives. It follows that one of the most valuable things any parent can impart to their children is a lifelong love of learning. If you can encourage your children to take pleasure from learning and developing as individuals, they will be far better placed to live happy, healthy and successful lives. If nothing else, you will probably reduce their chances of being unemployed and help to boost their lifetime earnings.

In view of its obvious desirability, developing a lifelong love of learning should be one of the prime objectives of education. However, children face an array of pressures that almost seem designed to put them off. The regime of testing, assessment, public exams and league tables leaves some children feeling impatient to leave school – and learning – behind them as soon as possible. Anxious parents can add to the problem by pushing their children to perform even when they are not ready to.

Psychology has an important lesson to offer here. People can be motivated to do something, such as studying, because they receive some form of external reward such as money or praise. Or they can be motivated to do something for its own sake, because they enjoy it or find it intrinsically satisfying. Psychological experiments have shown that *intrinsic* motivation (doing something for its own sake) is in many respects more robust and more enduring than *extrinsic* motivation (doing something for an external reward).

The problem with relying too much on extrinsic motivation is that if the external reward is removed, the motivation tends to disappear as well. In the context of education, this means that children who have been trained to jump the hurdles of tests and exams may become too reliant on extrinsic motivation. Take away those hurdles and they are no longer motivated to learn or perform. They have not acquired an intrinsic motivation to learn for its own sake.

As a parent, you have only limited control over what happens to your children once they are in the education system. But you can still do a lot to help them at home. The key here is to kindle a sense of pleasure and fun in the learning process. If you can leave your children feeling there is more to learning than just passing exams, and that learning is both worthwhile and enjoyable in its own right, then you will have done them a favour that will stand them in good stead for the rest of their lives.

Are my beliefs about boys and girls correct?

One of the enduring myths of parenthood is that girls are generally more vulnerable than boys, and that parents should worry more about the safety of their daughters than of their sons. The truth is rather different. Looking back over the 40 top worries, you can see that boys actually fare worse on average than girls on many different counts.

Among other things, boys are significantly *more* likely than girls to:

- die (at every age throughout their lifespan)
- be knocked over by a vehicle
- be murdered
- commit suicide
- develop some form of mental health problem
- have a serious or fatal accident in the home
- be the victim of crime
- commit crime
- be injured or physically assaulted during a robbery
- end up on a child protection register
- become a sexual abuser of children
- be physically bullied
- bully others
- be excluded from school
- have problems learning to read and write
- do badly at GCSEs
- develop behavioural problems
- find it hard to communicate with their parents
- take drugs
- have an unhealthy diet
- consume excessive amounts of caffeine
- consume excessive amounts of alcohol
- be diagnosed with ADHD
- take unnecessary risks
- do little or no housework

Girls do come off worse in a few areas, but compared to boys the list is short. Girls are more likely than boys to:

- start smoking during adolescence
- be sexually abused
- deliberately harm themselves (short of committing suicide)
- develop a serious eating disorder

- be physically inactive
- be verbally bullied

Why these differences arise is beyond the scope of this book, and often far from clear. What is clear, however, is that parents have no cause to feel more confident about the safety or well-being of a child just because he is a boy.

Am I enjoying being a parent?

Few parents seriously regret having children. That said, being a parent isn't always easy and it certainly isn't always fun. Parenthood can be something of a rollercoaster ride, with moments of intense joy punctuated by periods of anxiety, stress, fatigue or irritation. The overall effect may be one of satisfaction and fulfilment, but there will nonetheless be days (or weeks) when it can all seem rather trying.

Moreover, life for parents in the UK has in some respects become harder over the past few decades, with the decline of the extended family. Fewer parents now have ready access to the practical and emotional support that would once have come from grandparents, siblings, cousins or other relatives living close by. The burden has increasingly fallen on the parents alone. On top of that, a far higher proportion of families now comprise either a lone parent or two working parents.

And parents do pay a price. For example, research has found that most married couples' feelings of satisfaction with their marriage decline significantly following the arrival of children. Having kids can put a strain on the relationship.

This may be one of the reasons why a growing number of people in the UK and other wealthy nations are choosing to have no children at all, while those who do have children are starting later and having fewer of them.

The average British family now has 1.8 children. Less than 1 in 20 couples have three or more children, while more than a quarter of married or cohabiting couples are childless. It is estimated that 1 in 4 women born in the early 1970s will be childless in their mid-40s.

One possibly comforting thought for anxious parents is that their behaviour is not the only influence in a child's life. The individual child's temperament, the friends they make, the school they attend, the genes they inherit, the neighbourhood in which the family lives, and many other factors besides will affect how a child turns out. For example, a child's social interactions with other children will have an important impact on his or her development. Parents are a crucial influence, but they are not the only one. So, every tiny detail of what you do with your children will not always have a big and irreversible impact on them. You can have your occasional bad days without necessarily doing them irreparable harm.

Another possibly comforting thought is the philosophical distinction between pleasure and happiness. Pleasure is about how you feel in the here-and-now. Happiness depends more on how you view your life as whole: it is about satisfaction and fulfilment as well as immediate pleasure. Harassed and exhausted parents may feel stressed or down in the dumps because their children are giving them a hard time, but that need not mean they are unhappy in the more profound sense, or that they regret becoming parents. Some bad days do not make a bad life.

Being a parent is profoundly satisfying; it can be fun (at least some of the time) and it is the most important thing that most of us will ever do in our lives. The added incentive for enjoying parenthood more is that it will make you an even better parent.

Final Thoughts

In Part 2 we looked at the 40 top worries of Britain's parents, and assessed each of them in terms of their Chances, Consequences and Control – in other words, the likelihood of that particular worry coming true, the worst impact it could have if it did happen, and the ability of parents to do something reasonable to reduce or eliminate the risk.

You might not agree with how we rated every worry on these three dimensions. But we hope you will agree that, taken together, they highlight three simple but important points.

1. You might not always worry about the right things.

Parents rarely have access to enough information to make considered judgements about the seriousness of various risks. We all have to rely mainly on our experience, impressions and instinct. Most of the time we probably get it about right, but sometimes we end up worrying too much about things that are actually very unlikely to happen, or being complacent about things that in fact pose a significant risk. For example, our survey found that murderous strangers are a bigger cause of concern to parents than accidents in the home. The evidence suggests that it should be the other way round. In fact, domestic accidents kill and injure far more children every year than violent attackers.

2. Many of the biggest risks lie close to home.

All of us have a psychological tendency to worry more about exotic or unusual risks and to pay less attention to familiar, everyday hazards, especially those we believe we can control. That is one reason why shark attacks and plane crashes get far more attention from the media than the daily carnage on our roads. Parents, like everyone else, are prone to this inherent bias.

The evidence often paints a different picture. Many of the real dangers to children come from familiar, everyday sources: children are much more likely to be physically abused or murdered by a parent or close relative than by a stranger, for example, and they are much more likely to die in an accident at home than on a school trip. When it comes to risk, we should all try to avoid allowing familiarity to breed contempt.

3. There's a lot you can do to reduce or eliminate risks.

Our focus group research revealed a tendency for parents to feel that there is little they can do about many of the problems they see facing their children. Often, they look to the school or the government for a solution. However, we found ourselves reaching a different conclusion after we had rated each of the 40 top worries for Control (defined as the extent to which a parent could reasonably do something to protect their child without making matters worse).

To our surprise, nearly every single worry came out as Medium or High on Control. When we had stopped and thought about them, almost none of the top 40 worries seemed to us to warrant a Low rating (signifying that there is little or nothing a parent could reasonably do). For example, our research suggested that parents can actually do a fair bit to reduce the risks of their children being knocked over, becoming victims of crime, succumbing to peer pressure, lacking confidence, eating badly or having problems in school. And in some areas, such as watching too much TV, eating too much junk food or having a domestic accident, parents have quite a lot of control, provided they exercise it.

PART 3

About our Research

This section explains how we conducted our national survey to identify parents' top 40 worries. It also looks at some of the other things our survey revealed.

How was our survey conducted?

The topics covered in this book were not chosen by us on the basis of what *we* thought parents ought to know. Instead, they were determined by what parents told us they wanted to know.

We started with some exploratory research to form an idea of what parents wanted and needed from a parenting book, and to identify the main areas where they had concerns or worries. To do this, we carried out a nine-month programme of two-hour focus group meetings involving a total of more than 250 parents.

Phase two of our research was quantitative. In late 2002, we commissioned MORI to conduct the most comprehensive national survey ever carried out to establish what Britain's parents are most concerned about. At the end of 2002 and in early 2003, in homes across Great Britain, MORI held face-to-face interviews with a nationally representative sample of 1038 parents of children aged from four to 14 years. The interviews were all conducted on a one-to-one basis, which means that the interviewees were not subjected to conscious or unconscious pressure from partners, children or other people to respond in particular ways. (Social pressure can be a significant source of bias when people are interviewed in groups.) The sample included mothers and fathers, and the interviews took place in their homes in England, Scotland and Wales. A further sample of 144 parents was interviewed in Northern Ireland to allow regional comparisons.

The results revealed no clear, consistent differences between parents living in urban and rural areas, or between parents living in England, Scotland, Wales and Northern Ireland. This was reassuring, since it means that the results have broad relevance for British parents in general, and not just for specific regions. The figures reported here for the survey are drawn from the sample of 1038 parents in Great Britain. The findings from Northern Ireland were analysed separately and were found to be broadly comparable with those for the rest of the UK.

Each parent was presented with a list of 115 possible worries to choose from. The list was compiled by us on the basis of our preliminary research with the focus groups, and was intended to cover the widest range of possible issues. The worries were arranged under nine main subject headings: physical development, nutrition and environment, risks and accidents, social and emotional issues, learning, school, behaviour, sleep, and the family.

The 115 potential worries were presented to each parent on a series of cards. Each card related to one of the nine main headings, and listed up to 12 worries under that heading. The parent could choose as many, or as few, of the worries as they wished, so there was no pressure to pick any issues they were not actually concerned about.

What did parents tell us about their worries?

The data from all these interviews allowed us to rank-order the 115 worries according to how many parents chose them. The rank order therefore reflects the number of parents who expressed some concern about each issue; it says nothing about the strength or intensity of individual parents' concerns about particular issues.

We tackled the top 40 of these concerns in this book. They appear in Part 2 in the rank order determined by the survey results. The nation's number one worry (my child might be knocked over by a vehicle) was chosen by 465 out of the 1038 parents, or getting on for half the sample. The *least* common worry (my child masturbates) was picked by only eight parents, which was less than 1 per cent of the sample. Worry number 40, the least common worry discussed in this book, was chosen by 139 parents (13 per cent).

We recognise that the top 40 worries as chosen by parents are probably not the same 40 worries that experts would have chosen on the basis of, say, the severity of outcome. Moreover, if children had been asked to pick *their* top 40 worries, we would probably have ended up with something different again. But this is a book for parents.

What were parents *not* worried about?

The results of our national survey showed that some subject headings – notably risks and accidents, and nutrition – featured more prominently than others.

One slight surprise for us was the relatively small number of worries among the top 40 that were about education and schooling. Out of the 115 possible choices, 29 worries related to learning, education or school, but only seven of these featured in the final top 40. Among the worries that did *not* appear in British parents' top 40 were:

My child ...

- Is suffering because his/her lessons are disrupted by other students (41st)
- Is under too much pressure from testing and exams (54th)
- Is not being pushed hard enough in school / is in a school that is not academic enough (55th)
- Has a poor teacher/teacher they don't get on with (58th)
- Has too much homework (65th)
- Dislikes school and is reluctant to go (66th)
- Is at a poor school (89th)
- Is being pushed too hard in school / is in a school that is too academic (108th)

We expected more of the top 40 worries to be about education, largely because this topic seems to feature so prominently in the media, political debate and the everyday conversations of parents. We can only speculate as to why parents are less worried about this than we might have assumed.

Another surprise was that relatively few parents expressed concern that their child might be smoking, taking drugs or abusing alcohol. 'My child is, or might be, smoking' came 86th overall, having been selected by only 7 per cent of parents. 'My child is, or might be, taking drugs' came 97th, and 'my child is, or might be, drinking alcohol' came 98th, with only 5 per cent of parents choosing either. The explanation for these low rankings might lie partly with the age range of the children concerned (4-14 years). Worries about drugs, alcohol and smoking might have been much more prominent among the parents of, say, 14 to 18-year-olds.

Something else we would not have predicted was the relative lack of concern expressed about family issues such as working parents and divorce. A worry that children might be suffering because their parents were, or would be, divorced or separated was chosen by only 8 per cent of parents and came 81st in the overall ranking. Bear in mind that 2 out of 5 marriages end in divorce and more than 1 in 4 children in the UK will experience parental divorce by the age of 16 (see Divorce, p. 113). Even fewer parents were worried about the possible consequences of one or both parents working. 'My child will suffer because his/her mother works' came 94th, and 'my child will suffer because his/her parents both work' came 95th, with each selected by only 6 per cent of parents.

Our advisory panel

Dr Howard Baderman OBE qualified in medicine at University College Hospital, London, where he later became the first Accident & Emergency consultant in the UK. He was the first Chairman, and is now a vice president, of the Child Accident Prevention Trust (CAPT). He was the consultant adviser in Accident & Emergency Medicine to the Chief Medical Officer at the Department of Health for nine years, until he retired from clinical work in 2000. As Chair of an inner London Family Proceedings Court from 1985–2001, he was closely involved with the protection of children at risk. He continues to work for the Department of Health on advisory teams assisting failing hospitals.

Jacquie Coulby is head teacher of a primary school in Bath, where she lives with her husband and two teenage children, and has many years' experience in education. She has been the head teacher of two London schools, taught on a children's psychiatric ward, worked in the behaviour support team for schools in Tower Hamlets, and has taught nursery, primary and secondary school children in both mainstream and special schools. She has written about positive behaviour management and lectures on this subject to student teachers.

Professor Philip Graham is Emeritus Professor of Child Psychiatry at the Institute of Child Health, University of London. He held the Chair of Child Psychiatry from 1975 to 1994 and was Dean of the Institute of Child Health, London from 1985 to1990. He was President of the European Society for Child and Adolescent Psychiatry from 1987 to 1991. From 1994 to 2000 he was Chairman of the National Children's Bureau and from 2001 to 2003 Chairman of the Association of Child Psychology and Psychiatry. He has written widely on emotional and behaviour problems of childhood and adolescence, both in academic journals and for the general public. His many publications include the textbook *Child Psychiatry: a developmental approach*.

Dr Harvey Marcovitch, a consultant paediatrician, is the press and public relations adviser to the Royal College of Paediatrics and Child Health, editor of *Black's Medical Dictionary*, syndication editor for BMJ Journals and a member of the General Medical Council's professional conduct committee. He was until recently editor of the journal *Archives of Disease in Childhood*. He has had a long career as a medical journalist, both writing for lay and medical journals and writing and producing video teaching material for doctors. He is medical adviser to the BBC TV series *Holby City*. He has previously held academic posts at London and Bristol Universities and Harvard Medical School.

Dr Harriet Martin is Head of Educational Psychology and Learning Support for a county council. After reading Psychology & Philosophy at Oxford University, she trained as a teacher at Sussex University and taught for a few years. She then took a PhD in developmental psychology at Cambridge University and did postdoctoral research at Stanford University, before a career break to have three children. She qualified as an educational psychologist at the Institute of Education, University of London, and has worked for several years as a practising educational psychologist. She is co-author of *Behaviour and Social Organisation*.

Selected references

We have listed here a representative sample of the sources from which we obtained the information in this book. This is by no means a full list.

Worry 1:
Might be knocked over by a vehicle

Child Accident Prevention Trust, *Child Pedestrians* (London, CAPT, 2002)

Child Accident Prevention Trust, *Child Road Accidents,* (London, CAPT, 2002)

Child Accident Prevention Trust, *Cycle Safety* (London, CAPT, 2002)

Department for Transport, *Child Casualties in Road Accidents: Great Britain 1998* (London, DfT, 1999)

Department for Transport, *Casualties: by age band, road user, type and severity, 2001* (London, DfT, 2001)

Department for Transport, *Travel to School in GB* (London, DfT, 2003)

Department for Transport, *Transport Statistics Bulletin. Road Casualties in Great Britain. Main Results: 2002* (London, DfT, 2003)

Worry 2:
Might be abducted or murdered

Creighton S.J., *Child Protection Statistics 5: Child Deaths* (London, NSPCC, 2002)

NSPCC, *Protecting Babies and Toddlers* (London, NSPCC, 2003)

NSPCC, *Child Killings in England and Wales* (London, NSPCC, 2003)

Worry 3:
Eats too much sugar and sweet foods

British Nutrition Foundation: www.nutrition.org.uk

Butchko, H. et al., 'Aspartame: review of safety', *Regul. Toxicol. Pharmacol.*, 35, S1 (2002)

Campbell, K., et al., *Interventions for preventing obesity in children* (Cochrane Review). In: *The Cochrane Library, Issue I* (Oxford, Update Software, 2002)

Food Commission: www.foodcomm.org.uk

Food Standards Agency: www.foodstandards.gov.uk

Gregory, J. et al., *National Diet and Nutrition Survey: young people aged 4 to 18 years* (London, Stationery Office, 2000)

Laing, P., 'Childhood obesity', *Paediatr. Nurs.,* 14, 14 (2002)

Wolraich, M. et al., 'Effect of sugar on behavior or cognition in children', *JAMA*, 274, 1617 (1996)

Worry 4:
Spends too much time watching TV or playing computer games

Coon, K.A. & Tucker, K.L., 'Television and children's consumption patterns', *Minerva Pediatr., 54,* 423 (2002)

Eisenmann, J.C. et al., 'Physical activity, TV viewing, and weight in US youth', *Obes. Res.,* 10, 379 (2002)

Gunter, B., *The effects of video games on children* (Sheffield, Academic Press, 1998)

Johnson, J.G. et al., 'Television viewing and aggressive behaviour during adolescence and adulthood', *Science,* 295, 2468 (2002)

Lu, L. & Argyle, M., 'TV watching, soap operas and happiness', *Gaoxiong Yi Xue Za Zhi, 9,* 501 (1993)

Towler, R. *The Public's View 2001* (ITC/BSC, 2001)

Worry 5:
Is growing up too fast

Graber, J. et al. 'The antecedents of menarcheal age', *Child Dev., 66,* 346 (1995)

Herman-Giddens, M. et al., 'Secondary sexual characteristics and menses in young girls seen in office practice', *Pediatrics, 99,* 505 (1997)

Kanazawa, S., 'Why father absence might precipitate early menarche', *Evol. Hum. Behav., 22,* 329 (2001)

Neisser, U. (ed.), *The Rising Curve* (American Psychological Association, 1998)

Wellings, K. et al., 'Sexual behaviour in Britain', *Lancet, 358,* 1843 (2001)

Wellings, K. et al., *Sexual Behaviour in Britain* (London, Penguin, 1994)

Whincup, P.H. et al., 'Age of menarche in contemporary British teenagers', *BMJ, 322,* 1095 (2001)

Worry 6:
Might be the victim of crime

Crimestoppers: www.crimestoppers-uk.org

Smith, J. *The Nature of Personal Robbery* (London, Home Office, 2003)

Victim Support, *Crime Against 12- to 16-year-olds* (London, Victim Support, 2003)

Worry 7:
Eats too much junk food or convenience food

British Nutrition Foundation: www.nutrition.org.uk

Bundred, P. et al., 'Prevalence of overweight and obese children between 1989 and 1998', *BMJ, 322,* 1 (2001)

Department of Health, *Health survey for England 2001* (London, Stationery Office, 2003)

Food Commission: www.foodcomm.org.uk

Food and Drink Federation: www.fdf.org.uk

French, S. et al., 'Fast food restaurant use among adolescents', *Int. J. Obesity, 25,* 1823 (2001)

Gregory, J. et al., *National Diet and Nutrition Survey: young people aged 4 to 18 years.* (London, Stationery Office, 2000)

Mintel, *British Lifestyles 2003* (Mintel, 2003)

Worry 8:
Has friends who are or could be a bad influence

Coggans, N. & Watson, J., 'Drug Education', *Drugs-Educ. Prevent. Policy, 2,* 211 (1995)

Jang, S. 'Age-varying effects of family, school, and peers on delinquency', *Criminology, 37,* 643 (1999)

Jessor, R. & Jessor, S., *Problem Behaviour and Psychosocial Development* (NY, Academic Press, 1977)

Pearson, M. & Michell, L., 'Smoke rings', *Drugs-Educ. Prevent. Policy, 7,* 21 (2000)

Simons-Morton, B. et al., 'Peer and parent influences on smoking and drinking among early adolescents', *Health Educ. Behav., 28,* 95 (2001)

Wang, M.Q. et al., 'Smoking acquisition', *Psychol. Rep., 86,* 1241 (2000)

Worry 9:
Might get a serious illness

Armstrong, J. et al., 'Breastfeeding and lowering the risk of childhood obesity', *Lancet, 359,* 2003 (2002)

Kay, T. et al., 'The effect of diet on risk of cancer', *Lancet, 360,* 861 (2002)

Lissauer, T. & Clayden, G., *Illustrated Textbook of Paediatrics* (London, Mosby, 2002)

Meltzer, H. et al., *Mental Health of Children and Adolescents in Great Britain* (London, Stationery Office, 2000)

National Statistics, *Social Focus in Brief: Children* (London, ONS, 2002)

National Statistics, *Child Health Statistics* (London, ONS, 2000)

Rudolf, M. & Levene, M., *Paediatrics and Child Health* (Oxford, Blackwell Science, 1999)

World Health Organisation: www.whi.int/en/

Worry 10:
Might be the victim of physical violence

Cawson, P. et al., *Child Maltreatment in the United Kingdom* (London, NSPCC, 2000)

Creighton, S., *Physical Abuse* (London, NSPCC, 2002)

Creighton S.J., *Child Abuse Trends in England and Wales 1988–1990* (London, NSPCC, 1992)

Department of Health, *Referrals, Assessments and Children and Young People on Child Protection Registers Year ending 31 March 2002* (London, DoH, 2002)

Egeland, B., 'A history of abuse is a major risk factor for abusing the next generation'. In: *Current controversies on Family Violence* (ed. by R. Gelles & D. Loseke) (London, Sage, 1993)

Kidscape, *Long-term Effects of Bullying* (Kidscape, 1999)

Victim Support, *Crime against 12- to 16-year-olds* (London, Victim Support, 2003)

Worry 11:
Might be abused by an adult

Cawson, P. et al., *Child Maltreatment in the United Kingdom* (London, NSPCC, 2000)

Creighton, S., *Child Protection Statistics. 2. Child Protection in the Family* (London, NSPCC, 2001)

Department of Health, *Children and Young People on Child Protection Registers* (London, DoH, 1999)

Erooga, M., *Adult Sex Offenders* (London, NSPCC, 2002)

NSPCC Inform: Summary of Child Protection Register Statistics 2002. www.nspcc.org.uk/inform/statistics/Protect2001.asp

NSPCC, *Protecting Children from Sexual Abuse in the Community* (London, NSPCC)

NSPCC, *Protecting Children from Sexual Abuse in the Family* (London, NSPCC)

Worry 12:
Will only eat a narrow range of food/has food fads

Drewnowski, A., *Taste, Genetics and Food choices*. www.danoneinstitute.org/danone_institutes_initiatives/pdf/02_drewnowski.pdf

Eating Disorders Association: www.edauk.com

Fox, C. & Joughin, C., *Eating Problems in Children* (Royal College of Psychiatrists, 2002)

Haliborange, *Report of the Haliborange Food Fight Survey* (Haliborange, 2000)

Worry 13:
Has difficulty concentrating/paying attention

Cosgrove, P.V.F., Attention Deficit Hyperactivity Disorder, A UK Review (1997). www.btinternet.com/~black.ice/addnet/addnetmain.html

Gottlieb, S. '1.6 million elementary school children have ADHD', *BMJ, 324*, 1296 (2002)

Kewley, G., 'Attention deficit hyperactivity disorder is underdiagnosed and undertreated in Britain', *BMJ, 316*, 1594 (1998)

Martin, P., *Counting Sheep* (London, HarperCollins, 2003)

Taylor, E. et al., *The Epidemiology of Childhood Hyperactivity* (London, Oxford University Press, 1991)

Worry 14:
Will not be successful in adult life if he/she does not do well at school

Department for Education & Skills, *Youth Cohort Study: The Activities and Experiences of 16 Year Olds* (London, DfES, 2003)

Department for Education & Skills, *Youth Cohort Study: The Activities and Experiences of 18 Year Olds* (London, DfES, 2003)

Goleman, D., *Emotional intelligence* (NY, Bantam Books, 1995)

McIntosh, S., *Further Analysis of the Returns to Academic and Vocational Qualifications* (Centre for Economic Performance, London School of Economics, 2002)

Salgado, J.F., 'The five factor model of personality and job performance in the European Community', *J. Appl. Psychol., 82*, 30 (1997)

Veenhoven, R., *Happiness in Nations* (Erasmus University, Rotterdam, Netherlands, 1992).

Worry 15:
Does not get enough sleep

Chervin, R. et al., 'Symptoms of sleep disorders, inattention, and hyperactivity in children', *Sleep, 20*, 1185 (1997).

Dahl, R. & Lewin, D., 'Pathways to adolescent health', *J. Adolesc. Health, 31*, 175 (2002)

Glaze, D., 'Toward a practical definition of pediatric insomnia', *Curr. Ther. Res., 63*, B4 (2002)

Liu, X. et al., 'Prevalence and correlates of sleep problems in Chinese schoolchildren', *Sleep, 23*, 1053 (2000)

Martin, P., *Counting Sheep* (London, HarperCollins, 2003)

Mindell, J. et. al., 'Developmental features of sleep', *Child Adolesc. Psychiatr. Clin. N. Am., 8*, 695 (1999)

Pilcher, J. et al., 'Sleep quality versus sleep quantity', *J. Psychosom. Res., 42*, 583 (1997)

Rosen, C. et al., 'Pharmacotherapy for pediatric sleep disturbances', *Curr. Ther. Res., 63*, B53 (2002)

Worry 16:
Doesn't tell me what he/she is really thinking or feeling

Anderson, M. et al., *Relatively Speaking* (London, BT Future Talk, 2000)

Aldridge, M. & Wood, J., 'Talking about feelings', *Child Abuse Negl., 21*, 1221 (1997)

Catan, L. et al., *Getting Through* (London, BT Forum, 1996)

National Family and Parenting Institute, *Teenagers' Attitudes to Parenting* (London, NFPI, 2000)

Smith, P. & Turner, R., *Listening to the Nation* (London, BT Forum, 1997)

Sroufe, L., *Emotional Development* (Cambridge, Cambridge University Press, 1997)

Worry 17:
Won't go to bed

Adams, L. & Rickert, V., 'Reducing bedtime tantrums', *Pediatrics, 84*, 756 (1989)

Blader, J. et al., 'Sleep problems of elementary school children', *Arch. Pediatr. Adolesc. Med., 151*, 473 (1997)

Owens, J. et al., 'Television-viewing habits and sleep disturbance in school children', *Pediatrics, 104*, (1999)

Pollak, C. & Bright, D., 'Caffeine consumption and weekly sleep patterns in US seventh-, eighth-, and ninth-graders', *Pediatrics, 111*, 42 (2003)

Ramchandani, P. et al., 'A systematic review of treatments for settling problems and night waking in young children', *BMJ, 320,* 209 (2000)

Worry 18:
Is at risk if he/she goes on a school trip

Department for Education and Skills, *Health and Safety of Pupils on Educational Visits* (DfES, 1998)

Royal Society for the Prevention of Accidents, *Guide to Health and Safety at School. Out and About – School Trips* (RoSPA, 1998, 2001)

Royal Society for the Prevention of Accidents, *The School Minibus* (RoSPA, 1998)

Teacher Support Network, *School Trips.* http://www.teacherline.org.uk/index.cfm?p=1507

Worry 19:
Is reckless and not sufficiently aware of dangers

Child Accident Prevention Trust, *Child Accident Facts* (CAPT, 2002)

Child Accident Prevention Trust, *Children and Accidents* (CAPT, 2002)

Department for Transport, *Children's Knowledge of Danger, Attentional Skills and Child/Parent Communication* (London, DfT, 1999)

DiLillo, D. et al., 'Predictors of children's risk appraisals', *J. Appl. Dev. Psychol., 19,* 415 (1998)

Millstein, S. & Halpern-Felsher, B., 'Perceptions of risk and vulnerability', *J. Adolesc. Health, 31S,* 10 (2002)

Zuckerman, M., 'Sensation seeking and risk taking'. In: *Emotions in Personality and Psychopathology* (ed. by C. Izard) (NY, Plenum, 1979)

Worry 20:
Has tantrums

Leung, A. & Fagan, J., 'Temper tantrums,' *Am. Fam. Pract., 44,* 559 (1991)

National Family and Parenting Institute, *Over the Top. Behaviour in the Under Tens* (London, NFPI)

Needlman, R. et al., 'Psychosocial correlates of severe temper tantrums', *J. Dev. Behav. Pediatr., 12,* 77 (1991)

Stevenson, J. & Goodman, R., 'Association between behaviour at age 3 years and adult criminality', *Br. J. Psychiatry, 179,* 197 (2001)

Worry 21:
Won't get up, get dressed and get ready in the mornings

Blader, J. et al., 'Sleep problems of elementary school children', *Arch. Pediatr. Adolesc. Med., 151,* 473 (1997)

Epstein, R. et al., 'Starting times of school', *Sleep, 21,* 250 (1998)

Fukuda, K. & Ishihara, K., 'Age-related changes of sleeping pattern during adolescence', *Psychiatry Clin. Neurosci, 55,* 231 (2001)

Giannotti, F. et al., 'Circadian preference, sleep and daytime behaviour in adolescence', *J. Sleep. Res., 11,* 191 (2002)

Rosenthal, N. et al., 'Seasonal affective disorder in children and adolescents', *Am. J. Psychiatry, 143,* 356 (1986)

Szymczak, J. et al., 'Annual and weekly changes in the sleep-wake rhythm of school children', *Sleep, 16,* 433 (1993)

Worry 22:
Is shy/lacks confidence

Bogels, S. et al., 'Familial correlates of social anxiety in children and adolescents', *Behav. Res. Ther., 39,* 273 (2001)

Crozier, R., 'Shyness as anxious self-preoccupation', *Psychol. Rep., 44,* 959 (1979)

Feinstein, L., *The Relative Economic Importance of Academic, Psychological and Behavioural Attributes Developed in Childhood* (London, Centre for Economic Performance, 2000)

Henderson, L. & Zimbardo, P., 'Shyness'. In: *Encyclopaedia of Mental Health.* (San Diego, Academic Press, 1998)

Schneier, F. et al., 'The social anxiety spectrum', *Psychiatr. Clin. N. Am., 25,* 757 (2002)

Tremblay, M. et al., 'The relationship between physical activity, self-esteem, and academic achievement in 12-year-old children', *Pediatr. Exercise Sci, 12,* 312 (2000)

Worry 23:
Squabbles with/is too jealous of his/her siblings

Bateson, P. & Martin, P. *Design for a Life* (London, Vintage, 2000)

Dunn, J. & Plomin, R., *Separate Lives* (NY, Basic Books, 1990)

Goodwin, M. and Roscoe, B., 'Sibling violence and agonistic interactions among middle adolescents', *Adolescence, 25,* 451 (1990)

Green, A., 'Child abuse by siblings', *Child Abuse Negl.*, 8, 311 (1984)

Molgaard, V. *Sibling Rivalry* (Iowa State University, 1998)

Quittner, A. & Opipari, L., 'Differential treatment of siblings', *Child Dev.*, 65, 800 (1994)

Walker, A. et al., *Living in Britain* (London, HMSO, 2002)

Worry 24:
Won't listen to me/is disobedient

American Academy of Pediatrics, 'Guidance for effective discipline', *Pediatrics, 101,* 723 (1998)

Barber, B., 'Cultural, family, and personal contexts of parent–adolescent conflicts', *J. Marr. Fam., 56,* 375 (1994)

Baumrind, D., 'Parental disciplinary patterns and social competence in children', *Youth Soc., 9,* 239 (1978)

Rice, F., *Human Development* (Upper Saddle River, NJ, Prentice Hall, 2001)

Straus, M.A., 'Spanking and the making of a violent society', *Pediatrics, 98,* 837 (1996)

Worry 25:
Doesn't eat enough

Fairburn, C. & Harrison, P., 'Eating disorders', *Lancet, 361,* 407 (2003)

Hill, A. and Silver, E., 'Fat, friendless and unhealthy', *Int. J. Obes., 19,* 423 (1998)

Patton, G. et al., 'Onset of adolescent eating disorders', *BMJ, 318,* 765 (1999)

Ricciardelli, L. & McCabe, M., 'Children's body image concerns and eating disturbance', *Clin. Psychol. Rev., 21,* 325 (2001)

Smolak, L. et al., 'Parental input and weight concerns among elementary school children', *Int. J. Eat. Disord., 25,* 263 (1999)

Turnbull, S. et al., 'The demand for eating disorder care', *Br. J. Psychiatry, 169,* 705 (1996)

Worry 26:
Isn't reading or writing as well as he/she should

Beard, R., *National Literacy Strategy* (Suffolk, DfEE, 2000)

Brooks, G., 'Trends in standards of literacy in the United Kingdom, 1948–1996', *Topic, 19,* 1 (1998)

Department for Education and Employment, *The National Literacy Strategy* (London, DfEE, 1998)

Department for Education and Skills *Learning to Read and Write at Home and at School:* www.dfes.gov.uk/ltraw/

National Literacy Trust, *Parental Involvement and Literacy Achievement* (London, National Literacy Trust, 2001)

National Literacy Trust, *Statistics* www.literacytrust.org.uk

Peer, L., *Research Reviews.* British Dyslexia Association: www.bda-dyslexia.org.uk/main/research/index.asp

Twist, L. et al., *Reading All Over the World* (Slough, NFER, 2003)

Worry 27:
Is bored or under-stimulated at school

Blatchford, P. et al., 'A study of class size effects in English school reception year classes', *Br. Educ. Res. J., 28,* 169 (2002)

Boaler, J. et al., 'Students' experiences of ability grouping', *Br. Educ. Res. J., 26,* 631 (2000)

Department for Education and Skills: www.dfes.gov.uk

Department for Education and Skills, *Pupil Characteristics and Class Sizes in Maintained Schools in England* (London, DfES, 2003)

Gamoran, A., *Standards, Inequality and Ability Grouping in Schools CES, 25,* (2002)

National Association for Gifted Children: www.nagcbritain.org.uk

Worry 28:
Is being bullied

Bullying Online: www.bullying.co.uk

Creighton, S.J., *Child Protection in the Community* (London, NSPCC, 2001)

Kidscape, *Long-term Effects of Bullying* (Kidscape, 1999)

Kidscape, *Preventing Bullying!* (Kidscape, 2001)

Oliver, C. & Candappa, M., *Tackling Bullying* (London, DfES, 2003)

Worry 29:
Is disorganised/loses things

BBC parenting: *You and Your Family. Family Finance* www.bbc.co.uk/parenting/

Crimestoppers Youth Survey (2002) : www.crimestoppers-uk.org

Simmons, J. et al., *Crime in England and Wales 2001/2002* (London, Home Office, 2002)

Worry 30:
Might be harmed by mobile phone masts or overhead power cables

Independent Expert Group on Mobile Phones, *Mobile Phones and Health* (London, Stationery Office, 2000)

Hyland, G., 'Physics and biology of mobile telephony', *Lancet, 356,* 1833 (2000)

Rothman, K.J., 'Epidemiological evidence on health risks of cellular telephones', *Lancet, 356,* 1837 (2000)

UK Childhood Cancer Study Investigators, 'Exposure to power-frequency magnetic fields and the risk of childhood cancer', *Lancet, 354,* (1999)

Youbicier-Simo, B., & Bastide, M., 'Pathological effects induced by embryonic and postnatal exposure to EMF radiation by cellular mobile phones', *Radiat. Prot., 1,* 218 (1999)

Worry 31:
Might have an accident in the home

Child Accident Prevention Trust, *Children and Accidents* (CAPT, 2002)

Child Accident Prevention Trust, *Child Accident Facts* (CAPT, 2002)

Child Accident Prevention Trust, *Home Accidents* (CAPT, 2002)

Royal Society for the Prevention of Accidents, *Child Safety in the Home:* www.rospa.com

Worry 32:
Does not get enough physical exercise

Anderssen, N. & Wold, B., 'Parental and peer influences on leisure-time physical activity in young adolescents', *Res. Q. Exer. Sport, 63,* 341 (1992)

Ebbeling, C.B. et al., 'Childhood obesity', *Lancet, 360,* 473 (2002)

Fisher, K., *Chewing the Fat* (Colchester, Institute for Social and Economic Research, 2002)

Gregory, J. et al., *National Diet and Nutrition Survey: young people aged 4 to 18 years* (London, Stationery Office, 2000)

Malina, R.M., 'Tracking of physical activity and physical fitness across the lifespan', *Res. Q. Exerc. Sport, 67,* S48 (1996)

Sport England, *Addressing the Health Agenda* (London, Sport England)

Sport England, *Young People and Sport* (London, Sport England, 2003)

Worry 33:
Won't help with household chores

Harding, D.J., 'Measuring children's time use', *Center for Research on Child Wellbeing, Working paper #97-01* (1997)

MORI Poll Digest, *Children Are Well Paid for Household Chores* (2002): www.mori.com/digest/2002/pd020517.shtml

National Family and Parenting Institute, *Work and the Family Today* (London, NFPI, 2001)

National Statistics, *The UK 2000 Time Use Survey* (London, ONS, 2001)

Walker, A. et al., *Living in Britain* (London, HMSO, 2002)

White, L. & Brinkerhoff, D., 'Children's work in the family', *J. Marr. Fam., 43,* 789 (1981)

Worry 34:
Is always asking for things or money

Dammler, A. & Middelmann-Motz, A., 'I want one with Harry Potter on it', *Int. J. Advert. Market. Children. 3,* 3 (2002)

Dittmar, H. & Pepper, L., 'To have is to be', *J. Econ. Psychol., 15,* 233 (1994)

Goldberg, M. et al., 'Materialism among youth,' *J. Consum. Psychol., 13,* 278 (2003)

John, D., 'Consumer socialization of children', *J. Consum. Res., 26,* 183 (1999)

Mischel, W. et al., 'Delay of gratification in children', *Science, 244,* 933 (1989)

Nestle Family Monitor, *Money in the Contemporary Family* (Nestle UK, 2001)

Young, B.M., *The Child's Understanding of the Intent Behind Advertising* (ITC, 2003).

Worry 35:
Doesn't get enough vitamins from his/her normal diet

British Nutrition Foundation: www.nutrition.org.uk

Food Standards Agency, *New FSA advice on safety of high doses of vitamins and minerals* www.foodstandards.gov.uk/news/pressreleases/vitsand minspress

Food Standards Agency, *Vitamins and Minerals A–Z* www.foodstandards.gov.uk/healthiereating/vitaminsmin erals/vitsminsaz/

Gregory, J. et al., *National Diet and Nutrition Survey: young people aged 4 to 18 years* (London, Stationery Office, 2000)

Van Straten, M. & Josling, P., 'Preventing the common cold with a vitamin C supplement', *Adv. Ther., 19,* 151 (2002)

Worry 36:
Won't do his/her homework

Cooper, H., 'Homework research and policy', *Res. Pract., 2,* (1994)

Davidson, C. & Powell, L., 'Effects of easy-listening background music on the on-task-performance of fifth-grade children', *J. Educ. Res., 80,* 29 (1986)

Department for Education and Skills, *Homework.* www.dfes.gov.uk/homework

Forster, K., 'Homework', *Iss. Educ. Res., 10,* 21 (2000)

Sharp, C. et al., *Homework* (Slough, NFER, 2001)

Sui-Chu, E. & Willms, J., 'Effects of parental involvement on eighth-grade achievement', *Sociol. Educ., 69,* 126 (1996)

Worry 37:
Is not safe on public transport

Crime Concern for Merseytravel: Public Transport in Merseyside, *Children and Young People* (Crime Concern, 1995)

Department of the Environment, Transport and the Regions. *Focus on Public Transport* (London, Stationery Office, 1999)

Department for Transport, *Young People and Crime on Public Transport* (London, DfT, 1999)

Department for Transport, *Travel to School in GB* (London, DfT, 2003)

Department for Transport, *A Bulletin of Public Transport Statistics* (London, DfT, 2002)

Worry 38:
Might get into trouble with the authorities or commit a crime

Crime and Criminal Justice Unit, *Criminal Statistics England & Wales 1998* (London, Home Office, 2000)

Department for Education and Skills, *Permanent Exclusions from Schools and Exclusion Appeals, England 2001/2002* (DfES, 2003)

East, K. & Campbell, S. *Young Offenders* (London, Home Office, 1999)

Flood-Page, C. et al., *Youth Crime, Findings from the 1998/99 Youth Lifestyles Survey* (London, Home Office, 2000)

Youth Justice Board, *Youth Survey 2002* (Youth Justice Board, 2002)

Youth Justice Board, *Risk and Protective Factors Associated with Youth Crime and Effective Interventions to Prevent it* (Youth Justice Board, 2001)

Worry 39:
Isn't as good at maths as he/she should be

A Fresh Start, 'The report of the Working Group chaired by Sir Claus Moser': www.lifelonglearning.co.uk/mosergroup/index.htm

Ashcraft, M. & Kirk, E., 'Relationship among working memory, math anxiety and performance', *J. Exp. Psychol. Gen., 130,* 224 (2001)

Department for Education and Skills, *Numeracy:* www.parentcentre.gov.uk

Department for Education and Skills, *What Your Child Learns:* www.parentcentre.gov.uk

Office for Standards in Education, *The National Numeracy Strategy* (London, Ofsted, 2002)

Worry 40:
Is only assessed on narrow academic achievements, not broader abilities

Bandura, A. et al., 'Self-efficacy beliefs as shapers of children's aspirations and career trajectories', *Child Dev., 72,* 187 (2001)

Barton, K. et al., 'Personality and IQ measures as predictors of school achievement', *J. Educ. Psychol., 63,* 398 (1972)

Gardner, H., *Frames of Mind* (NY, Basic Books, 1983)

Hoyle, R.B. & Robinson, J.C., 'League tables and school effectiveness', *Proc. R. Soc. Lond., DOI* 10.1098/rspb.2002.222, (2002)

Juang, L. & Silbereisen, R., 'The relationship between adolescent academic capability beliefs, parenting and school grades', *J. Adolesc., 25,* 3 (2002)

La Paro, K. & Pianta, R., 'Predicting children's competence in the early school years', *Rev. Educ. Res., 70,* 443 (2000)

FACE THE FACTS

The Top 10 Risks Worldwide
World Health Organisation, *The World Health Report 2002* (WHO, 2002).

Alcohol
Drug Use, Smoking and Drinking Among Young People in England in 2002 (London, Stationery Office, 2003)

IAS Factsheet, *Young People and Alcohol* (Institute of Alcohol Studies, 2002)

Smoking
ASH, *Young People and Smoking* (ASH, 2003). www.ash.org.uk

ASH, *Smoking and Disease* (ASH, 2002). www.ash.org.uk

Drug Use, Smoking and Drinking Among Young People in England in 2002 (London, Stationery Office, 2003)

Working Parents
Duffield, M., 'Trends in female employment 2002', *Labour Market Trends, Nov, 605* (London, ONS, 2002)

Ermisch, J. & Francesconi, M., *The Effect of Parents' Employment on Children's Lives* (London, Family Policy Study Centre, 2001)

HM Treasury and Department of Trade and Industry, *Balancing Work and Family Life* (London, HMSO, 2003)

National Family and Parenting Institute Factsheet 3, *Work and the Family Today* (London, NFPI, 2001)

Drugs
Drug use, smoking and drinking among young people in England in 2002 (London, Stationery Office, 2003).

Drug use, smoking and drinking among young people in England in 2001 (London, Stationery Office, 2002)

Updated Drug Strategy 2002 (London, Home Office, 2002)

Divorce
National Statistics, *Divorce Increases* (London, ONS, 2002)

National Statistics, *Children of couples divorced, 1971, 1981, 1991, 1998–2001* www.statistics.gov.uk/STATBASE/xsdataset.asp?vlnk=6187

National Statistics, *Divorces in 2002: England and Wales* (London, ONS, 2003)

Rodgers, B. & Pryor, J. *Divorce and Separation* (Joseph Rountree Foundation, 1998)

Smacking
Ghate, D. & Daniels, A., *Talking About My Generation* (London, NSPCC, 1997)

Ghate, D. et al., *The National Study of Parents, Children and Discipline in Britain* (London, Policy Research Bureau, 2003)

National Family and Parenting Institute, *Is it Legal?* (London, NFPI)

Mobile Phones
NOP, *Half of 7–16s now have a Mobile Phone* (2001). www.nop.co.uk/news/news_survey_half_of_7-16s.shtml

The Law
National Family and Parenting Institute, *Is it Legal?* (London, NFPI)

And Ten Questions From Us
Bateson, P. & Martin, P., *Design For A Life* (London, Vintage, 2000)

Furedi, F., *Paranoid Parenting* (London, Allen Lane/Penguin Press, 2001)

Index

abduction by a stranger 12-15
academic skills, overemphasis on 215-19
accidents
  and lack of sleep 83
  as cause of death in children 49
  in the home 103, 166-70
  outside the home 103
  prevention 102-6
  risk factors for children 103, 104
  types of 167-8
ADHD (Attention Deficit/Hyperactivity Disorder) 71, 73-4 see also hyperactivity
  and bedtime resistance 94
  and risk of accidents 104
  and sleep problems 83
  and tantrums 110
adolescents see also teenagers
  ability to judge risk 104
  communication with 87
  concerns about public transport 198-202
  lack of sleep 81, 82-3, 94
  reluctance to get up in the mornings 114, 115
  school schedules and sleep deprivation 115-16
adults, violence between 57, 58
adventure centres, licensing for school trips 98-9
advertising
  aimed at children 181-3
  and smoking 48
  effects on diet 37, 40
  influences on children 29
age, and risk of being hit by a vehicle 8
aggression, learning to control 58
alcohol
  facts about 31
  talking to children about 45-6
alcohol use, and lack of sleep 83
allergies, and early diet 52
anger, teaching children about 111-12
anger management 58
anorexia nervosa 67, 135, 136-9

antisocial behaviour 73-4
  and excitement-seeking personalities 104
anxiety
  and lack of sleep 82-3
  and shyness 120
  and sleep problems 83
arthritis, in children 50
artificial sweeteners 19
aspartame 19
assaults on children see violence against children
assessments
  formal academic 215-19
  teacher 217, 218
asthma, in children 49, 50
Attention Deficit/Hyperactivity Disorder see ADHD (Attention Deficit/Hyperactivity Disorder)
attention seeking, and tantrums 108, 109-10
attention span, short 71-5

babies, risk of being murdered 12, 13-14, 15
bed, reluctance to get up in the mornings 114-18
bed wetting, and sleep problems 83
bedroom curtains, light exclusion 96
bedtime resistance 92-6
  and ADHD 94
bedtime routine 94, 95, 96
bedtime tantrums 94, 96
bedtimes, inconsistent 92, 93
behaviour, rewarding good behaviour 111
behaviour problems
  and bedtime resistance 93, 94
  and lack of sleep 82-3
  and tantrums 108, 109, 110
  and tiredness 83
behavioural intervention, for ADHD 74
biological clocks, changes in adolescence 92, 94
biological rhythms, and sleep patterns 115

birth order, links with personality 125-6
blind children, and sleep problems 83
body image, preoccupation with 135-9
boredom in school, reasons for 146-50
boys
  as perpetrators of 'street crime' 34
  as victims of 'street crime' 34
  consumption of caffeine 93
  effects of sedentary lifestyles 23
  effects of violent images 23
  likelihood of developing behavioural disorders 110
  risk factors which are higher than girls 227-8
  risk of accidents 103
  risk of accidents in the home 166, 167
  risk of being hit by a vehicle 8
  risk of being murdered 13
  risk of developing ADHD 73
brain tumours, childhood 49
breastfeeding
  health benefits for the mother 52
  long term health benefits for the child 52, 53
breathing disorders, sleep apnoea 83, 84
bulimia 67, 135, 136-9
bullying 55, 57, 59, 151-6
  consequences of 152-3
  forms of 152
  in or around school 55, 59
  responses to 153-6
  signs of 152

caffeine
  and bedtime resistance 92, 93-4
  and difficulty with getting up 114, 116
  and sleep problems 83, 84
  cutting down on 95, 117
  sources of 93-4

calcium
food sources 191
requirements 189, 191
cancer
as cause of death in children 49
childhood 49, 52
survival rates 49
cancer risk
and breastfeeding 52
and diet 52
and obesity 19, 39
cannabis 48, 107
car design, and injuries to
pedestrians 9, 11
car pooling 11
car speeds
and pedestrian safety 10-11
effects on severity of injuries 8-9
carers
assessing suitability of 14-15
children as 28-9
disciplining children 58
murder by 13, 14-15
violence against children 55-6
cars, risks to children travelling in
9-10
Chances (of a worry coming true)
4-5
child carers 28-9
child cyclists
risk of being hit by a vehicle 8
what you can do about safety
10
child pedestrians
risk of being hit by a vehicle 7-11
what you can do about safety
10
child protection register
and physical abuse 56
and sexual abuse 60, 61
childhood
allowing children to have 223-4
value of 28-30
childhood obesity see obesity in
children
children
always knowing where they are
200
average number per family 127
being paid to do housework
179
Calories required per day 136
complex busy lives 178
effects of divorce 113

helping with housework 176-80
lack of physical exercise 171-5
not eating enough 135-9
personal safety awareness 35, 36
pressures on 225
safety on public transport 198-202
teaching personal security 201
unable to talk to parents 86-90
use of mobile phones 161-5
children's bedrooms, TV in 93, 95-6
children's diet, getting enough
vitamins and minerals 187-92
chocolate
caffeine in 93, 94
sugar in 18
consumption in Britain 18
choking accidents, involving
children 167
chronic fatigue syndrome, in
children 50
circadian rhythm (waking and
sleeping cycle) 115
coffee, caffeine content 93
communication
between parents and children
222-3
non-verbal 87
within families 86-90
community orders, for criminal
behaviour 204-5
computer games
and shyness 122
and violent behaviour 21
as obstacle to communication
88
spending too much time playing
21-3, 24
concentration problems 71-5
due to lack of sleep 82, 84
Conduct Disorder (CD) 110
confidence, lack of 119-22, 225
conflict in families
causes 129-30
strategies for dealing with 130-2
congenital heart disease 50
Consequences (of a worry coming
true) 5
consumerism in children 181-6
Control (what you can do about a
risk) 4, 5
convenience food, eating too much

37-42
coronary heart disease, and obesity
19
corporal punishment, and
disciplining children 56-7, 58
crime see also 'street crime'
and materialism 184
children as victims of 32-6
formal punishments for children
203, 204-6
rise in 'street crime' 32-6
criminal behaviour 203-7 see also
'street crime'
and excitement-seeking
personalities 104
risk factors for 206
criticism, not undermining
confidence 225
custodial sentences, for young
offenders 205-6
cycle helmets, to reduce risk of
head injury 8, 10
cyclists
risks on the roads 8
what you can do about safety
10

danger, lack of awareness of 102-6
death
causes of 49
in the family, and disruptive
behaviour 109
top ten risk factors worldwide
(World Health Organisation) 16
delinquent behaviour 203-7
depression
and emotional abuse 61
and lack of sleep 82-3
and poor concentration 72-3
in children 50
diabetes
in adolescents 39
in children 50
diabetes risk
and diet 52
and obesity 19, 37
diet
effects of advertising 37
effects on health 52
food refusal 67
getting enough vitamins and
minerals 187-92
inappropriate texture of food for
age 67

influence of TV viewing 23
restricted 66-70
restrictive eating 67
selective eating 67
'diet' soft drinks, caffeine content 93-4
dieting
and supplements 190
by children who are not overweight 135-9
diphtheria 51
discipline 56-7, 58
effective strategies 130, 131, 132
ineffective methods 129-33
and tantrums 108
disobedience 129-33
disorganisation 157-60
disruptive behaviour, causes of 109-10
divorce 113
and disruptive behaviour in children 109
dressing in the mornings, refusal or very slow at 116
drinking (alcohol)
facts about 31
talking to children about 45-6
drivers
safety considerations 10-11
speeding and pedestrian accidents 7, 8-9
drowning accidents, involving children 167-8, 170
drugs see also medication
and excitement-seeking personalities 104
cannabis 107
Class A 107
facts about 107
lack of sleep and 83
peer-group influences 45-6
smoking and 107
talking to children about 45-6
dyscalculia 211
dyslexia 140, 142-3
and dyscalculia 211

eating disorders 67, 135-9
education see also school
parents worries about 76-80
pushing children too hard 223-4
starting too young 224
emergencies, teaching children

what to do 15
emotional abuse of children 61
signs of 62
emotional development 30
and life experiences 28-9
in relation to physical development 28
emotional instability, and lack of sleep 82-3
emotional intelligence, and career prospects 79
employment prospects
and numeracy skills 210
and qualifications 76, 77, 78
entrepreneurs, skills required 76, 78
environment, providing love and security 224-5
epilepsy, in children 50
examinations (academic) 76, 77, 78
excitement-seeking personalities 102, 104, 105
exclusion from school, and smoking 48
exercise see physical exercise

falls, as cause of injury to children 167
family health history, and potential risk factors 53
fashion, and peer groups 45
fast food, eating too much 37-42
father substitutes, violence against children 57
fathers, violence against children 57, 58
feelings, inability to deal with 108, 109
fires, in the home 167, 169
first aid training, for adults and older children 169
fizzy drinks see soft drinks (fizzy)
food fads 66-70
food intolerance 67
food refusal 67, 68
formal assessment, narrow focus of 215-19
friends
as a bad influence 43-7
as a source of support 44
fruit
guidelines for children's diets 39-40, 41
health benefits of 52

frustration, as cause of tantrums 109
fussy eaters see food fads

games consoles see computer games
German measles see rubella
getting up in the morning, difficulty with 114-18
gifted children 146, 148-50
girls
effects of sedentary lifestyles 23
mineral deficiency risk 189, 191
risk factors which are higher than boys 228
risk of being murdered 13
risk of developing eating disorders 135, 136, 137-8
violence among 55, 57
gratification, delayed or instant 183-4
growth, and sexual activity 27-8

Haemophilus influenzae (Hib) immunisation 51
happiness, and money 78
health, encouraging good habits 226
hearing problems, and poor concentration 72, 75
heart disease, congenital 50
heart disease risk
and breastfeeding 52
and diet 52
and obesity 37, 39
and salt in the diet 37, 39
height (adult), increase over time 27
high blood pressure risk
and obesity 19, 39
and salt in the diet 37, 39
high-voltage power cables, health concerns about 161-4
HIV 51
home, as source of many serious risks 231
homework
home-school agreements 195
purposes of 193, 194-5
reluctance to do 193-7
house fires, cause of death and injury to children 167, 169

household chores, disputes over 176-80
hyperactivity see also Attention Deficit/Hyperactivity Disorder (ADHD)
    and sleep problems 83
    and sugar in the diet 19

illness
    and supplements 188, 190
    chronic 50
    in childhood 50
    serious 49-54
immunisation 50-2
income, and qualifications 77-8
independence, and bedtime 92
infectious diseases 50-2
injuries, accidental 103
insomnia 83
    in primary school-age children 94
intelligence
    and breastfeeding 52
    various forms of 216-17
Internet
    teaching children how to use it safely 15, 62-3, 64
    use by paedophiles 61, 62-3
IQ (intelligence quotient)
    increasing over time 28
    limitations of tests 216-17
iron
    food sources 191
    requirements 189, 191

jealousy among siblings 123-8
junk food 37-42

language skills, and concentration 72
larks (morning type circadian rhythm) 115
law, facts relating to children 208
learning, lifelong love of 227
learning difficulties, and tantrums 108, 109
leukaemia, childhood 49, 52
lifelong learning, encouraging a love of 227
listening, by parents 86, 88-9, 222-3
listening skills, and concentration 72

literacy skills 140-5
losing things 157-60
lymphomas, childhood 49, 52

materialism in children 181-6
maths
    anxiety about 209-14
    lack of basic skills 209-14
'maths phobia' 209, 210-11
maths teaching 211-13
mealtimes see diet; food fads
measles 51-2
medication
    as source of caffeine 93
    for ADHD 74
    Ritalin (Methylphenidate) 74
men, and excitement-seeking personalities 104
meningitis 51, 52
meningococcal septicaemia 51
mental illnesses, in children 50
mental wellbeing, effects of lack of sleep 82-3
Methylphenidate (Ritalin), for concentration problems 74
minerals
    getting enough in the diet 187-92
    requirements 188, 189
    supplements 187, 188, 189-90
MMR vaccine 51-2
mobile phone masts, health concerns about 161-4
mobile phones
    as target for 'street crime' 33-4, 35
    facts about 165
    health concerns for children 161-4
money
    and happiness 78
    saving 182
    spending 182
    teaching how to manage 184, 185
mornings
    allowing more time 117-18
    reluctance to get up 114-18
mothers, working 91, 178
motivation
    and career prospects 76, 78-9
    intrinsic and extrinsic 227
mugging see 'street crime'
mumps 51-2
murder
    by a stranger 12-15
    by parents 12-15

neglect of children 61
nicotine, and sleep problems 94
nightmares, recurrent 83
numeracy
    and earning power 210
    anxiety about 209-14
    lack of basic skills 209-14
Nutrasweet (E951) 19
nutrition see diet

obesity in children
    and convenience food 37, 38-9
    and excessive sugar consumption 17, 18-19
    and junk food consumption 38-9
    and lack of exercise 21, 172-3, 174
    and low self-esteem 39
    and TV viewing 21, 23
    health risks of 18-19, 38-9, 52
only-child families, increase in 123, 126-7
Oppositional Defiant Disorder (ODD) 110
organisations skills, poor 157-60
over-protected children 14, 103
owls (evening type circadian rhythm) 115

packed lunches 20, 38
paedophiles 61
    use of the Internet 61, 62-3
parent-child relationships, and peer-group influences 45
parental consent for school trips 97, 98, 100
parenting styles
    and bedtime resistance 93, 94
    and children's development 130-1
    and disobedience 130-1
    and tantrums in children 109-10
parents
    ability to reduce or eliminate risks 231
    acknowledging a child's feelings 88, 89
    as role models for taking more exercise 171, 174
    as role models to counter materialism 183, 185
    as role models for healthy living 226

as role models for self-management 157, 158-9
as teachers of social skills 120-1
beliefs about boys and girls 227-8
building a child's self-confidence 120-2
children unable to talk to 86-90
communication with children 222-3
concerns about children under-eating 135-9
coping with sibling rivalry 126, 127-8
difficulties faced by 228-9
drinking and drugs as cause of accidents 166, 168, 170
enjoying parenthood 228-9
having tantrums 110
helping children to be good communicators 87
helping children with concentration problems 74-5
importance of listening 109-10, 222-3
inability to listen to children 86, 88-9
influence on children's attitudes towards food 135, 137-9
influence on children's educational performance 77, 78, 79
managing risk 3-5
managing their own anger 111-12
methods of dealing with fussy eaters 68-9
murder by 12-15
need to understand the child's world 225
paying children to do housework 179
poor social skills and shyness in children 120
providing love and security 224-5
pushing children to be academically precocious 29
setting a good example 226
spending enough time with children 221-2
supporting children with homework 194, 195, 196-7
supporting maths teaching 209, 213-14
supporting reading and writing at home 140, 141, 143-4

survey of worries 2, 233-4
unfair comparisons between siblings 125, 128
violence against children 55-6
working, facts about 91
working hours 178
parents relationship, and sibling rivalry 125, 128
pedestrians
    accidents involving vehicles 7-11
    what you can do about safety 10
peer-group influences 43-7
peer preference 43, 44-5
peer pressure 43, 44-5
personal safety awareness 35, 36
personality, and career prospects 78-9
physical abuse of children 55-9, 61
    signs of 62
physical exercise
    benefits of 52, 172-3
    excessive (and eating disorders) 137
    lack of 21, 22, 23, 171-5
    to help concentration 75
physical inactivity
    and obesity 172-3, 174
    dangers to health 172-3, 174
physical violence, against children 55-9 see also bullying
play
    and accidents 103
    importance for development 223-4
    safety of 105
playground injuries 103
pneumonia 51
pocket money 182
poisoning, accidental 103, 167, 169
polio 51
ponds, dangers of 167-8, 170
possessions, appreciating the value of 158-9
postnatal depression 13-14
power cables (high-voltage), health concerns about 161, 163-4
pregnancy, unplanned 28
pre-school children, risk of accidents in the home 166, 167
processed food see convenience food
protecting children, downsides of excessive measures 14

puberty 27
public transport, safety concerns 198-202

qualifications
    and employment prospects 76, 77, 78
    and income 77-8
    benefits of having 76, 77
    overemphasis on 215-19
'quality time' 221-2

radiofrequency radiation, concerns about 161-4
reading problems, reasons for 141-2
reading skills, concerns about 140-5
relatives
    murder by 13, 14-15
    violence against children 55-6
rewards, for good behaviour 131
risk factors, top ten worldwide (World Health Organisation) 16
risk management 3-5
risk-taking, and peer groups 45
risk-taking personalities 102, 104, 105
risks
    children's ability to judge 102, 103-4
    learning to deal with 104, 105
    parents' ability to reduce or eliminate 105, 231
    talking to children about 45-6
Ritalin (Methylphenidate), for concentration problems 74
road safety 7-11
robbery see also 'street crime'
    child victims and offenders 158
rubella (German measles) 51-2

saccharin 19
safety, excessive concern about 223
salt
    health risks of high intake 37, 39
    hidden in foods 39
SATs (Standard Assessment Tests) 216, 218
saving money 182
scalds and burns, injuries to

children in the home 167, 170
school see also education
    and academic precocity 29
    boredom with 146-50
    bullying 55, 59, 151, 153-6
    children being driven to 9-10
    children cycling to 9
    exclusion and crime 34, 35
    exclusion and smoking 48
    homework 193-7
    recognition of gifted children 146, 148
    reduction in physical activities 173
    truanting and crime 34, 35
school children
    Calories required per day 41
    lack of sleep 81, 82-3
    literacy problems 140-5
    numeracy problems 209-14
school lunches 20
school moves, and disruptive behaviour in children 109
school performance
    and computer games 21
    and lack of sleep 81, 82
    and TV viewing 21, 24
school problems, and reluctance to get ready 116
school schedules, and sleep deprivation 115-16
school trips
    activities involving water 97, 98-9, 100
    adventure activities 98-9
    benefits and risks 97-101
    DfES safety guidelines 98, 100
    international 97, 100
    lack of support and training for teachers 99-100
    risks during transportation 97, 99, 100
    staffing 98
    your child's emotional concerns 100
Seasonal Affective Disorder (SAD) 116-17
self-confidence
    building 120-2
    lack of 119-22
self-esteem
    and friends 44
    and obesity 39
    and peer groups 45-6
    and sleep pattern 82
    supporting your child 46-7

sex, talking to children about 30, 46
sexual abuse of children 60-5
    by a stranger 60, 62
    by other children 62
    by parents 60, 62
    by siblings 62
    by someone known to the child 60, 62, 64
    characteristics of abusers 62
    signs of 61-2
    untrue allegations of 63
sexual activity, starting younger 27-8
sexuality, influences of advertising 29
shyness 119-22
    and parents social skills 120
    assessing 120
    in adults 120
    pre-disposition for 120-1
sibling rivalry 123-8
    and age gap between siblings 123, 125, 126
    and new babies 123, 124-5, 128
    causes 124-5
    in adolescence 125
    in dysfunctional families 125, 128
siblings
    and sleep problems 95
    differences between 123, 125
    links between birth order and personality 125-6
    'niche picking' 125
    positive influences on one another 123, 126
    sexual abuse by 62
    time alone to talk to parents 90
    violence between 57, 58, 124
sleep
    lack of 81-85
    stressing the importance of 95, 117
    weekend lie-ins 116
sleep apnoea 83, 84
sleep deficit
    and bedtime resistance 93
    and poor concentration 72, 75
    due to TV or computer games 22, 23, 24
sleep deprivation, effects of 82-3
sleep problems 83
    adolescents 94
    and ADHD 83

and anxiety 83
and bed wetting 83
and caffeine 83, 93
and obesity 39
blind children 83
Delayed Sleep Phase Syndrome 95
diagnosis of 84
due to siblings 95
insomnia 83
recurrent nightmares 83
reluctance to get up in the mornings 114-18
sleep apnoea 83, 84
visually impaired children 83
sleep requirements 94-5
sleep schedule, establishing 84
sleeping and waking cycle (circadian rhythm) 115
smacking children 56-7, 58
    facts about 133-4
    long term concerns 131
smallpox 51
smoke alarms 169
smokers, vitamin C requirements 188
smoking
    and drug use 107
    and excitement-seeking personalities 104
    and lack of sleep 83
    and peer groups 45
    and sleep problems 94
    death toll in the UK 48
    facts about 48
    health risks for children 52
    talking to children about 45-6
snacking
    and junk food consumption 41
    and tooth decay 19, 20
snoring 84
social pressures on children 29, 30
social skills
    development of 28, 29, 30, 119, 120, 121
    parents as teachers and role models 120-1
soft drinks (fizzy)
    caffeine content 93-4
    sweeteners in 19, 20
speeding, and pedestrian accidents 7, 8-9, 10-11
sport, benefits of 172-3, 174
sports injuries 103
stepfathers, violence against children 57

strangers
  abduction by 12-15
  fear of 13, 14, 15
  murder by 12-15
'street crime' see also crime;
  criminal behaviour
  and exclusion from school 34,
  35
  and truanting from school 34,
  35
  fall in age of victims and
  offenders 34
  increase in 32-6
  offenders mainly male 34
  victims mainly male 34, 35
stress, and violence against
  children 57
stroke, high salt intake as a risk
  factor 39
sucralose 19
sugar
  and hyperactivity in children 19
  excessive intake of 17-20
  hidden in foods 18, 20
  in the British diet 18
suicide, and emotional abuse 61
suicide rates 50
supplements
  for young children 190
  vitamins and minerals 187,
  188, 189-90
survey of parents' worries 2,
  233-4

talented children 148 see also
  gifted children
tantrums 96, 108-12
  and behavioural disorders 109,
  110
  and lack of emotional
  development 108, 109
  and lack of language
  development 108, 109
  and parenting styles 109-10
  at bedtime 94, 96
  causes of 108, 109-10, 111
  dealing with 111-12
  forms of 109
  in older children 108, 109
  testing boundaries 109
taste, development of sense of 67-
  8
tea, caffeine content 93
teaching methods, and boredom in
  school 147-8

teenage sex 27-8
teenagers see also adolescents
  committing crime 203-7
  concerns about public transport
  198-202
  lack of sleep 81, 82-3
  peer group influences 44
  reluctance to get up in the
  mornings 114, 115
television see TV
theobromine, in chocolate 94
'time out' rule 58, 131
tiredness
  and tantrums 108, 109
  effects on children's behaviour
  83
toddlers, depression in 50
tooth decay, and excessive sugar
  consumption 17, 18, 19, 20
truanting
  and poor educational
  performance 78, 79
  and smoking 48
tuberculosis (TB) 51
TV, in children's bedrooms 23, 24,
  95-6
TV viewing
  and bedtime resistance 92, 93
  and difficulty with getting up
  114, 116
  and lack of exercise 23
  and lack of sleep 22, 23, 24,
  84, 93
  and personal relationships 24
  and risk of becoming obese
  173, 174
  and school performance 24
  and shyness 122
  and violent behaviour 21, 22-3
  influence on diet 23
  influence on risk-taking
  behaviour 103
  obstacle to communication
  88
  spending too much time on
  21-25
'tweenies' (9-12 age group),
  spending power 182

university education 77

vaccination 50-2, 53
vegan diets 190, 191
vegetables

guidelines for children's diets
  39-40, 41
  health benefits of 52
vegetarian diets 190, 191
vehicle design, and injuries to
  pedestrians 9, 11
vehicle speeds, and injuries to
  pedestrians 8-9, 10-11
vehicles, risks to children
  travelling in 9-10
video games see computer games
violence against children 55-9
  and family structures 57
  and stress 57
  bullying 55, 57, 59, 151-6
violence between adults, risks to
  children 57, 58
violence between siblings 57, 58,
  124
violent images, effects of 21, 22, 23
viral infections 51
visual impairment
  and poor concentration 72, 75
  and sleep problems 83
vitamins
  getting enough in the diet 187-
  92
  requirements 188-9, 189-90
  supplements 187, 188, 189-90

waking up in the mornings,
  difficulty with 114-18
weight, and health 53 see also
  obesity in children
winter, difficulty with getting up
  114, 116-17
'winter blues' 117 see also
  Seasonal Affective Disorder
  (SAD)
working mothers 91, 178
working parents 91
  and family relationships 88, 91
worries
  managing risk 3-5
  not worrying about the right
  things 231
  survey of parents 2, 233-4
writing skills, concerns about
  140-5

zinc
  food sources 191
  requirements 189, 191